The UK Monetary and
Financial System

The UK Monetary and Financial System

An introduction

John Gilbody

London and New York

First published 1988
by Routledge
11 New Fetter Lane, London EC4P 4EE
29 West 35th Street, New York, NY 10001

Reprinted 1991

© 1988 John Gilbody

Phototypeset by Input Typesetting Ltd, London
Printed and bound in Great Britain by
Mackays of Chatham PLC, Chatham, Kent

British Library Cataloguing in Publication Data

Gilbody, John, *1939–*
    The UK Monetary and Financial System: An
    Introduction.
    1. Great Britain. Monetary system
    I. Title
    332.4'941

    ISBN 0–415–00435–7
    ISBN 0–415–00095–5 Pbk

Contents

Contents

Preface

The origins of this book lie in a first-year course that I was drafted to teach at the University College of Swansea, the group involved constituting both intending Honours students in economics and a variety of non-specialists reading some economics in the context of other schemes of study. The existence of this course stems from a belief that the monetary and financial system is of sufficient interest and importance in its own right to warrant a somewhat more detailed treatment at an introductory level than is possible in the standard course on macroeconomic theory which students pursue in parallel. Thus the goal of this textbook is to provide the reader with a broad introduction to the operation, mechanics, and structure of the monetary and financial system within the United Kingdom, emphasizing its institutions, markets, and instruments.

Although the book contains a brief survey of some relevant monetary theory in the context of a discussion of monetary policy, it is intended as a complement, rather than a substitute, for the many excellent introductory texts available which deal primarily with macroeconomic theory and policy and the book will be read most profitably by undergraduates with some knowledge of basic economic principles. The level of exposition is such, however, that aspects of it may appeal to students pursuing the standard A-level economics curriculum in schools, to students pursuing business studies courses in colleges of further education and to part-time students studying monetary economics as an element in professional examinations.

As is well known, in recent years the financial services sector has been one of the fastest growing sectors of the economy and, at the same time, has undergone fundamental institutional change. A further objective in writing this book has been to provide a reasonably up-to-date account of such changes, but the reader should perhaps be warned that the sheer pace of institutional change presents problems for any would-be textbook writer hoping to present a snapshot picture of the financial system at a point in time. While certain general principles underlying the operation of the system remain fairly constant, the continuing process of competition and structural adjustment may render certain descriptive parts of this book obsolete within a very short space of time.

In writing this book I have benefited considerably from the discussions I have had with three generations of students in tutorial situations; their perceptive questions have prompted me to clarify my own thoughts in a number of areas and I am extremely grateful to all of them. I have also benefited from the comments made on an original draft of the manuscript by two anonymous referees who, apart from picking up errors, suggested ways in which the exposition might be strengthened and clarified. Any errors which remain are, of course, my sole responsibility. Most of all, I am deeply indebted to Miss Siân Davies and to my wife Judith who both cheerfully deciphered some extremely illegible handwriting and produced the typescript with what can only be described as superb efficiency. Finally I apologize to all my family – to whom this book is dedicated – for a great deal of neglect that they suffered during the course of this enterprise.

J. H. Gilbody
March 1988

Part one

Introduction

Chapter one

The nature of a monetary economy

Money and exchange

The United Kingdom economy in common with practically all
other economies is a monetary economy. The importance of
money for the everyday business of life may seem to be self-
evident, but an appreciation of the precise role which the institution of money performs in the workings of the modern economy
requires initially some consideration of certain fundamental
characteristics of economic organization.

All economic activity involves the use of resources, such as
labour time, land, machines, and buildings, to produce a variety
of goods and services which are consumed or used by individual
members of society. The process of production is organized within
an institutional framework which varies in detail between different
countries, but a fundamental characteristic of all economies is
that, to a greater or lesser extent, the ownership and control
of resources is dispersed among those individuals, or groups of
individuals, who collectively comprise society; each individual (or
family unit) at any point in time can be considered as having a
given endowment of human and non-human resources over which
he or she possesses private property rights. The institution of
private property usually depends on the existence of some governmental authority to guarantee and enforce private property rights
within a clearly defined system of law, but within the framework
of law that is established individuals have the freedom to use their
endowments as they themselves choose.

Within the basic framework of private property rights each
individual is free, if he so chooses, to use the resources he controls
primarily to produce goods and services for his own direct use
and, to some extent, elements of direct production for own
consumption are observed in modern society, as is evidenced by

the unpaid services of housewives and numerous 'do it yourself' activities such as gardening, house decorating, or car maintenance.

However, whenever economies have progressed beyond the stage of primitive subsistence agriculture, the institution of private property has been accompanied by a further dominating characteristic of economic life, namely that of specialization or the division of labour. Individuals do not attempt to use their resources to produce goods and services directly for their own immediate use – rather they specialize as producers of certain goods and services and then obtain the wider range of goods and services they desire to use by voluntary exchanges with other individuals. Generally speaking, as societies have developed in the economic sphere, the degree of specialization has intensified and most production is undertaken not for the direct satisfaction of the wants of the producers themselves, but for the proximate purpose of exchange with other individuals.

It is the phenomenon of voluntary exchange which gives rise to the use of money in the economy. As a general rule, in any economy where voluntary exchange is prominent, barter trades – where goods are directly exchanged or swapped for other goods – are not typically observed. The producer of a specific good or service, say good A, who seeks to obtain another good or service, say good B, through trade, will rarely exchange A directly for B; instead what usually happens is that the individual concerned exchanges, or sells, A in return for the receipt of something we generally term money and then subsequently uses his money receipts from this sale to buy B. A single direct exchange of goods is decomposed into two separate transactions involving the use of money. This method of conducting voluntary exchange is so ubiquitous that one can state formally a further fundamental feature of most economies which leads to their characterization as 'monetary economies': as a general rule in such economies 'goods buy money and money buys goods – but goods do not buy goods in any organized market.'[1]

As with most generalizations there are usually exceptions and it is true that a limited amount of barter trade does take place in modern economies. For example, it is a common practice for sellers of new cars to accept used cars in part-exchange, and it also is common for employers to remunerate employees for labour services rendered in part by various non-monetary 'perks' such as the private use of company cars, telephones, etc. However such barter exchange constitutes only a minute fraction of the total transactions that are mediated via an exchange of money.

Why money not barter?

The dominance of monetary exchange can be explained in a general way by consideration of the difficulties which would arise in conducting exchanges in a hypothetical barter economy.[2] The simplest system of barter one can envisage would be a system where each individual attempts to obtain in exchange goods to which he attaches some immediate value in use. The problem with such a system, however, is that the basis of any successful transaction rests on what is called a 'double coincidence of wants' between any two transactors; this is the necessity for the two parties to an exchange to want simultaneously that which the other party is offering.

A moment's reflection reveals that such a system would be unlikely to accommodate many of the exchanges we observe in a modern economy which has developed intricate forms of specialization. How could the modern business firm specializing in the production of a certain specific commodity, say sulphuric acid, employ workers by offering commodities of immediate use value in return for the use of their labour? Is it likely that a stockbroker could strike a bargain with the average taxi-driver by offering stockbroking services in exchange for the provision of transportation? Clearly a direct barter system is likely to be feasible, if at all, only in very primitive economies where a fairly small number of basic subsistence goods are being produced, but even in such an economy an individual attempting to trade would be likely to incur substantial costs simply in locating a trading partner with exactly matching requirements and in reaching agreement about the precise quantities of commodities that are to be exchanged; these costs might be so substantial as effectively to prohibit trade (the costs involved in exchanging goods and services, as opposed to the costs involved in producing them, are generally termed in economics as 'transactions costs').

Probably if a barter economy were to function at all in any way compatible with voluntary exchange, it would have to involve a certain amount of indirect barter, where individuals would accept in exchange intermediate commodities, i.e. commodities not required for their immediate use value to the individual concerned, but which have possible value in subsequent exchange. By then engaging in a sequence, or chain, of transactions individuals might eventually acquire their desired commodities. To illustrate, suppose we had four individuals A, B, C, and D who, at a given time, were offering to trade certain commodities for other commodities in the manner depicted in Table 1.1. If each indi-

Table 1.1   Desired trades of four individuals

Individual	Offers	Wants
A	Butter	Wool
B	Apples	Butter
C	Bread	Apples
D	Wool	Bread

vidual attempted to trade by direct barter there would be a double coincidence of wants problem and no trade would be feasible. However, the problem can be resolved if individual A, for example, was prepared to accept intermediate goods in exchange. A can trade with B accepting apples in exchange for butter, he then trades with C exchanging apples for bread and finally with D exchanging bread for wool (his desired good). While such a system might overcome the double coincidence of wants problem, it would again be formidably expensive in terms of transaction costs; the required exchange chains might be very long and every link in the chain would involve the cost of searching out trading partners with specific requirements, reaching agreement on the volume and terms of trade, etc. Moreover, some individuals, in this example A, are subject to the risk that the arranged sequence of exchanges does not in fact take place as planned, so that they are left holding commodities not desired for their own sake.

It is fairly obvious that a significant saving in transaction costs can be effected if, by some process, a single commodity (or other entity such as a banknote) becomes generally accepted by all traders as an intermediate good in exchange for the delivery of all other commodities, i.e. if some entity can perform the role we have ascribed to money. In this instance the longest exchange chain faced by any individual seeking to transform one commodity into another by trade is reduced to just two transactions; the ultimate requirements of the opposite party in any transaction become an irrelevant consideration and the costs and risks involved in long exchange chains are greatly reducedd. The general explanation for the use of money is, therefore, that individuals perceive the advantages of money in the facilitation of voluntary exchange, with its attendant advantages of increased specialization and productivity, and somehow come to adopt the convention that certain entities become socially sanctioned as exchange intermediaries.

It is, of course, rather more difficult to explain the exact process whereby particular things become adopted as money. If one considers the generality of historical experience an amazing variety of specific objects have been used as money in different times and in different places. The list would comprise amongst others, cowrie shells, stones, salt, olive oil, copper, tin, silver, gold, bales of tobacco, cigarettes, and brandy.[3] The main thing that all these objects had in common, apart from certain convenient properties such as durability, ease of transmission between individuals, fairly homogeneous quality and divisibility, was simply the fact of their general acceptability in exchange, the foundations of which lie in a rather peculiar interdependence between the subjective beliefs and expectations of all the individuals comprising the population at large.

Consider for example the present Bank of England £5 note. In terms of intrinsic value (value in immediate use) the note is virtually useless and the promise enshrined on it in the words 'I promise to pay the bearer on demand the sum of five pounds' is now meaningless; all one is likely to get in exchange for a £5 note would be another, perhaps newer, note or some coins which, if illegally melted down, would sell for considerably less than £5 as metal. Why then should Bank of England notes be accepted in exchange when similar bits of paper are not? The brief answer is that an individual will accept a £5 note because he expects with more or less complete certainty that everyone else will – £5 notes arc accepted because everyone believes they will be accepted, and everyone believes they will be accepted because according to their past experience they invariably have been accepted. Thus money can be described as a pure social convention; once firmly established such conventions are remarkably durable, but it has to be admitted there is an element of mystery regarding how they develop from their original usage by a few individuals into widely held conventions.

The acceptability of certain forms of money may be enhanced by the fact that they are fiat monies issued by a government and designated as legal tender (the legal tender property means that the government has decreed that certain entities be regarded by the courts as an acceptable method of settling debts of unlimited amounts). However, the legal tender designation is not a necessary characteristic of money, many forms of money have not been a result of compulsion by the state but have evolved in a spontaneous fashion through the actions of private individuals. Similarly there are numerous historical examples where individuals have rejected legal tender money for private transactions and have invented their own money, or used other countries' money.

The role ascribed to money in acting as an intermediate instrument in transactions is traditionally summarized by the phrase that 'money acts as a medium of exchange'. Recently however some writers have drawn a distinction between the role of money as a medium of exchange and a somewhat narrower role of money as a means of payment.[4] The argument here is that there are other instruments which are often provisionally acceptable by individuals in exchange, and an offer of such instruments may allow a transaction to be conducted; however only when an exchange of money has taken place will the two partners involved regard the transaction as being settled, or finalized, in the sense that it can be relegated to past history with neither of the partners having a claim on the other.

The distinction being drawn can be illustrated with reference to a modern innovation in the practice of shopping, namely the use of credit cards. If an individual possesses a credit card, he or she can enter many shops, choose an article for purchase, produce the card, sign a form and then leave the shop with the chosen article – clearly an exchange has been conducted. What happens is that in issuing a credit card, the credit card company simultaneously issues a promise to shopkeepers that it will ultimately pay them money for goods acquired by the card-holder. Because of the reputation of the credit card company, many shopkeepers are prepared to accept such promises in exchange for the delivery of goods to customers so that, in effect, these promises are serving as a medium of exchange. The initial exchange, however, is obviously not the end of the story. The shopkeeper will subsequently present the signed form representing his claim on the credit card company for settlement in terms of money and only when payment is received will the transaction be regarded as finalized. Likewise, the purchaser has incurred a debt to the credit card company which eventually he must liquidate by a payment of money, if he wants to avoid prosecution in the county courts. The general point is that many exchanges proceed via the use of credit arrangements of various types, where purchasers explicitly or implicitly make promises to pay later and sellers are prepared to accept such promises as the basis for a delivery of goods and services. Such credit represents a medium of exchange and in this sense money is not unique. Credit, though, does not lead to the completion of a transaction, it merely serves to postpone completion which will be accomplished only when payment has been made by an actual transfer of money.

Other functions of money

While the existence of money can be generally explained by its role in facilitating voluntary exchange, once the institution of money is established in an economy it also performs certain other distinguishable joint functions.

Money as a store of value

The use of money as a means of payment necessarily implies that money also acts as a store of value. In a money economy, transactions are decomposed into separate selling and buying transactions – individuals receive payments for goods and services sold at particular moments in time and then subsequently make payments for goods and services purchased at succeeding moments in time. Receipts and payments are thus non-synchronized and it therefore follows that for certain time intervals money is acting as a store of value of the goods and services sold, prior to the realization of this value in terms of the purchase of other goods.

This point can be illustrated by considering the position of most workers in the modern economy. Workers render labour services to employers on a credit basis and receive payments of money in arrears as wages or salaries at discrete intervals of time, typically weekly or monthly. These money receipts are then used to make payments for goods in the time intervals between wage or salary dates. Admittedly, if a worker receives his wages on a Friday afternoon and is in the habit of visiting supermarkets and other shops in 'late night' shopping excursions on a Friday evening, the average delay between receipts and payments might not be very long, but nevertheless for finite time intervals, however small, money is acting as a store of the value of the labour services that the worker has supplied. Clearly, if money did not serve as a store of value, nobody would accept it in payment for delivery of goods and services.

Money, of course, can also serve as a store of value for periods of time much longer than the usual interval between periodic receipts of money income. The possession of money provides individuals with purchasing power, or a stock of claims on goods and services, but they can delay the immediate exercise of such claims by accumulating money balances over time. Money can thus act as a convenient instrument for saving, i.e. a means of transferring consumption of goods and services from the present to the future. Money in this sense may therefore be described as a financial asset, in contradistinction to real or tangible assets.

Introduction

Real assets are material entities, such as houses, machines, vehicles or consumer durables, that are specialized in form and whose value is derived from a capacity to yield streams of specific goods and services in future periods. A financial asset, in contrast, is a claim to the consumption, or utilization of, goods and services in general; it gives its holder the potentiality of consuming an unspecified good or service at an unspecified time and can be described as generalized wealth. In a barter economy, saving on the part of an individual would have to involve the storage of real assets which, given the difficulties of storage and the fact that many material entities deteriorate with age, would constitute an inconvenient method of holding wealth.

Money as a unit of account

The functions of money in acting as a means of payment or a store of value result from the existence of money in 'concrete' or tangible form. An additional function of money which can be distinguished is the abstract function of acting as a unit of account. This refers to the use of money as a common denominator, in terms of the units of which the prices of all other goods and services can be expressed. Normally the units in which the circulating concrete money is embodied will also serve simultaneously as the abstract unit of account: prices are expressed in terms of pounds and pence, dollars and cents, etc.[5]

The advantage of using a common unit of account is that it greatly reduces the number of prices that have to be explicitly formulated to allow economic decision-takers to make pairwise comparisons of the exchange ratios of particular goods. With n commodities, one of which is acting as a unit of account, there will need to be only $n-1$ explicit prices to allow for pairwise comparisons between all commodities; thus for 1,000 commodities there need be only 999 prices. Without a common unit of account there would need to be a separate explicit exchange ratio between each pair of commodities; for n commodities there would be $\frac{1}{2}n(n-1)$ exchange ratios, thus for 1,000 commodities there would be 499,500 separate exchange ratios.

The existence of a unit of account immensely simplifies the appropriate buying and selling decisions of consumers and producers. Armed with knowledge of the various money prices of commodities, a consumer, for example, can subjectively translate the money price of any particular commodity into an alternative bundle of commodities which must be foregone if the commodity in question is to be purchased. The money price of a commodity can thus serve as an abstract summary measure of the exchange value of a commodity in terms of all other commodities. The use of money in acting as a measure of exchange value is readily appreciated if one considers the mental thought processes of UK citizens when travelling abroad; in deciding whether commodities whose prices are quoted in francs or pesetas are 'cheap' or 'expensive', we often subjectively convert the foreign currency prices back into pound prices, the standard with which we are more familiar, at any rate, initially, until we have acquired more information about the foreign currency prices of various commodities.

In addition, of course, all the numerous aggregate measures employed in practice in economic life, such as income, wealth, profits, costs, value added, etc., depend on the existence of a common unit of account.

Forms of money in the United Kingdom

Probably the most common way of distinguishing entities that serve as money from other assets is to define money with reference to its role in facilitating voluntary exchange, i.e. money is usually defined as 'anything that is generally acceptable as a means of payment, or in complete and final settlement of a debt'. This definition, of course, is somewhat imprecise – how 'general' does the acceptability of an entity as a means of payment have to be in order to classify it as money? The fact is that not all entities that are accepted by some individuals in some transactions at any point in time will be accepted by all individuals for all transactions. At the present time, for example, low-value coins struck by the Royal Mint are legal tender only up to certain upper limits and can, and probably will, be refused by sellers as a means of settlement of high-value transactions. Moreover, the means of payment used in various countries evolve through time; new means of payment are adopted and the transition from a stage where a certain means of payment is used by a relatively small group of individuals, to a stage where it is used by the majority of the population may take a long period of historical time. The point at which the acceptability of a particular means of payment is deemed to be sufficiently general to warrant classification as money is, therefore, a subjective matter on which different observers will often disagree. We can illustrate some of the problems involved in making definitive statements as to what money actually is by a brief survey of the historical evolution of means of payment in the UK.

Introduction

The commodity money stage

For most of the recorded history of the UK stretching back to antiquity the means of payment took the form of precious metals, usually silver, circulating in the form of coins. The coins contained a standardized quantity of metal guaranteed by kings or other ruling authorities in the form of a recognizable imprint or superscription placed upon them. By specifying a certain weight of precious metal for each coin, the issuing authorities established a monetary standard, and the unit which each coin represented came to serve as the unit of account in terms of which prices were expressed. After the Norman Conquest, for example, William the Conqueror established the standard that 240 silver pennies would comprise 1 lb weight in terms of silver and for accounting purposes 240 pennies were deemed equal to one pound;[6] this standard came to be referred to as the 'pound sterling'. In time the amount of silver in the coinage was gradually reduced by the issuing authorities (so that the coins consisted of a mix of silver and cheaper base metal) but despite this debasement of the monetary standard there was continuity in the use of pounds and pennies as the unit of account. Although gold coins were originally minted by Edward III in 1343 they did not come into common use until the eighteenth century. Eventually in 1816, the silver standard was abandoned and gold became the exclusive monetary standard, the value of a standard ounce of gold being set at £3 17s 11½d. Gold sovereigns of value equal to one pound containing an equivalent weight of gold became the principal coins, while other coins circulating became token money, i.e. coins whose intrinsic value in metallic content was below their face value.

The development of paper money

The use of paper money dates from the late seventeenth century and emerged as a by-product of the growth of a formalized banking system in the City of London. From the individual wealth-holder's viewpoint, although coinage constituted a convenient store of wealth, there were certain problems of storage, arising not so much from physical difficulties, but from the danger of theft. Accordingly the practice developed whereby wealthy individuals deposited coins with goldsmiths – craftsmen who worked with gold – and who by the nature of their trade were equipped with secure vaults. As evidence of deposit, individuals were given warehouse receipts stating their title to quantities of coin which were repayable on demand by the issuing goldsmith.

Although goldsmiths charged fees for such safe-deposit services, they became aware at an early stage that their business operations opened up further profitable opportunities. They came to realize that as the number of depositors grew the actual stocks of coin they were holding tended not to fluctuate a great deal; a law of large numbers tended to operate, the withdrawals of coin being made by some individuals in a given period were largely counter-balanced by new deposits being made by others, so that the net withdrawals of coin were small and predictable in relation to their holdings. Given that there existed in London at this time a community of traders prepared to pay interest for the privilege of borrowing coin, the goldsmiths took advantage of this stability in their stocks of coin by lending out a fraction, while retaining a sufficient quantity as reserves to meet probable net withdrawals. The goldsmiths thus evolved into what we now term as 'fractional reserve banks'; in balance sheet terms their liabilities in the form of promises to pay coin on demand were not fully backed by assets in the form of coin, a fraction of their assets would be tied up in the form of loans which were repayable only after some average time delay. The essence of the goldsmiths' banking operations was, of course, the judgement that up to a certain point the profitability of lending was sufficient to outweigh the risk that sufficient depositors would turn up during any particular period demanding redemption of their warehouse receipts for coin, in excess of the reserves actually being held.

In the initial period of the operations of these early banks, deposit receipts were assigned to particular named individuals. Towards the end of the seventeenth century, however, a crucial change occurred when receipts started being issued in the form of negotiable bearer certificates or promissory notes – a banker would pay coin to anyone presenting a note. Consequently deposit receipts evolved into bank notes; as an alternative to the rather cumbersome process whereby a purchaser of some commodity might make a payment by withdrawing coin from a bank and then physically transferring the coins to a seller, transactions could now be carried out by a simple exchange of bank notes, providing, of course, that the seller was prepared to accept them.

The spread of banking from London to the rest of the country took a considerable period of time and developed on a substantial scale only after 1750; with this gradual development bank notes started to circulate increasingly as a means of payment alongside commodity money. Obviously, the key to the wider acceptance of bank notes was the confidence held by individuals in their ability to convert the notes issued by private bankers into coin on

13

demand. Once any doubt developed regarding a banker's ability to redeem his notes, confidence often collapsed and the result was a bank run where numerous individuals holding notes attempted to withdraw coin. In these circumstances the conditions under which a fractional reserve bank could operate as a solvent going concern evaporated, the bank would be forced to suspend repayments and its notes consequently became worthless as a means of payment. This was not merely a theoretical possibility, the early history of banking in the UK and in other countries is replete with numerous examples of bank runs and failed banks. Moreover, the failure of an individual bank often led to a collapse of confidence in other banks and hence to widespread periodic crises for the banking system as a whole. The rather unstable nature of the banking system for a long period inhibited the wider acceptance of bank notes as a means of payment.

The emergence of deposit money

During the eighteenth century a further development in banking practice took place in London where the issues of private bank notes in circulation became increasingly dominated by those of a single bank – the Bank of England. From its inception in 1694 the Bank enjoyed a substantial reputation as the government's bank and, unlike other banks, which at the time were restricted to operate as private partnerships of no more than six partners, the Bank was constituted as a joint-stock company. Given the reputation of the Bank, its notes came to be regarded as more or less equivalent to coin with a similar risk of theft. Accordingly, other competing bankers gradually ceased to issue their own notes and developed business operations on the basis of Bank of England notes themselves deposited with them for safe-keeping; instead of issuing their own notes as receipts, customers were simply provided with written statements acknowledging that a bank had incurred a debt of a certain amount to the customer concerned, which was entered in the bank's ledgers and was redeemable either in Bank of England notes or coin on demand.

Given this development, the next natural step was to make these book entries transferable between individuals, in the same way as bank notes earlier had been made transferable. Depositors were permitted to write cheques on their accounts (i.e. written instructions to a bank to pay notes or coin to a specified person or bearer of the cheque) and the recipient of a cheque, if he also had a bank account, could present the cheque to his bank requesting that his account be credited with the stated amount. If the two parties to a transaction happened to have accounts at the same bank, the bank would then simply make book entries debiting the payer's account and crediting the payee's account. In effect, therefore, bank deposits started to circulate as a means of payment without any physical transfer of notes and coin being involved.

Obviously, there were certain complications with this procedure if the two parties involved kept accounts at different banks. Suppose an individual X with an account at bank A wrote a cheque for £50 in favour of an individual Y who held an account at bank B. Before creating a deposit for Y, bank B needed an equivalent asset in the form of notes and bank B would present the cheque to bank A for payment of £50 in notes; conditional on such a transfer bank B would credit Y's account, while bank A correspondingly would debit X's account. Thus an exchange of bank deposits between individuals often involved counterpart exchanges of Bank of England notes between banks. This physical transfer of notes was somewhat cumbersome and a logical next step was for the banks themselves to open deposit accounts at the Bank of England as a convenient means of effecting inter-bank settlements; payments could then be made by an appropriate debiting and crediting of banker's balances held at the Bank.

As early as 1773 the arrangements for inter-bank settlement were formalized further when the London banks established the Clearing House. Each business day banks would send representatives to the Clearing House and net positions between banks would be established. For example, if bank A was in possession of cheques to the value of £1,200 written on bank B, whereas B was in possession of cheques to the value of £1,000 written on A, then in net terms A had a claim on B for £200 and inter-bank settlement was then effected by an appropriate transfer of £200 from B's to A's account at the Bank of England. As payments by cheque grew in importance, the banks kept smaller quantities of notes and coin in tills to meet withdrawals by customers and larger accounts at the Bank to cover the ebbs and flows of inter-bank settlements; over time an increasing fraction of bank reserves constituted claims on the Bank.

Evolution in the nineteenth and early twentieth centuries

At the beginning of the nineteenth century, coins, Bank of England notes, bank notes issued by numerous provincial banks, and bank deposits were all serving to some extent as a means of payment, with considerable variation in the general acceptability of different instruments in different parts of the country. It was not surprising, therefore, that at this juncture there was considerable disagreement as to exactly what constituted money in the UK. By the end of the century, however, the monetary system had evolved in such a fashion as to produce more widespread agreement that in addition to coins, Bank of England notes and bank deposits had a sufficient degree of general acceptability to be classified as money. A number of developments contributed to this clearer situation.

1. During the early years of the nineteenth century the solvency of the Bank of England had been threatened on a number of occasions by crises of confidence in the banking system, but under the terms of the 1844 Bank Charter Act, the Bank, as far as the issue of notes was concerned, reverted largely to being a 'cloakroom bank' issuing notes only on receipt of a deposit of gold coin or bullion and conversely cancelling notes whenever a withdrawal of gold was made. Apart from a limited fiduciary issue of notes backed by government securities, Bank of England notes were fully backed by gold and thus the convertibility of the notes into coin was more or less guaranteed.

2. The 1844 Act restricted the note issue of other banks to the amounts in circulation at the time and the rights to this limited issue were to be forfeited and partially transferred to the Bank of England if a bank were forced to suspend payment, or merged with another bank to form a unit of more than six partners. In order to encourage greater stability in the banking system the government had relaxed the rules on the formation of joint-stock banks in Acts passed in 1826 and 1833, and in the years following 1844 banking business was reformulated along the lines of the purely deposit banks which had emerged previously in London. Throughout the second half of the nineteenth century the structure of banking was transformed by a series of mergers, which accelerated dramatically after 1890 to produce a highly concentrated structure. By 1914 commercial banking in England and Wales, apart from the Bank of England, was dominated by five large nationwide banks with extensive branch networks. By 1921 the paper currency in the UK was exclusively Bank of England notes apart from some notes still issued by the Scottish and Irish banks.

3. The acceptability of bank deposits as a means of payment was additionally enhanced by the adoption by the Bank of England of the role of 'lender of last resort' to the rest of the banking system. This role evolved pragmatically during a number of general crises of confidence in the banking system, when it was

discovered that if, in the early stages of a run on certain banks, the banks could continue to redeem their liabilities freely in the face of substantial net withdrawals of coin and Bank of England notes, then the very fact that they were redeeming their liabilities tended to assuage the fears of the public and restore confidence in the banks concerned. In order to maintain payments in such circumstances, fractional reserve banks needed to convert their non-reserve assets quickly (in the nineteenth century bank lending primarily took the form of discounting bills of exchange) into generally acceptable notes. As the ultimate source of such notes was the Bank of England, the appropriate tactic was for the Bank to buy (or rediscount), such assets from the banks in exchange for notes, or to lend freely to the banks on the security of such assets. The first instance of the Bank acting in this way was during a severe crisis in 1825 and by 1875 its role in this respect was clearly recognized by the Bank's directors;[7] this commitment underwrote the convertibility of bank deposits into notes.

The monetary system finally emerged in a close approximation to its modern form when in 1914, on the outbreak of World War I, the convertibility of Bank of England notes was suspended and gold coins were withdrawn from circulation. The suspension of convertibility meant that the paper currency became a purely token currency with no commodity money backing, but by this juncture the belief that notes constituted purchasing power had become more or less inbred in the minds of the population and the inconvertibility of notes made no difference to their general acceptability.

A classification of money for the present UK economy

A definition of money based on the means of payment criterion can be made somewhat more precise if, following Professor G. L. S. Shackle,[8] we define money as the generally accepted means of strictly simultaneous payment, i.e. it consists of the stock of various entities which would enable the holders to make payments at a given moment in time without receiving, or counting upon, the payments to be made to them from others.

According to this definition we would certainly include Bank of England notes and coin and there is now near unanimous agreement that current account deposits in banks (accounts on which cheques can be written) have a sufficient degree of general acceptability to be classified as money. There is, however, much less agreement on whether other types of bank deposit, such as traditional deposit accounts which nominally require seven days notice of withdrawal, should be so classified. Technically, cheques cannot be written on deposit accounts so that, strictly speaking, they are not a means of payment. On the other hand, it can be argued that, in practice, banks will transfer funds from deposit accounts into current accounts more or less on demand (albeit with a loss of seven days' interest) and all that is required is a book-keeping entry in the bank's accounts. Moreover, banks are often prepared to honour cheques drawn on current accounts with a zero balance, providing the account holder has a sufficiently large balance in a deposit account; many economists therefore would include seven day deposits on the grounds that the practical distinction between them and current accounts is nowadays negligible.

A further point of dispute in recent years concerns the question of whether it is now appropriate to include certain shares and deposits in building societies in the stock of means of payment. A case for inclusion can be made on the grounds that, in practice, many building society shares can be withdrawn on demand and hence many individuals probably regard them as essentially equivalent to deposit accounts in banks. Against this view, it can be argued that the inclusion of building society liabilities would not satisfy the criterion of simultaneity. Building society liabilities as such are not generally acceptable as a means of payment, and in order for an individual to spend by drawing down a building society account the building society must first provide the individual with notes and coin or current account bank deposits. In this case, a payment must be received by the individual before he can make a payment and the inclusion of building society liabilities in the stock of money would thus involve double counting.

According to Shackle's criterion we would thus, at this point in time, not count building society liabilities as money. This is so even though nowadays the holders of certain building society accounts are provided with cheque books. The writing of a cheque on a building society does not directly transfer a building society share account to another individual – rather the cheque is written on the building society's current account deposit in some bank; this arrangement therefore merely short circuits the more cumbersome process whereby, if an individual wished to make a payment, the building society would write a cheque on its bank in favour of the individual who would then pay the cheque into his own bank, before writing his own cheque.

Inevitably, though, there is some fuzziness at the margin in classifying money according to the means of payment criterion.

The importance of a precise definition, however, depends on the purpose in hand and an approximate classification of money as constituting notes and coin plus short maturity bank deposits, is sufficiently meaningful to be useful for purposes of describing the structure of the monetary and financial system. The need for a precise empirical definition of money becomes most important in the context of monetary policy, where the monetary authorities are seeking to influence the aggregate monetary expenditure of the community and have reason to believe that the stock of certain financial assets can exert predictable effects on this variable. For control purposes the authorities may therefore include certain assets in what can be termed an 'operational measure' of the money supply, and the criteria relevant for the construction of such an aggregate are wider than the simple means of payment criterion. We relegate further discussion of the problems involved in an empirical definition of money for monetary policy purposes to Chapter 12.

The value of money

A common complaint of UK citizens with memories stretching back to before World War II is that a pound isn't worth what it used to be. What they mean by this is that the quantity of real goods and services they could buy with a given sum of pounds was much greater then, than it is today, or, in other words, that the general purchasing power of money over goods and services, or the 'real value' of money, has declined markedly.

In practice, changes in the purchasing power of money over time can be gauged in a general fashion by observation of various general price indices that are compiled by government statisticians. A general price index is constructed by selecting a hypothetical bundle of given quantities of goods and services and then observing the money expenditure needed to purchase the bundle at periodic intervals. A particular date is chosen, known as the base date, and the money expenditure required to purchase the bundle on that date is assigned an index value of 100. The index value for future dates is then calculated by expressing the required money expenditure required to purchase the chosen bundle on those dates as a percentage of that required on the base date. For example, if on the chosen base date the required money expenditure was £204, while on a subsequent date the required money expenditure was £220, then the value of the price index for the subsequent date would be:

$$\frac{£220}{£204} \times 100 = 107.8$$

The change in the value of money over a given period will be the inverse of the change in the price index; obviously, if the money expenditure required to purchase a given bundle of goods and services increases, then the purchasing power of a given sum of money has correspondingly declined.

Percentage changes in the price level relative to the base date are easily ascertained; if the price index rises from 100 to 120 we know the average price of the goods included in the index has increased by 20 per cent. If we wish to ascertain the percentage change in the price level between any two dates other than the base date then the relevant formula is:

$$\Delta P = \frac{P_1 - P_0}{P_0} \times 100$$

Where ΔP is the percentage change in the price level, P_1 is the value of the price index at the end date and P_0 is the value of the price index at the starting date.

Consider a practical illustration from recent UK economic history. On 19 March 1974 the value of the General Index of Retail Prices stood at 102.6, while one year later on 18 March 1975 the index stood at 124.3. Thus, over the year, the percentage change in the price level (or the percentage decline in the real value of money) as measured by this index was:

$$\frac{124.3 - 102.6}{102.6} \times 100 = 21.2\%$$

The measurement of the change in the real value of money by any price index can only be an approximation. This is because the prices of the various goods and services included in an index rarely, if ever, move in exactly the same percentage fashion between any two dates. The movement of an index is therefore sensitive to the exact composition of the representative bundle of goods and services, the greater the relative quantity of a specific good in the bundle, the greater is the importance, or 'weight', attached to the movements in the price of this good in influencing the overall movement of the index. The choice of a different bundle will therefore usually produce a different result for the change in the value of money between any two dates. The most commonly used price indices in the UK are

1. *The General Index of Retail Prices* (RPI). The bundle of goods is designed to reflect the average expenditure patterns of UK households on consumer goods. The RPI is the basis for the calculation of the 'official' inflation rate in the UK which is calculated on a moving basis by comparing the value of the index, when published each month, with its value twelve months earlier; the inflation rate announced in October 1988 is thus the percentage change in the RPI since October 1987.
2. *The Wholesale Price Index*. This measures changes in the wholesale prices of various commodities ranging from raw materials to finished goods.
3. *The Implied Deflator for Gross Domestic Product* (GDP). This index includes, not only the prices of goods sold to consumers, but the prices of all final goods included in the calculation of GDP. The weight of particular goods in the index depends upon the quantities produced within the UK in the base year.

Money and other financial assets

Even in the most simple economies the existence of money permits individuals, in any given period, to separate their spending on real goods and services from the income they derive from their role as producers, or, equivalently, it breaks the rigid link between decisions to save and decisions to invest in real assets. Individuals can choose to save by restricting their spending to amounts less than their current incomes, holding over money balances to a future period while, equally, individuals with accumulated money balances held over from previous periods can spend amounts on goods and services greater than their current incomes by running their money balances down. During any period of time, therefore, there may co-exist two groups of individuals:

1. Those whose current money incomes exceed their total spending on real goods, both consumer goods and capital goods, who can be described as having a financial surplus. Equivalently, the savings of this group exceed their investment.
2. Those whose total spending on real goods exceeds their current incomes, who can be described as having a financial deficit. Equivalently, the investment expenditure of this group exceeds their savings.

The institution of money thus permits some specialization between individuals at any time in the acts of saving and investment. If money was the only financial asset as distinct from real assets the degree of specialization which could be achieved in this respect would, at the same time, be somewhat restricted; the deficit spending which individuals could undertake in any period would be limited by the size of their accumulated money balances. A further degree of specialization is possible in this respect, however, if there are no legal restrictions (as there have been at various times in the past) on loans of money from one individual to another. If there exist individuals who can perceive advantages in engaging in spending amounts greater than their current incomes and accumulated money balances, then there is scope for mutually advantageous transactions between such individuals and those who have financial surpluses or who hold accumulated money balances. By the offer of a certain price – some rate of interest – then individuals may be prepared to transfer money to other individuals in return for a promise (or more generally a prospect) of the delivery of money at some future date, or dates. By a 'rate of interest' is meant some stipulation in the terms of the loan agreement whereby, in return for making a loan of a certain sum for a given period, an individual will receive at the due date a larger sum of money constituting the return of principal with interest. Interest can thus be described as the rental price of money and is usually expressed as an annual percentage of the sum of money borrowed; if, say, a sum of £100 is lent for one year after which time a sum of £108 is due to be repaid, then the annual rate of interest is 8 per cent.

As a counterpart to the process where money is lent from one economic unit to another, there came into existence what can be termed as 'non-monetary financial claims', which in physical forms are records or documents of some sort defining the future claim which one party has on another. In balance sheet terms, such claims constitute a liability of the borrower and an asset for the lender and therefore constitute an alternative method of holding wealth, as distinct from holding money itself or real assets. This terminology is used to emphasize the fact that while certain financial claims constitute claims to future money, they do not themselves circulate as a means of payment and are thereby distinct from money within the general category of financial assets.

An alternative terminology often used to describe a loan transaction is to say that a borrower 'issues' or 'sells' a financial claim on himself, which is correspondingly 'purchased' by a lender;

when the borrower redeems the loan he subsequently 'repurchases' the claim from the lender.[9]

Historically speaking, the practice of money lending in various forms has occurred whenever economies have used money, and the essential role of the complex of institutions and markets which comprise the financial system is one of facilitating the transfer of funds (ultimately real resources) from financial surplus units to financial deficit units. The simplest form of financial transaction is the case where a borrower issues a financial claim purchased by a lender, in a single direct transaction between the two parties concerned, as where, for example, an individual acquires a bond issued by the government; in this instance the balance sheet effects of the transaction are confined to the two parties involved. In most economies, however, financial transactions are not always so straightforward owing to the interposition between ultimate borrowers and ultimate lenders of specialized financial intermediaries. Financial intermediation occurs when financial claims issued by ultimate borrowers – often referred to as primary financial claims – are purchased by financial institutions, who finance the acquisition of such assets by issuing separate claims on themselves – often referred to as secondary financial claims – which are then acquired by ultimate lenders. The relationship between ultimate borrowers and ultimate lenders thus becomes an indirect one via a financial intermediary, which both borrows and lends on its own account and, as a result, there come into existence financial assets and liabilities additional to those arising from the issue of primary claims by borrowers.

For example, an individual wishing to obtain funds for house purchase in the UK often transacts a mortgage loan from a building society, i.e. he issues a primary financial claim on himself, secured by the value of the relevant property, which is sold to the building society. The building society finances its acquisition of primary financial claims by the issue of secondary financial claims on itself, in the form of shares or deposits, which are then acquired by ultimate lenders. The liability the ultimate borrower incurs is not directly to the holder of building society shares, but to the building society itself; similarly the ultimate lender has a direct financial claim on the building society rather than the ultimate borrower.

The structure of financial claims in developed economies is often further complicated by the fact that (as our previous discussion of the evolution of forms of money in the UK established) the secondary claims issued by certain financial intermediaries, nowadays bank deposits, themselves circulate as a means of payment. A bank is clearly a financial intermediary in the sense we have defined it; it holds primary financial claims issued by borrowers and issues secondary financial claims on itself in the form of promises to repay notes and coin on demand or at short notice; an individual holding a bank deposit over time is, in effect, making a continual series of short term loans of notes and coin to a bank. However, when bank deposits become accepted as money, a crucial point to appreciate is that financial transactions involve not simply the lending of notes and coin, but of bank deposits themselves; a lender can make a loan by transferring a bank deposit to the ownership of the borrower in return for a promise of a future payment of, implicitly, a bank deposit. Thus, when bank deposits circulate as money, the financial claims issued by non-banks involve an additional 'tier', or 'layer', of credit – they constitute promises to deliver either notes and coin or bank deposits which, in turn, are the promises of banks to deliver notes and coin.

The tiered relationship involved in the structure of financial claims is the basis on which economists have traditionally distinguished banks from other financial intermediaries. Those institutions whose liabilities (at least in part) serve as a means of payment are classified as banks; non-bank financial intermediaries, such as building societies, insurance companies and unit trusts on the other hand, issue secondary financial claims that do not serve as a means of payment and their intermediary role involves the borrowing and lending (nowadays primarily) of the liabilities of banks.

We should note also that as financial systems develop in sophistication the structure of financial claims becomes even more complex, in that financial intermediaries borrow from and lend to other financial intermediaries; banks lend to other banks, insurance companies acquire securities issued by unit trusts, etc. The relationships between ultimate borrowers and lenders thus become even more indirect, involving more than one stage of intermediation.

Money, liquidity, and portfolio choice

In economies such as the UK with sophisticated financial systems a large number of non-monetary financial claims are issued and a recognition of this fact prompts a reconsideration of the role of money as a financial asset. Given that there are numerous alternative financial assets available, in addition to a decision as to the amount of financial wealth they plan to accumulate in a given period (the consumption-savings decision), individuals are faced with a further portfolio decision regarding the form in which they are going to hold their generalized wealth. What considerations will influence an individual's portfolio decisions and what role will money play as a financial asset?

At first sight other financial assets would seem to dominate money as a means of holding wealth, in that normally there exists a positive differential between the returns (or prospective returns) obtainable on other assets compared to those obtainable on money; thus non-monetary assets typically offer a prospect of greater appreciation in wealth over a given holding period. Money, however, does have advantages which must be weighed against its disadvantages in this respect (indeed it is postulated that the advantages of holding money explain why other assets exhibit positive interest differentials). To induce individuals to substitute other assets for money some incentive must be offered them to forego these advantages. The specific advantages involved in holding money are usually summarized by the global term 'liquidity'. Liquidity is a somewhat elusive concept which is often used by different writers in somewhat different ways, but generally speaking indicates the joint possession by an asset of two separable attributes which are termed as 'exchange convenience' and 'capital certainty' (or 'safety').

Exchange convenience

This refers to the ease with which specific forms of wealth may be converted into other forms of wealth or the consumption of specific goods and services without delay or loss of value. Because money is what it is, it can be transformed into something else with minimum time delay and minimum transaction costs (minimum loss of value in this sense) and thus has maximum exchange convenience. This attribute may be desired by wealth-holders simply because they plan to undertake a series of predictable expenditures in the time intervals between their periodic income receipts and they are holding wealth as a strictly temporary store of purchasing power. It may also be desired because the future is inherently uncertain and a variety of unforeseen contingencies or opportunities may arise where the individual desires a rapid conversion of generalized wealth into specific goods and services.

Other assets, it is postulated, are inferior to money as exchange convenient assets because they can only be 'spent' if they are first exchanged for money and, hence, some additional time delay or transaction costs will be involved. The additional time and costs will vary according to the particular asset being considered but might, for example, constitute

1. some period of time before a lender can demand repayment of a loan or complete the sale of a negotiable asset to someone else;
2. the personal time and effort involved in converting the asset into money, such as a visit to a branch office of a building society;
3. explicit costs in the form of payments to brokers for the quick sale of negotiable assets, such as stocks and shares, which can often amount to a significant fraction of the money receipts of a sale, particularly if the value of the assets being sold is fairly small;
4. the loss of value involved if an asset is sold quickly.

Capital-certainty

This attribute refers to the absence of the risk of fluctuations in the capital value of financial assets, or their general future purchasing power in terms of goods and services. The assumption here is that wealth-holders will value this attribute because, as a general rule, they are risk-averse (i.e. dislike taking risks) and thus have an intrinsic preference for financial assets which have highly predictable future purchasing power.

In general, an activity is considered to be risky in the economic sense if there is a range of variation in the possible financial outcomes. Suppose, for example, an individual is offered two alternative ways of being rewarded for carrying out an economic activity:

1. He can choose to receive a sure sum of £100 – no more, no less.
2. He can choose to be rewarded by the opportunity to participate in a lottery where he can draw either of two tickets; with the first ticket he receives £50, with the second he receives £150.

The second alternative offers the individual the same average return (or expected value) as the first in that if he performed the same activity a large number of times on average he would receive £100 per time – half the times he would draw a £50 ticket and half the times he would draw a £150 ticket. The second alternative is, however, more risky – for any single one-off performance of the activity the individual has a 50 per cent chance of receiving either £50 or £150. In these circumstances a risk-averse individual will always choose the first alternative. This does not imply that a risk-averse individual will never take risks, but will only do so if the average return he is offered is sufficient to overcome his inherent dislike of risk.

Again, at first sight, the characteristics possessed by money would seem to make it an asset with perfect capital-certainty – the future money value of £100 stored in the form of a bundle of £5 notes or a bank deposit will still be equal to £100 in the future, whatever the length of the holding period. Money, in this sense, would therefore seem to be clearly superior to certain financial assets like bonds or ordinary shares. Although the capital value of a bond is often fixed in terms of future money if the bond is held to maturity, there is a certain risk of default on the part of the borrower and, moreover, if the holder of a bond wishes to resell a bond prior to the redemption date, the price at which it can be sold cannot be guaranteed. The market price of a bond can alter dramatically over short periods of time and may rise above or fall below the price at which the bond was acquired, thus providing the holder with a realized capital gain or loss. Like bonds, ordinary shares are also subject to market fluctuations in their market value and thus are inherently risky assets in the capital value sense.

The status of money, however, as an asset with superior capital-certainty characteristics, does depend also on the risk of fluctuations in the future purchasing power of money. Constancy in the money value of an asset over time (or its nominal capital-certainty) is not sufficient to guarantee its real capital-certainty if the future general price level is unpredictable – if there is a rise in the general price level then anyone holding money or assets which promise to pay fixed sums of future money incurs a real capital loss and, in these circumstances, such assets can also be regarded as inherently risky assets. In periods when future inflation is regarded as uncertain, assets such as ordinary shares, which may be expected to maintain their real value in the face of inflation, or assets which are explicitly 'index linked' (i.e. assets where the sums of money for future delivery are adjusted to take account of changes in the general level of prices as measured by some price index) may come to be regarded as superior to money as regards their capital-certainty characteristics.

Near money assets

The concept of liquidity encompasses two characteristics of assets which may be ranked differently by different individuals and which are possessed in varying degrees by particular assets. The assess-

27

ment of the liquidity of an asset is therefore essentially a subjective exercise on the part of wealth-holders and it is not possible to rank different assets unambiguously on an objective scale.

None the less, certain assets would seem to have characteristics that render them only marginally inferior, if at all, to money in this sense and, as such, they are likely to be considered as extremely close substitutes for money as a means of holding wealth. Many types of building society shares are more or less equivalent in their capital-certainty properties to money, in that they carry the right to redemption of the sums originally deposited (there may be a certain risk of default on the part of the borrowing institution but this risk also applies to bank deposits), while various innovations in recent years have reduced what time delay and transaction costs were involved in converting such assets into money. As previously mentioned, many building society share holders are now provided with chequebooks and, in addition, have the facility of withdrawing notes in automatic machines outside normal office hours. Similarly a number of other assets such as National Savings Bank deposits, National Savings certificates and bonds very close to their redemption dates can likewise be regarded as only slightly inferior to money in terms of liquidity. In recognition of their very close substitutability to money proper as liquid assets, it is often common to refer to such assets as 'near money' or 'quasi money' assets, although again it is difficult to draw a precise boundary line separating such assets from other assets.

Notes

1 This aphorism is attributable to Clower, R. W. (1969) in the 'Introduction', Clower, R. W. (ed.) *Readings in Monetary Theory*, to Harmondsworth: Penguin Books, p. 14.
2 The term 'hypothetical' is used because examples of real world barter economies have never been recorded in history. Whenever voluntary exchange occurs so does the institution of money.
3 Cigarettes and brandy were widely used in practice as a means of payment in the aftermath of World War II in Germany.
4 For example, Goodhart, C. A. E. (1981) *Money, Information and Uncertainty*, London: Macmillan Press, p. 3.
5 This is not always the case. For example some prices in the UK were quoted for a long period in guineas even though no guinea coins or notes were circulating.
6 At this juncture no pound coins were minted given the weight of metal involved.
7 The Bank of England's role in this respect was rather inconsistent

with the provisions of the 1844 Bank Charter Act which restricted its powers to issue notes. In practice the provisions of the Act were not strictly adhered to and the government permitted the fiduciary issue on occasions to increase above the stipulated maximum.

8 Shackle, G. L. S. (1971) in Clayton, G., Gilbert, J. C., and, Sedgwick R. (eds) *Monetary Theory and Monetary Policy in the 1970s*, Oxford: Oxford University Press, p. 32.

9 This terminology has some advantages because it can encompass transactions in certain financial claims like perpetual bonds or ordinary shares where there is no obligation on the part of the receiver of funds to repay the sum initially subscribed by the provider of funds.

Further reading

Coghlan, R. (1980) *The Theory of Money and Finance*, London: Macmillan, Chapter 1.

Dennis, G. E. J. (1981) *Monetary Economics*, London: Longman, Chapter 1.

Harris, L. (1981) *Monetary Theory*, London: McGraw Hill, Chapters 1 and 14.2.

Harrod, R. F. (1969) *Money*, London: Macmillan, Chapter 2.

Moore, B. J. (1968) *An Introduction to the Theory of Finance*, New York: The Free Press, Chapters 1 and 4.

Morgan, E. V. (1969) *A History of Money*, revised edition, Harmondsworth: Penguin Books, Chapters 1, 2 and 3.

Appendix: Financial claims

A financial claim can be generally defined as a claim to the payment of a sum of money at some future date or dates. It may also, as in the case of bank deposits, constitute a claim to a future payment of a certain form of money such as notes and coin. The primary ways in which the contractual obligations associated with particular financial claims can vary are as follows:

1. A claim may specify payment of a single terminal sum of money winding up the contractual obligation on some future date known as the 'redemption date', or a sequence of periodic payments of money over some future interval of time, or both. For some claims no redemption date may be specified, only a promise of a sequence of periodic payments for the indefinite future.

2. Where a redemption date is specified the time difference between the original issue of the claim and the redemption date can vary; this time difference is described as the 'original maturity' of the claim, while the time difference between the present date

and the redemption date is described as the 'term to maturity'. For some claims the redemption date may be at the option of the holder or it may be a specific future date.

3. The future payments of money associated with particular claims may or may not be fixed at the time of issue – a stipulation may be built into a contract whereby the borrower or lender has the right to vary the payments involved. With some claims there is no definite promise of the payment of future sums of money, only a prospect of such payments.

4. Some claims when issued are non-negotiable and must be held to the redemption date by the original lender; others can be sold to different individuals prior to the redemption date.

These differing characteristics can be illustrated with reference to some of the main types of financial claims observed in practice.

Deposits

A deposit is simply a record of the liability of a financial institution to pay a fixed sum of money (or specifically notes and coin) to an individual or an institution in the future. Some deposits are payable at the option of the holder either on demand ('sight' deposits) or after a given period of notice; for other deposits there may be a fixed redemption date which in some cases is as long as five years from their original date of issue. Many fixed-term deposits are non-negotiable, but large-scale deposits in commercial banks are nowadays issued in the form of negotiable certificates of deposit. In this instance a depositor of a sum of money in a fixed-term deposit is given a certificate acknowledging the obligation of the institution concerned to the holder of the certificate; the original depositor has the option of selling the certificate to a third party and redemption of the deposit will be made to anyone holding the certificate at the maturity date.

Bills

A bill, or more precisely a bill of exchange, is a claim to a fixed future sum of money, known as the bill's face or 'par value', payable on a given date usually with an original maturity of under a year; commonly the redemption date of bills is three months after the date of issue. A bill bears no explicit statement about interest payable but as a bill is invariably issued at a discount on its par value the holder of a bill earns an implicit interest return or 'yield'. For example, if a bill with a par value of £100 and a maturity of three months is issued at £98 and held to maturity, the holder receives a yield of approximately 2 per cent per three months, or slightly more than 8 per cent per annum; the implicit interest rate is often termed the 'discount rate'.

Bills of exchange have a long ancestry as financial instruments and developed primarily as a way of formalizing trade credit granted by one merchant or manufacturer with respect to goods delivered by another. To illustrate: suppose company A supplies goods to company B on the understanding that B be given three months' delay before payment. To formalize the arrangement A (the drawer of the bills) sends a bill to B (the drawee), the wording of which would specify B's obligation to pay a certain sum of money after three months. B then accepts the bill by signing it and returning it to A. If A then wants money immediately rather than in three months' time he sells the bill, at a price of course below its par value, to another person or institution who is described as having discounted the bill and who then becomes entitled subsequently to receive payment from B. In effect the third party involved is making a short-term loan to the original debtor, and, in practice, bills may be rediscounted several times before they mature. Unless the reputation of company B is well known, the saleability of the bill is often enhanced by the further endorsement of the bill by a reputable financial institution. For a certain commission banks and other financial institutions are willing to provide a guarantee that the payment of the stated sum will be made in the event of default on the part of the debtor. In anticipation of the enhanced saleability which acceptance by a reputable financial institution provides, it is often the practice for companies to arrange for bills to be drawn directly on a bank.

Bills of this type arising from transactions involving the delivery of specified commodities are commonly described as 'trade bills'. A second type is known as a 'finance bill', which is simply a promise of future payment issued by borrowers seeking to raise short-term funds for unspecified reasons. The major types of finance bills issued in the UK are those issued by central government, known as Treasury bills, and bills issued by the local authorities.

Bonds

A bond is a claim which promises to pay future sums of money as interest at regular intervals over a number of years; the regular payments of money are known as 'coupon payments'. The promises may apply for a fixed number of years, at the end of which the bond is redeemed by payment of a terminal sum known again as the bond's par value. On the other hand, no terminal date may be precisely specified; for example, bonds known as 2½ per cent consolidated stock (popularly known as 2½ per cent consols) which were issued by the UK government in 1888 carried a promise that redemption would be 'on or after 5th April 1923 and, as yet, have not been redeemed. In other cases a range of dates may be specified for redemption. In the UK bonds are issued by the central government, local authorities, public corporations and private sector companies. Those issued by governmental authorities are commonly referred to as 'stocks' while those issued by private companies are described as 'debentures' or 'loan stocks'. Bonds, like bills, are negotiable claims and can be resold by their holders prior to their maturity.

Until fairly recently it was invariably the case that the coupon payments on bonds were fixed sums of money and par values were equal to the sums of money originally borrowed when the bonds were issued. If a purchaser of such a bond at the time of issue holds the bond to maturity, the yield, or annual rate of interest in money terms, is therefore fixed and equal to the annual coupon expressed as a percentage of the bond's par value. If, however, an individual purchases existing bonds and holds them to maturity, the yield, while fixed thereafter, will depend on the price at which the bonds were purchased and will vary inversely with the price.

The inverse relationship between the yield of a bond and its market price can be demonstrated most simply with reference to an undated stock such as 2½ per cent consols. If we assume that an investor purchasing a consol plans to hold the bond for ever, then he is buying the right to receive an annual coupon of £2.50 in perpetuity and the yield in this instance is derived purely from the annual coupon. The yield is then the annual coupon expressed as a percentage of the market price; if the price of a consol was £50 a coupon of £2.50 would represent a yield of 5 per cent, whereas if the price fell to £25 the yield would increase to 10 per cent. More generally, for a perpetual bond the yield is given by the formula:

$$r = \frac{100 \times C\%}{P}$$

where r is the yield, C the coupon and P is the market price. In this case, as the price of the bond varies, the percentage increase in yield is equal to the percentage decrease in price and vice-versa.

In the case of bonds with fixed redemption dates, the same inverse relationship between the price of a bond and the yield if held to maturity will apply, but the relationship is more complex as the terminal sum paid on the maturity of the bond must be taken into account. For example, a government guaranteed stock known as transport 3 per cent with a redemption date in 1988 was quoted on the market in August 1982 at a price of £75. The annual coupon on the stock is £3 but an individual holding a bond at the redemption date will receive repayment of the par value of £100. An investor purchasing a unit of stock in August 1982 and holding it to maturity thus makes a capital gain of £25 which, in effect, is equivalent to an annual yield over the six-year holding period additional to that represented by the coupon of £3 per annum. The shorter the term to maturity the greater is the yield equivalent to any given terminal capital gain; therefore a given percentage change in the market price of a bond produces a greater percentage change in the yields of bonds with shorter terms to maturity compared to those with longer terms to maturity.

It should be stressed that the yields on bonds whose coupons and par values are fixed in money terms are fixed only if the bonds arc held to maturity. Given that bonds compete with other financial assets as a means of holding wealth, the yields obtainable for prospective purchasers of bonds must be broadly comparable to interest rates on other financial assets. Thus if interest rates generally rise in a particular period, then the market price at which existing bonds can be sold must fall to a level sufficient to guarantee a purchaser a yield commensurate with the interest rate obtainable on other assets. If, therefore, interest rates display a tendency to fluctuate in an unpredictable fashion over time there will be similar fluctuations in the market prices of existing bonds. Thus the holder of a bond who sells it prior to maturity has no guarantee that the selling price will be equal to the price at which the bond was originally purchased and hence there is the possibility of a capital gain or loss; the yield on bonds for holding periods shorter than the time to maturity is thus subject to risk.

In recent years bonds have been issued with characteristics which differ from traditional bonds. Both the UK government and private borrowers have issued bonds on which the annual coupons are not fixed sums of money but vary in line with the current interest rate available on some other financial instrument. The UK government has also issued low coupon bonds at prices at a discount below par values so that the yield if held to maturity largely arises in the form of a terminal capital gain (such bonds are particularly attractive for taxpayers with high marginal rates of income tax as capital gains on government bonds are tax-exempt). Specifically in the UK a major innovation has been the introduction since 1981 of government index-linked bonds. The idea underlying the introduction of such bonds is to offset the disadvantages inherent in holding traditional fixed interest bonds in periods when the general price level is increasing. In these circumstances the real yield derived from holding bonds is reduced below the nominal yield. Although the nominal yield to maturity in money terms of a bond at a given time might, for example, be 10 per cent, if prices are rising at a rate of 8 per cent per annum the real yield – the appreciation in the bondholder's purchasing power over goods and services – would be only approximately 2 per cent per annum.

The characteristics of such bonds can be illustrated with reference to a government stock issued by tender in July 1986 known as 2½ per cent Index-Linked Treasury Stock 2016. The nominal par value of the stock is £100 but the actual par value in money terms is altered continually to maintain its real purchasing power constant as indicated by the General Index of Retail Prices. Suppose, for example, that the price index (with the base year of 1974) stood at 460 in 1993 compared to its actual value at the time of issue of 380. The par value of the stock in 1993 would then be 460/380 × £100 = £121.05 which constitutes the sum of money in 1993 which would have the same purchasing power as £100 had in 1986. The annual coupons paid in money terms in any particular year are equal to 2½ per cent of the adjusted par value appropriate to that year – in 1993, assuming that the price index stood at 460, the coupon would be 0.025 × £121.05 = £3.03. Likewise, the actual sum of money paid on redemption of the stock in 2016 depends on the value of the price index in that year. Thus the future sums of money promised to holders of the stock rise in such a way as to offset the diminishing purchasing power of money, thus leaving the real yield to maturity unaffected by inflation (symmetrically, of course, if the price level actually fell, the par value and annual coupons in money terms would be adjusted downwards). Index-linked bonds, like conventional bonds, can be resold before the date of maturity and the market price can fluctuate over time in the same fashion. Fluctuations in the market price of index-linked bonds will, however, be related to fluctuations in real interest rates rather than purely nominal interest rates, i.e. nominal interest rates minus the rate of inflation expected by holders of financial assets.

National savings certificates

National Savings certificates are a form of non-negotiable promissory note issued by the UK government which can be redeemed
at a time of the holder's own choosing. With traditional certificates
the sums payable on redemption after specified periods are fixed
in money terms; for example, if the rate of interest on a particular
issue is set at 8 per cent the purchaser of a £100 certificate is
guaranteed a sum of £146.9 if the certificate is held for five years.
Since 1975, National Savings certificates have also been issued in
index-linked form with redemption values being revised monthly
in the light of movements in the retail price index relative to the
date of purchase (when originally issued, index-linked certificates
became popularly known as 'granny bonds' as the right to buy
was initially restricted to old age pensioners, but in 1981 this right
was extended to the whole population). Index-linked certificates
are superior to index-linked bonds as assets with real capital-
certainty as the terminal index-linked redemption value is paid to
the holder whatever the length of his holding period in excess of
one year. Index-linked bonds are redeemed only on a certain
future date and an investor wishing to convert his bonds into
money before maturity must sell bonds in the market for whatever
price he can get.

Shares

This type of financial claim arises from the existence of joint-stock
companies who play a central role in the organization of the
modern UK economy. The purchase of an ordinary share issued
by a company, unlike that of the debenture, does not constitute
a loan with a fixed date of repayment; rather, it is a claim to the
ownership of a share of the real or financial assets of the company
which carries the right to a similar pro-rata share of any profits
earned by the company in a given period. Normally, but not
always, the possession of ordinary shares, or 'equities' as they are
often called, entitles the owner to voting rights at a company's
general meeting which, theoretically, is the sovereign body to
which corporate management is accountable and where issues of
company policy are decided. In practice, within the formal appar-
atus established by company law, corporate management often
has considerable discretion to formulate policy without frequent
consultation of shareholders.

The annual sums of money paid as dividends on ordinary shares
which constitute the distribution of profits to shareholders are thus

35

not fixed sums agreed in advance, but are contingent on a variety of circumstances which can affect the financial performance of a company. In practice, also, the sums distributed as annual dividends will depend on the decisions of corporate management as to the proportion of overall profits to be retained within the company as reserves – a normal procedure of most companies is the retention of profits to finance the acquisition of additional real assets.

A company is under no obligation to repay shareholders at any time the original sum subscribed when the shares were issued (in fact in the UK, company law severely limits a company's discretion to repay shares) and even in the event of liquidation there is no guarantee of any sum being repaid. On the other hand, if when a company is liquidated the sale of a company's assets is not sufficient to redeem the company's outstanding debts, the individual shareholder under the limited liability provisions of company law is not personally liable for any debts which may remain. A shareholder in a public limited company, however, is not irrevocably committed to holding any shares purchased – he can sell his claim to any other individual without the prior approval of the company. As with marketable bonds, though, the market price of particular shares can fluctuate considerably over time and a shareholder may incur capital gains or losses on his shareholding. A holder of ordinary shares is thus subject to risk with regard both to income and capital.

Within this general category of financial claim there are a variety of types of share with differing contractual entitlements. In some companies preference shares are issued which bear a specified rate of dividend which must be paid before any dividends are distributed to the ordinary shareholders; such shares usually do not carry voting rights, or at best, only limited ones. Preference shares are often cumulative – if dividends are not paid fully in a particular year the deficiency must be made good in subsequent years.

In recent years certain financial claims issued by companies have become popular which do not fit precisely into the general categories discussed hitherto.

Convertibles

These are issues of loan stocks which carry with them the option for the holder to convert them into ordinary shares of the issuing company on specified terms in the future. For example, in 1982 the UK company Habitat issued a 9½ per cent convertible loan-stock in the course of a takeover of the Mothercare chain of retail stores; the stock is redeemable in four equal instalments from

1998 to 2001 but before then the holder has the right to convert the stock into ordinary shares at the rate of £145 per 100 shares – the right being exercisable on 30 November in any of the years from 1985 to 1998. The advantage of convertible debt to the issuing company is that where the option of conversion to equity exists the coupon can be set lower than the going redemption yields on existing bonds.

Warrants

Warrants are options which give the holder the right to buy shares in a company at a given price in the future and are often issued with loan-stocks – when warrants are exercised new shares in a company come into being. Through time they usually become detached from the stocks with which they are issued and trade as securities in their own right.

Part two

An Overview of the Monetary and Financial System

Chapter two

Banks and the creation of money

Bank lending and the creation of bank deposits

In Chapter 1 we defined money in the modern UK economy as constituting notes and coin together with bank deposits and, in fact, the large majority of transactions, in terms of value, are conducted via an exchange of bank deposits. In the present chapter we explore the general processes which cause bank deposits to come into and go out of existence. A key point we seek to establish is that the commercial banking system, as a by-product of its normal business operations, can create bank deposits to an extent which far exceeds the amount of notes and coin being explicitly deposited in the banking system by the general public in any period. The determination of the money supply can thus be regarded as being, in part, dependent on the discretion of the commercial banking system and the general public, as well as on the decisions being made by the monetary authorities regarding the issue of notes and coin ('banks' in this discussion refer to institutions whose liabilities serve unambiguously as a means of payment).

To illustrate the essentials of the process of deposit creation by the banking system we can consider a simple example, where we compress institutional detail by assuming that fractional reserve banks hold just two categories of assets in relation to their deposit liabilities:

1. *Cash*, i.e. notes and coin held in tills, plus balances at the Bank of England which constitute claims which can be redeemed for notes and coin on demand.
2. *Loans*, by which we mean any financial assets acquired by a bank in transactions with the non-bank private sector of the economy. In reality (as described in a later chapter) banks hold a mix of different financial assets in their asset portfolios, but the

monetary effect of a bank's acquisition of any financial asset from the private sector of the economy is equivalent – it is a matter of indifference in this context whether, for example, a bank purchases an existing bond from a private individual, or makes an advance of money to that individual.

A fractional reserve bank will structure its balance sheet between these two asset categories by balancing its perceptions of risk against the profitability of lending and will choose what it considers to be an optimal portfolio. For numerical sumplicity we assume that each bank chooses to hold a prudential reserve of cash in the ratio of 10 per cent to its deposit liabilities, to cover contingent withdrawals of cash by customers and the demands of other banks in the course of inter-bank settlements. We assume also that there is a competitive banking system comprising a number of banks.

Assume initially that a member of the public makes a deposit of £1,000 in notes in a certain bank A at a time when the cash ratio is at the desired 10 per cent. The initial change in bank A's balance sheet is as follows:

BANK A

Liabilities		Assets	
Deposits	+£1,000	Cash	+£1,000
		Loans	0
	+£1,000		+£1,000

A bank deposit of £1,000 has come into existence, but this could be described as a 'passive' creation of deposits by the bank in response to the initiative of the member of the public. The monetary effect is neutral, the increase in bank deposits being exactly balanced by a reduction in the amount of notes in circulation outside the banking system. The increment of cash, however, earns the bank nothing and, as a profit-making concern, it will quickly seek to expand its earning assets and, on the basis of its optimal portfolio decision, will seek to make additional loans of £900, retaining £100 in cash as a reserve against its additional deposit liability of £1,000.

Assume bank A makes contact with a borrower and makes an advance of £900. The way this loan is arranged can vary, but assume that the bank creates in its books a deposit of £900 for the borrower on which he is given the right to draw cheques.

Momentarily, the change in the bank's balance sheet is transformed to:

BANK A

Liabilities		Assets	
Deposits	+£1,900	Cash	+£1,000
		Loans	£900
	+£1,900		+£1,900

However, the borrower will inevitably have some spending purpose in mind and presumably he will write a cheque for £900 in favour of another individual. What subsequently happens then depends upon how the recipient of the cheque acts. If he presents the cheque to bank A for payment in notes, cash immediately leaves the bank and the subsequent change in the balance sheet position becomes:

BANK A

Liabilities		Assets	
Deposits	+£1,000	Cash	+£100
		Loans	£900
	+£1,000		+£1,000

At this point the process stops, but by its initiative in making a loan the bank has increased the amount of notes in circulation by £900 which therefore constitutes a net increase of £900 in the money supply. Suppose, alternatively, that the recipient of the cheque has an account with bank B and pays the cheque into his bank, requesting that his account be credited. Bank B creates an additional deposit of £900 but will demand £900 in cash from bank A in the course of inter-bank settlement. Cash therefore again leaves bank A and its balance sheet position is identical to the case where the cheque was presented for direct payment in cash. The change in bank B's balance sheet now becomes:

BANK B

Liabilities		Assets	
Deposits	+£900	Cash	+£900
		Loans	0
	+£900		+£900

43

The banking system has thus actively created an additional £900 bank deposit. Bank B will similarly seek to expand its earning assets and if, as assumed, its desired cash ratio is 10 per cent, it will seek to lend an additional £810, retaining £90 as a cash reserve against its additional deposit liabilities of £900. If we assume again that the borrower writes a cheque for £810 in favour of someone who does not bank with bank B, cash leaves bank B and the change in its balance sheet position becomes:

BANK B

Liabilities		Assets	
Deposits	+£900	Cash	+£90
		Loans	+£810
	+£900		+£900

A further round in the expansionary process is thus initiated. If, during this process, no additional cash is withdrawn from the banking system by depositors, then the additional deposits created upon the increase in bank lending will be a diminishing series of increments equal to:

$$£900 + £(900 \times 0.9) \div £(900 \times 0.9^2) + £(900 \times 0.9^3) + \ldots$$
$$= £900 + £810 + £729 + £651.6 + \ldots$$

This is a convergent geometric series whose sum is equal to:

$$£900 \times \frac{1}{1-0.9} = £9,000$$

Thus, on the basis of an initial deposit of £1,000 of notes, the banking system has actively created additional deposits equal to £9,000 (so that in total bank deposits have increased by £10,000), with, of course, the connivance of the general public who are prepared to borrow sums from, or sell financial assets to the banks equal to this amount and who are prepared to hold the additional deposits created. In the course of the expansion, each individual bank increases its lending only after receiving a new deposit which has increased its cash and lends only a fraction of the cash received, but the banking system as a whole has 'manufactured' additional deposits.[1]

This simple sequence example should not be interpreted as a precise description of what happens in reality, as a number of complicating factors have been assumed away. In reality, increments of cash and deposits are likely to accrue simultaneously to several banks within the system, as are the subsequent gains of cash and deposits arising from bank lending; some lending may not involve cash leaving an individual bank if the borrower makes a payment to another customer of the same bank. These complications, however, do not affect the logic of the process as long as each bank tries to reduce the cash it is holding as a reserve against deposits to what is considered to be an optimal cash ratio. More importantly, the illustration assumes that the general public are content to hold all the additional bank deposits created (as opposed to withdrawing some of the increment to hold in the form of notes and coin) and, also, that there are always individuals willing to provide the banking system with the financial assets it desires to acquire. By making these assumptions we have thus ignored the question of the terms the banking system would have to offer to induce behaviour of this kind on the part of the general public, and thus avoided the question of whether it would be profitable for the banking system to engage in the creation of additional deposits to the numerical extent demonstrated. None the less, the example has pedagogic value as a general illustration of the process whereby a layer of bank deposits can emerge on the basis of a smaller underlying quantity of notes and coin.

On the basis of this illustration one can make a conceptual distinction between two processes giving rise to the creation of bank deposits.

1. If the general public makes net deposits of notes and coin in the banking system, then what one can call primary bank deposits are created; as a result the banking system's holdings of cash increase. The direct effect on the total money supply (i.e. the quantity of notes and coin plus bank deposits) held by the non-bank public in this instance is neutral.
2. Whenever the banking system makes advances to, or acquires assets from the general public, then secondary or derivative bank deposits are created.

The destruction of bank deposits

Symmetrical to the process of the creation of bank deposits is a reverse process by which bank deposits can go out of existence.

1. If notes and coin are withdrawn by depositors from the banking system there is a decrease in the cash held by the banks. Primary

bank deposits decrease, with again a neutral direct effect on the money supply.

2. If the general public buys assets from the banking system, or repays bank loans, or pays interest on bank loans by writing cheques on bank deposits, then the stock of secondary bank deposits decreases.

Consider, for example, a sale of bonds by a bank to a private individual. If the purchaser writes a cheque on a deposit held with the bank concerned, then the reduction in the bank's assets (i.e. bonds held) is matched by a simple cancellation of its deposit liabilities to the purchaser. If the purchaser pays by means of a cheque written on another bank, then the selling bank's deposits remain unchanged – the fall in its assets being held in the form of bonds being matched by an equivalent increase in its cash gained in the course of inter-bank settlement with the purchaser's bank. The purchaser's bank, however, loses cash and its deposit liabilities to the purchaser fall by a matching amount. Considering the banking system as a whole, therefore, cash is transferred between one bank and another leaving the cash position of the banking system unaffected, but there is a net decrease in bank deposits.

In practice, there are continual two-way transactions between the banking system and the general public. Bank lending in the aggregate thus increases bank deposits only to the extent therefore that it constitutes net lending in excess of repayments of loans, etc.

The direct influence of the Bank of England on the creation of bank deposits

Our analysis, thus far, has illustrated how net deposits of notes and coin by the general public result in the creation of primary bank deposits which, by also affecting the banking system's ability to lend, plausibly results in a further expansion in secondary bank deposits. Thus, even if the total supply of notes and coin is fixed, by inducing the public to hold a greater fraction of its assets in the form of bank deposits and a lower fraction in the form of notes and coin, the banking system can initiate increases in the money supply.

An expansion in primary bank deposits can also arise as a result of Bank of England transactions with the rest of the private economy outside the commercial banking system (i.e. the non-bank private sector). Suppose the Bank purchases existing financial assets in what are termed 'open-market operations'. The Bank pays for the assets purchased by cheques written upon itself and assume that the sellers of the assets pay the cheques into accounts held with commercial banks. The commercial banks create deposits for the recipients of the cheques and matching this increase in their liabilities the banks hold additional assets in the form of claims on the Bank. Recall that the commercial banks keep balances in the Banking Department of the Bank (Banker's deposits) which constitute part of their effective cash reserves; thus when the cheques in the banks' possession are presented to the Bank, the inter-bank clearing mechanism results in the Bank crediting Banker's deposits, and the banks' cash reserves are increased. As this increment of cash for the banking system does not diminish the cash held by the non-bank private sector, in this instance the increment in primary bank deposits constitutes a net direct increase in the money supply. Note that as the Bank of England is no longer required to redeem its notes for commodity money and can print notes in whatever quantities are necessary to redeem its deposit liabilities, there is now technically no limit to the additional claims it can issue upon itself in this way. Clearly an open market purchase of financial assets by the Bank – in the same way as net deposits of cash by the general public – may initiate a further multiple expansion of secondary bank deposits if the banks attempt to convert the increment of cash acquired into additional earning assets.

The Bank of England may also purchase financial assets from the banks themselves; there is, however, a difference between such transactions compared to Bank transactions with the non-bank private sector. In this instance, the Bank writes cheques on itself directly in favour of the banks concerned and the effect of such transactions is confined to the assets side of the banks' balance sheets – their cash balances at the Bank increase, while their holdings of other financial assets decrease in a matching fashion. There is thus a change in the composition of the banks' asset portfolios but no change occurs in their deposit liabilities and, hence, there is no direct effect on the money supply.

Symmetrically, open market sales of financial assets to the non-bank private sector or to the banks themselves exert effects working in the reverse direction.

Central government transactions and the creation and destruction of bank deposits

As described in the previous chapter, the Bank of England has, since its inception, served in the UK as banker to the central government – the vast majority of central government payments and receipts arising from transactions with the rest of the economy are channelled through accounts held in the Banking Department (public deposits). This institutional arrangement[2] has the important consequence that, in the UK, central government transactions with the non-bank private sector of the economy (or the rest of the public sector which banks with the commercial banks) result in the automatic creation or destruction of primary bank deposits.

Suppose, for example, the Department of the Environment makes a payment to a construction company of £5 million on the completion of a road project. The Department makes the relevant payment by writing a cheque for £5 million on the Bank of England and the construction company will almost certainly pay the cheque into an account held with a commercial bank; the bank creates an additional deposit of £5 million for the company concerned and at the same time in the course of inter-bank settlement, is credited with an additional £5 million in its balance at the Bank. Thus any payment made by the central government to the non-bank private sector, in itself, automatically increases bank deposits in a direct fashion while simultaneously increasing the cash reserves of the banking system (assuming, of course, that the recipients of the cheques do not redeem them directly for notes and coin – if they do, then the increase in the money supply takes the form of additional notes and coin in circulation outside the banks).

Symmetrically, of course, any payment made by the non-bank private sector to the central government, whether it be with respect to the payment of taxes, or purchases of newly-issued government securities, or purchases of shares in privatized government enterprises, in itself, will have an opposite automatic effect on bank deposits. In this instance cheques will be written on the banks in favour of the government and the result is a direct decrease in bank deposits with an equivalent matching decrease in the banks' cash reserves.

In the same way as in our previous discussion of Bank of England open market operations, we can also make a distinction between central government transactions with the non-bank private sector and transactions with the banks themselves.

Suppose the government redeems maturing government securities held by the banks. In this case the effects of the payment made by the government are again confined to the assets side of the banks' balance sheets – bank balances at the Bank are increased but this increase in cash is matched by a decrease in their holdings of government securities; hence such transactions have no direct effect on bank deposits. In the reverse case where the banks make payments to the government, say, with respect to the acquisition of newly issued government securities, the result is that the banks hold less cash and more government securities, but again their deposit liabilities are not directly affected.

In the UK the institutional position in this latter respect is complicated (but not fundamentally affected) by the fact that the banks do not usually transact directly with the government to acquire certain newly issued short-term government securities such as Treasury bills. Instead, as described more fully in a later chapter, the banks make short-term loans to intermediaries known as discount houses who use the funds to tender for newly issued bills. Technically, therefore, government borrowing from the banks is often indirect and results in an increase in the commercial banks' balance sheet item 'money at call and short notice' rather than directly in their holdings of government securities; the banks' cash reserves, however, decrease in the same way as if they had acquired newly issued bills directly.

Central government budget deficits and the money supply

The principles established in the previous section can now be applied to consider the monetary effects of central government budget deficits, i.e. situations where the government's expenditure on goods and services, transfer payments, etc., exceeds in some period the tax revenues that it is receiving.

Considered in itself, a government budget deficit will have an automatic effect tending to increase directly the stock of bank deposits; the flow of payments being made by the government to the non-bank private sector (government expenditure) exceeds the flow of payments in the reverse direction (taxes) and, hence, the rate of creation of bank deposits exceeds the rate at which they are being extinguished. However, these automatic monetary effects of a budget deficit can be completely neutralized if the government borrows amounts from the non-bank private sector, by way of the issue of bonds or non-marketable debt such as national savings certificates, of exactly equal magnitude to the deficit involved. In this instance total payments made by the non-bank private sector to the government, which now comprise taxes plus payments for newly issued bonds, exactly match the payments being made by the government; therefore, the expansionary effect of government expenditure on bank deposits is completely offset by the contractionary effect of the flow of payments in the opposite direction; the net flow is zero and hence there is a zero overall effect on the stock of bank deposits. If, however, the magnitude of the budget deposit in any period exceeds the sums raised by government borrowing from the non-bank private sector, i.e. the government has what is sometimes termed a 'residual financial deposit', then it follows quite simply from the previous argument that as a consequence the stock of bank deposits must automatically increase.

Now in a situation where the government has a residual financial deficit, in a book-keeping sense it will be running down its account in the Banking Department of the Bank of England and must obtain funds from somewhere. All that technically need happen in these circumstances, however, is for the Bank to act as lender of last resort to the government by making it what is termed a 'wages and means advance'. In accounting terms what happens to the Banking Department balance sheet entries is that, as the government writes cheques, the liabilities entry bankers' deposits is increased as the banks present the cheques to the Bank and this increase is matched on the assets side of the account by an increase in the item 'government securities' (i.e. there is an increase in the nominal financial claims held by the Bank of England as a separate institution on the central government); in effect, the Bank permits the government to overdraw on its account. In these circumstances the increase in the stock of bank deposits is matched by an increase in the bank cash reserves and there is thus a possibility of additional secondary bank deposits being created if the banks respond to the increase in their cash ratios by attempting to increase their lending to the non-bank private sector.

The Bank as agent for the government may, however, depending upon the monetary policy stance it deems appropriate at the time, seek to finance a residual financial deficit by issuing securities which might be taken up by the banks, thus offsetting the increase in the banks' cash reserves which results from ways and means advances by the Bank itself. A common practice in the UK, for example, has been for residual financial deficits to be accompanied by the more or less simultaneous issue of Treasury bills taken up by the banks via the discount houses. The purchase of additional Treasury bills by the banking system offsets the increase in the banks' cash reserves that is automatically occurring as a result of the residual deficit, but as previously argued, such transactions affect the composition of the banks' assets and not their deposit liabilities. Thus the issue of additional Treasury bills does not offset the direct impact effect of such a deficit on the stock of bank deposits and in no way nullifies our previous conclusion that the stock of bank deposits must increase.

What the issue of Treasury bills plausibly affects,[3] however, in the monetary context is the existence and magnitude of any increase in secondary bank deposits arising from increased bank lending to the non-bank private sector. The issue of additional Treasury bills, other things being equal, will lead to changes in interest rates which can affect the portfolio preferences of the banks and the public and the banks' willingness and ability to make additional loans. Conceptually speaking, in certain limiting cases the secondary effects may be zero. Such a case is very simply illustrated in case 1 in Table 2.1, which shows some hypothetical balance sheet changes that might arise consequent upon a residual financial deficit of £100 million.

In the table, what is termed the 'impact effect' shows the immediate balance sheet changes, given an assumption that the emergence of a residual financial deficit is unforeseen by the Bank and is temporarily financed by a ways and means advance. The 'final effect' illustrates the position where we take into account a subsequent increase in the Treasury bill issue of £100 million together with an assumption that the banks choose to use the increment of cash entirely to make additional call loans to the discount houses which are used to purchase the additional bills on offer. All that subsequently happens in this instance is a switch in the asset portfolios of the banks; the final increase in bank deposits is equal to the initial increase, and the Treasury bill issue can be regarded as having completely absorbed the additional cash injected into the banking system. The conclusion in this regard would have been identical if the banks, as opposed to making additional loans to the discount house, chose to use the increment of cash entirely to purchase new issues of longer maturity government securities.[4] We should note, additionally, that the proceeds of the Treasury bill issue wipe out the technical indebtedness of the government to the Bank of England.

However, in a fractional reserve banking system there is obviously some probability that a residual financial deficit may initiate an expansion in bank lending to the non-bank private sector and hence an expansion in secondary deposits. For illustrative purposes one can again consider a simple example of such an

Table 2.1 Illustrative balance sheet changes consequent upon a residual financial deficit of the central government

---

Case 1   Zero secondary effect

Impact effect

Bank of England (Banking Dept)				Commercial banking system			
Liabilities		Assets		Liabilities		Assets	
Bankers'		Government					
Deposits	+100	Securities	+100	Deposits	+100	Cash	+100
....	......	....	......	....	......	....	......
	+100		+100		+100		+100

Final effect

Bank of England (Banking Dept)				Commercial banking system			
Liabilities		Assets		Liabilities		Assets	
Bankers'		Government					
Deposits	0	Securities	0	Deposits	+100	Cash	0
....	......	....	......	....	......	Money at call, bills	+100
....	......	....	......	....	......	....	......
	0		0		+100		+100

Case 2   Positive secondary effect

Final effect

Bank of England (Banking Dept)				Commercial banking system			
Liabilities		Assets		Liabilities		Assets	
Bankers'		Government		Deposits			
Deposits	+10	Securities	+10		+500	Cash	+10
						Money at call, bills	+90
....	......	....	......	....	......	Securities	+25
						Advances	+375
	+10		+10		+500		+500

All figures are in £ million.

expansionary process, similar to our earlier example, the end result of which is shown as case 2 in Table 2.1, where it is assumed that the impact effect is as in case 1. Here, anticipating a more detailed discussion of the asset structure of banks,[5] we assume that banks hold four categories of assets, but again unrealistically, we assume that they are held in rigid desired ratios to total deposits as follows: cash 2 per cent, money at call and bills 18 per cent, marketable securities 5 per cent, and advances 75 per cent. In considering the transition to the final effect it might be helpful to imagine the impact effect being concentrated on a single 'bank A' whose deposits and cash initially increase by £100 million. Bank A then responds to the increment of £100 million in its cash by allocating £2 million to cash, £18 million to money at call and bills, £5 million to securities and £75 million to advances. Assuming that the £18 million allocated to money at call is used by the Discount Houses to acquire newly issued Treasury bills, that the securities purchased by the banks are existing securities held by the non-bank private sector and that the ultimate recipients of the payments made by bank A and its borrowers bank with 'bank B', then bank B experiences an increase of £80 million in its deposits and cash. Bank B in turn allocates £1.6 million to cash, £14.4 million to money at call and bills, £4 million to securities and £60 million to advances, etc., etc., the limit of this process being the final effect shown in the table where deposits have increased by £500 million. In this case the banks indirectly would have taken up an additional £90 million of Treasury bills.[6]

Both cases 1 and 2 depicted in Table 2.1 can be regarded in practice as unlikely polar cases and the reality probably lies somewhere in between. None the less, they demonstrate the importance of distinguishing clearly between the direct effects of a government residual financial deficit and the secondary effects which may be initiated. It also follows that in the case where the sums raised by new issues of government securities to the non-bank private sector exceed the central government budget deficit then there is direct contractionary impact on the stock of bank deposits.

The external balance of payments and the money supply

The UK in reality is very much an open economy; UK residents buy and sell both goods and services and financial assets from and to overseas residents. Because different countries use different national monies then a payment made by a UK resident to a foreign resident will usually involve at some stage a transaction where foreign currency (meaning by 'foreign currency' primarily deposits in foreign banks rather than physical notes and coin) is purchased with domestic currency. If a UK importer, say, is making a payment for commodities purchased from a US exporter then, either the UK importer will buy dollars with sterling and make payment in dollars, or the US exporter may receive payment initially in sterling and subsequently buy dollars with sterling.

The actual mechanisms by which transactions between domestic residents and foreign residents are conducted invariably involve banks in the two countries concerned. There are various ways in which foreign payments may be arranged, but in the case above, for example, the UK importer might arrange with his local bank for payment to be made using telegraphic or cable transfer. UK banks have correspondent banks in the USA with whom they hold dollar accounts and a telegraphic transfer simply involves an instruction to a correspondent US bank to debit the dollar account of the UK bank concerned and to credit the dollar account of the US exporter in some US bank. The UK importer pays his bank for this dollar deposit by writing a cheque on his bank account, the amount of sterling involved being dependent on the current exchange rate determined in the 'wholesale' foreign exchange market where UK banks buy and sell dollar deposits held in the US banking system. It therefore follows that, in itself, any payment made by a UK resident to abroad involves the extinction of sterling bank deposits as the bank debits the account of the customer concerned, the reduction in the bank's sterling liabilities being matched by a reduction in its dollar assets.

Symmetrically, any payment received by a UK resident from abroad, in itself, will usually result in the creation of sterling bank deposits. Suppose a UK resident receives a payment from a US resident who simply mails a cheque drawn on a US bank. The UK resident, assuming he wants sterling, pays the cheque into his bank requesting that his account be credited with the sterling equivalent; in effect the UK resident sells dollars to the bank in exchange for a sterling bank deposit. The UK bank subsequently mails the cheque to its US correspondent bank requesting that its dollar balance be credited; the US bank concerned credits the UK bank's dollar account, at the same time presenting the cheque to the US bank on which it was drawn, hence receiving additional dollars in its account with the Federal Reserve System in the course of the US inter-bank clearing mechanism. Thus in this case the increase in sterling bank deposits is matched by an increase in the bank's dollar assets.

It therefore follows that whenever the total payments (i.e. both for 'current' transactions and 'capital' transactions involving financial assets) received by UK residents from abroad exceed the total payments being made by UK residents to abroad – whenever during a particular period there is a balance of payments surplus – then the stock of sterling bank deposits will increase. Vice-versa, if there is a balance of payments deficit then the stock of sterling bank deposits will decrease.

The extent to which the balance of payments, in practice, will affect the stock of sterling bank deposits depends ultimately on the attitude taken by the central monetary authorities. Suppose during a particular period the UK balance of payments with abroad started to run into deficit. In this instance, consideration of the international payments mechanism implies that the foreign currency deposits held as working balances by UK banks in correspondent foreign banks would be diminishing and, as such working balances are limited, individual banks will therefore be seeking to purchase additional foreign currency deposits in the wholesale market to implement the excess payments being made abroad by UK residents. As the banks collectively attempt to purchase additional foreign currency deposits, the result is excess demand for foreign currency in the wholesale market and consequently the sterling price of foreign exchange would increase (inversely the foreign currency price of sterling would decrease), the price in the market moving as necessary until the quantity of foreign currency being demanded from the banks was brought into equality with the quantity of foreign currency being supplied to the banks. If, in fact, exchange rates in the foreign exchange market were allowed to float freely then, apart from temporary disturbances capable of being absorbed by changes in the banks' working foreign currency balances, the balance of payments deficit (or surplus) would be constrained to zero and the stock of domestic bank deposits would not be subject to disturbance from this source.

If, however, the authorities wish to stabilize what would otherwise be frequent fluctuations in exchange rates, or they wish to minimize deviations from some chosen target exchange rate, they may intervene in the foreign exchange market. In the UK the official agency for intervention in the foreign exchange market is the Exchange Equalisation Account (EEA), operated by the Bank of England on behalf of the government, which holds foreign currency deposits, or other short-term foreign financial assets, constituting the official reserves. Suppose that during a certain period the authorities have some target exchange rate in mind, but that at this exchange rate there emerges a balance of payments deficit of £20 million. In these circumstances, to prevent the foreign exchange price of sterling depreciating, the authorities would have to intervene in the foreign exchange market selling to the banks £20 million of foreign currency deposits held by the EEA which the banks need to implement the desired net payments of UK residents to foreigners. The banks, in exchange for the foreign currency provided, make payments of £20 million in sterling to the EEA; thus, matching the direct reduction in sterling bank deposits there is now a reduction in Bankers' deposits at the Bank of England. Conversely, at the chosen rate there may emerge a balance of payments surplus. In this instance, the authorities would intervene in the foreign exchange market to prevent the foreign currency price of sterling appreciating by buying foreign currency deposits from the banks, which then constitute an addition to the official reserves held by the EEA. The EEA purchases involve cheques written on the Bank of England in favour of the banks; thus matching the direct increase in sterling bank deposits there is an increase in Bankers' deposits at the Bank. Therefore official exchange rate intervention simultaneously affects the stock of sterling bank deposits and the banks' cash reserves and, hence, results in changes in the bank's cash ratios. In addition to the direct impact on the stock of bank deposits, there is therefore the possibility of further changes in secondary bank deposits if the banks respond to their changed cash position by either increasing, or reducing, their lending to the non-bank private sector.

The external effects on the stock of domestic bank deposits therefore depend crucially on the attitude of the monetary authorities to the exchange rate. At the limit, under a fixed exchange rate regime, where the authorities aim to maintain implicitly the exchange rate at a certain value, then the state of the external balance of payments will constitute a significant influence on the stock of bank deposits. In the past, however, in periods when fixed exchange rate regimes have been in operation, the monetary authorities in various countries have often attempted to nullify the external effects on the domestic money supply by offsetting open market operations: such offsetting policies are termed sterilization policies. In the case of a balance of payments surplus, for example, the monetary authorities would simultaneously issue additional securities to the non-bank private sector, which, as we have seen, would exert contractionary effects on bank deposits, thus offsetting the expansionary effects of the balance of payments surplus. Whether or not sterilization could be successful in the long run in the face of continuing external imbalance is, however, a matter on which there is considerable disagreement.

Banks as financial intermediaries

The apparent powers of the banking system to create money by bank lending prompts the question of whether it is appropriate to regard banks as being essentially equivalent to other financial intermediaries in the sense defined in Chapter 1. In the example we used to illustrate the process of creation of secondary deposits, although each bank could regard itself as only lending out cash received by way of prior deposit from the public, the sum of these individual acts of bank lending resulted in a net creation of bank deposits by the banking system as a whole. This result seems to run counter to the notion that financial intermediaries are institutions which 'convey' or 'transmit' existing money balances released by net savers or financial surplus units to net spenders or financial deficit units – it now seems as if the banking system can lend and create funds for financial deficit units without prior saving on the part of other individuals in the economy.

This may be correct at the immediate moment when additional bank lending to financial deficit units takes place, but, eventually, bank intermediation must result in the emergence of financial surpluses somewhere in the economy to match the deficit spending being financed by bank lending. As a counterpart to a net increase in bank lending, additional financial assets – bank deposits – come into existence which, ultimately, must be willingly held by some individuals, and the acquisition of such assets requires additional savings on the part of the individuals concerned. As institutions for effecting transfers of claims on real resources, banks are thus functionally analogous to any other type of financial intermediary.

At the same time, we should note some peculiarities regarding intermediation by banks. In the first place, once bank deposits become widely used as a means of payment, some individuals receiving incomes in the form of transfers of bank deposits to their account from someone else's account, may choose to save by simply allowing their bank balances to accumulate. Suppose, for example, an individual receives a monthly salary of £1,000 paid by direct transfer to his bank account from his employer's bank account and that each month he writes cheques on his account equal to £800; he thus saves £200 a month in the form of an accumulating bank balance, but this act of saving, in itself, does not affect the ability of the banking system as a whole to make additional loans. The ability of the banking system to make loans is constrained by its prudential reserves of cash, but an individual's decision to save via accumulating a bank balance does not generate any additional cash for the banking system as a whole. All this individual act of saving does is to change the distribution of bank deposits between individuals (although in consequence there may also be redistribution of cash held in the banking system to the saver's bank at the expense of other banks). In these circumstances, the banking system may be powerless to intermediate between potential borrowers of funds and individuals who choose to save in this form if, for example, it regards its ratio of cash to deposits as being at the absolute minimum it considers necessary for prudential purposes and cannot obtain additional cash from the public at interest rates which would make additional bank lending profitable.

The banking system, however, may be able to intermediate in such circumstances if it can obtain additional cash profitably from the public, or as a result of the actions of the monetary authorities, or if it is in a position where the profitability of bank lending is such that it would be prepared to reduce its ratio of cash to total deposits. To match the bank deposits being accumulated by savers, the banking system can create new bank deposits for financial deficit units – thus in effect transferring the purchasing power from those who choose to save in this form to those who wish to spend.

On the other hand, the banking system may at particular junctures, dependent on its cash position, be in a position where it can make loans to financial deficit units initially in excess of the savings being made in the form of desired accumulations of bank deposits. The deficit units presumably will use the created deposits to buy goods and services; the sellers of such goods and services may accept bank deposits because they are a means of payment, but may not demand them in the sense that they desire to hold them as an increment to their desired stock of bank deposits, i.e. the stock they desire to hold on average over time. Instead they may spend the bank deposits received, transferring their deposits to other individuals, so that the spending of deficit units is not immediately matched by savings on the part of someone else in the form of bank deposits. Bank lending may therefore, in principle, initiate an increase in aggregate spending which, eventually, via changes in real income and/or prices will cause the quantity of bank deposits which individuals desire to hold to increase. At some point, some individuals will restrict their spending to accumulate the additional deposits created and, therefore, in an ex-post sense, the banking system will have intermediated between financial deficit and financial surplus units. The distinctive feature of banks (or at least some of the institutions nowadays described as banks) is that the secondary financial claims they issue serve as money and, as such, bank intermediation may plausibly have more significant macroeconomic effects than other types of financial intermediation – the point being that the ability of the banking system to make loans is not necessarily related at any moment in time to the amounts the community wish to save via accumulations of bank deposits.

The relationships between banks and other financial intermediaries

In Chapter 1 we argued that once bank deposits serve as money then the financial claims issued by non-bank financial intermediaries can be regarded as constituting an additional 'tier' of credit; what NBFIs borrow and lend are nowadays primarily bank deposits and not simply notes and coin. Thus when an individual acquires a secondary financial claim issued by an NBFI, the transaction often takes the form of the individual writing a cheque on his bank account transferring a bank deposit to the ownership of the NBFI concerned. The immediate consequence is a change in the ownership of bank deposits but no diminution in the total in existence. When an NBFI, in turn, acquires primary financial claims, then the institution concerned writes a cheque on its bank account transferring bank deposits to someone else; the banking system is involved in this process, but its role is essentially confined to that of administering the payments mechanism, i.e. simply one of transferring deposits in its ledgers.

The tiered relationship between banks and NBFIs is often a source of some confusion, but in Table 2.2 we construct a simple example to illustrate what happens when an individual deposits a certain sum in an NBFI, say a building society, by writing a cheque on a bank account. The first element in the table illustrates the initial balance sheet change following a deposit of £1,000 made by an individual A in a building society. The building society incurs additional liabilities in the form of A's deposit of £1,000 and acquires additional assets in the form of an increase of £1,000 in its bank deposit. The distribution of bank deposits has altered; A's deposit is reduced by £1,000, that of the building society is increased by £1,000, but there is no change in the total quantity of bank deposits (although if the building society has an account in a different bank, one bank will lose deposits and cash and another will gain deposits and cash). The building society thus has extra deposit liabilities on which it has to pay interest and will presumably seek to convert a fraction of its additional bank deposits of £1,000 into assets which earn higher returns. Assume that it subsequently makes an additional loan of £800 to an individual for house improvement, acquires £150 worth of existing government securities from members of the public and retains £50 as liquid reserves in bank deposits. The second element of the table illustrates the subsequent balance sheet changes: the distribution of the banking system's liabilities is again altered, the final increase in the building society's deposit becomes £50 while other

Table 2.2 An example to illustrate the effects of a switch by an individual from a bank deposit to a building society deposit

1. *Balance sheet changes consequent upon a deposit of £1,000 by individual A in a building society*

£

Banking system		Building society		
Liabilities	Assets	Liabilities		Assets
			Bank	
A's deposit −1,000		A's deposit +1,000	deposits	+1,000
Building society's				
deposit +1,000		....	....	....
0	0	+1,000		+1,000

2. *Subsequent changes as the building society lends*

£

Banking system		Building society		
Liabilities	Assets	Liabilities		Assets
			Bank	
A's deposit 0		A's deposit 0	deposits	−950
Building society's			Government	
deposit −950		....	securities	+150
			Mortgage	
Other +950		....	loans	+800
deposits 0	0	0		0

individuals to whom the building society has lent or from whom it has acquired government securities now hold additional bank deposits of £950. Thus the building society has acted as an inter-mediary transmitting existing bank deposits from individual A to other individuals but again there is no diminution in the stock of bank deposits.

This example needs some qualification, in that had the building society acted differently in certain ways, then there might have been some reduction in bank deposits. If the building society had chosen to hold additional liquid assets in the form of cash, i.e. notes and coin, as opposed to bank deposits then the banking system would have incurred some loss of deposits. In practice, building societies do hold reserves of cash but these are very small in relation to their holdings of bank deposits.[7] Equally, if the government securities acquired by the building society comprised newly issued securities rather than existing securities, so that the cheques written were in favour of the government, then this in itself would have caused bank deposits to diminish, although had the government subsequently spent the equivalent of the sums borrowed, bank deposits would be restored to their original level. The general principle is that, as long as the assets held as liquid reserves by NBFIs do not duplicate those held by the banks, there is unlikely to be a decline in the stock of bank deposits consequent upon the purchase of NBFI financial claims by bank depositors.

Although non-bank financial intermediation does not in general have much effect on the stock of money, this does not mean that such intermediation is incapable of initiating increases in aggregate spending in the same fashion as intermediation by banks. If the lending of NBFIs corresponds to inflows of funds that constitute current savings on the part of individuals, then the spending of borrowers receiving funds from NBFIs is immediately matched by a reduction in spending elsewhere and the effect on aggregate spending can be considered neutral. However, in certain periods, it is possible that individuals may acquire non-bank secondary claims as a result of portfolio switches where they substitute such claims for previously accumulated money balances being held idle; equally an NBFI can increase its lending in excess of any inflow of new funds if it is prepared to reduce the money balances that it is holding as a liquid reserve. Thus again, in principle, NBFIs can increase their lending to financial deficit units without there being equivalent matching financial surpluses and increases in aggregate spending can be initiated; in effect non-bank financial intermediation can increase the velocity of circulation of existing bank deposits. While this is so, many economists consider that the effect of bank intermediation in this respect is likely to be more significant, in that there is plausibly a much greater correspondence between NBFI lending and current savings than is the case with bank lending.

In practice in the UK, the distinction between banks and NBFIs in the sense defined here is now confused by the fact that the liabilities of some institutions referred to as 'banks' do not always circulate as a means of payment. Such banks, often classified as 'secondary' or 'wholesale' banks, issue liabilities which are promises to repay the deposits of other banks whose deposits do circulate as a means of payment in the way described hitherto; those banks who carry out the historical functions which emerged in the nineteenth century are now often referred to as 'primary' or 'retail' banks. There thus exists a tiered relationship between institutions within what is conventionally classified as the banking system and some banks can be considered as equivalent to what are defined here as NBFIs. Intermediation by NBFIs is often described as 'non-monetary financial intermediation' to emphasize the fact that the secondary claims they issue do not generally circulate as money.

Notes

1 Practical bankers in the past often held that such deposit creation was impossible because they could lend only after first receiving a fresh deposit. This argument however involves a 'fallacy of composition'; what is true as far as the individual bank is concerned is not necessarily so when the banks are considered collectively.
2 There is no particular necessity for governments to bank with the central bank. In the USA, for example, most of the Federal government's receipts and payments flow into and out of accounts held with private banks.
3 In a technical sense the financing of a residual financial deficit by sales of securities to the banking system makes the government indebted to the banks rather than to the Bank of England. There is, however, a certain cosmetic element involved here; in effect the deficit spending results in the Bank creating extra cash for the banks which is then lent back to the government. If the temporal sequence is slightly different so that the borrowing from the banks precedes the deficit spending the Bank can be regarded as recycling cash back to the banks.
4 Another hypothetical limiting case in this respect might occur if the non-bank private sector immediately extinguished its additional £100 million of bank deposits by withdrawing notes and coin. In this instance the increase in the money supply takes the form ultimately of additional notes and coin in circulation rather than additional bank deposits.
5 A more detailed discussion of the structure of the bank's asset portfolio is contained in Chapter 8.
6 In this case the banks financed only 90 per cent of the residual financial deficit. What often happened in practice in such a situation was a loan by the Bank of England directly to the discount houses enabling them to take up additional Treasury bills – thus the increase in the government securities item in the Banking Department balance sheet was replaced by an item representing increased loans to the discount houses.
7 At the end of 1985 building societies held £105 million in notes and coin compared to £6,937 million in the form of bank deposits.

Further reading

Carter, H. and Partington, I. (1984) *Applied Economics in Banking and Finance*, third edn, Oxford: Oxford University Press, Chapter 6.
Chick, V. (1983) *Macro Economics after Keynes*, Deddington: Philip Allen, Chapter 12.

Evitt, H. S. (1960) *A Manual of Foreign Exchange*, fifth edn, London: Pitman, Chapter IV.

Moore, B. V. (1968) *An Introduction to the Theory of Finance*, New York: The Free Press, Chapters 6 and 7.

Newlyn, W. T. and Bootle, R. (1978) *The Theory of Money*, 3rd edn, Oxford: Clarendon Press, Chapter II.

Revell, J. (1973) *The British Financial System*, London: Macmillan, Chapter 7.

Struthers, J. and Speight, H. (1986) *Money: Institutions, Theory and Policy*, London: Longman, Chapter 3.

Chapter three

Monetary circulation and financial flows of funds

The objective of this chapter is a clarification of the general role which the institutions and markets comprising the monetary and financial system play in the organization of the modern economy. Any discussion relating to the economy as a whole necessarily involves considerable simplification of what in reality is a very complex structure; the simplification we adopt here is that used in national income accounting, where the numerous individual components of the economy are aggregated into a small number of broad 'sectors'. Real economic activity can then be considered as resulting in flows of money around what can be visualized as an income-expenditure circuit linking the various aggregated sectors. What we seek to demonstrate is that, in addition to such flows, one can also visualize a financial circuit,[1] involving flows of money corresponding to sales and purchases of financial claims, which will interact with the income-expenditure circuit at various points and which will constitute a significant influence determining the actual flows of money income in the economy. The role of the financial system can then be visualized as one of facilitating the efficient transmission of funds in the financial circuit. To focus our ideas we start by considering a very simple unrealistic 'model' of the flow of money payments in an economy and then subsequently expand it to encompass more realistic features. Finally we describe some data relating to actual financial flows in the UK economy.

The circular flow of income and expenditure

A key simplifying concept in modern macroeconomics is that of the flow of income and expenditure around a hypothetical circuit. If, initially, we ignore the existence of a public sector and the fact that residents of any country make transactions with residents of other countries, then the basic simplification is that the economic units which conduct transactions can be aggregated into two distinct sectors termed 'households' and 'firms'. In a capitalist society all wealth is ultimately owned by individuals, or family units, who make up the household sector, but usually we observe a form of specialization where the proximate ownership and control of a large fraction of the nation's stock of real assets (land, industrial and commercial buildings, plant and machinery, vehicles, inventories of finished goods, and raw materials, etc.) is vested in distinct institutions we can describe as 'firms', by which we mean all forms of business units ranging from large joint-stock companies to small owner-managed enterprises. Rather than hold such real assets directly, households often hold financial claims on firms, such as ordinary shares or bonds.[2]

Firms then organize the production of real goods and services by hiring labour services and other resources from households to work in conjunction with the real assets under their control. In exchange, households receive a flow of money payments, constituting wages, salaries and rents, which provide money income for the recipients. In any given period there will usually also be a residual between a firm's receipts from the sale of goods and services produced and the contractual payments made to hired resources, which constitutes 'profits', or a return on the real assets controlled by the firm (profits, of course, in particular instances may be negative). There will thus be an additional flow of money payments from firms to households representing the distribution of profits in the form of dividends on ordinary shares or interest payments on bonds, etc. Households then largely use their current money incomes received in any period to purchase the goods and services that are being produced by firms and, hence, there will be a flow of money payments back from households to firms constituting household expenditure on goods which corresponds to firms' sales revenue which, in turn, is the source of the money incomes received by households. Consequently real economic activity can be visualized as leading to a circular flow of money payments around an income and expenditure circuit, corresponding to real flows of goods and factor services occurring in the reverse direction.

Under certain unrealistic assumptions, the flows of money income and expenditure can be depicted as the simple closed circuit depicted in Figure 3.1. This would be the case, for example, if

1. each individual household's expenditure on real goods and services in any period was equal to its money income;

Figure 3.1 The circular flow of income and expenditure

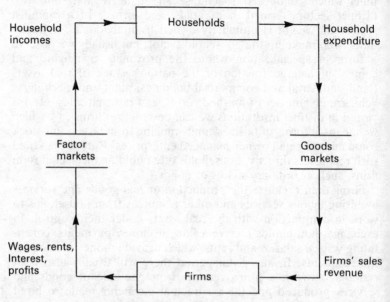

2. firms made no expenditure on real assets;
3. all firms' profits were distributed to households.

In the diagram we assume that households and firms will be holding stocks of money as their money payments and receipts are not perfectly synchronized and the circular flow can be visualized as flows into and out of these 'reservoirs' of money. Providing we consider a sufficiently long period of time then, given our assumptions, the inflows and outflows per period will be equal and there will be constant flow of money around the circuit – the aggregate monetary expenditure of households will equal firms' sales revenue which in turn will equal the total of households' money incomes.

We should note, of course, that in aggregating all firms in the economy into a single sector we are ignoring the considerable volume of transactions that take place in reality between firms. In effect, we are netting out all intermediate transactions and considering only the sales made by firms to final buyers.

Finance and the circular flow

In an economy with the characteristics just described, there would be no current role for any financial system to play. However, a role for a financial system is established once we take account of the fact that, in any period, households have the option of saving by restricting their expenditure on goods for immediate consumption to amounts less than their current money incomes. Typically, in real world economies households tend, in aggregate, to save a certain fraction of their money incomes in most periods but, given the forms of specialization in the economy, such savings are not usually matched by an equivalent desire to invest directly in real assets. Rather households have a relative preference for accumulating wealth in the form of financial assets, so that household savings exceed household investment and the household sector often has a financial surplus. Formally, we can write a financial identity[3] for any economic unit, or aggregated sector, as follows:

savings minus investment = financial surplus
                            = increase in financial assets minus increase in financial liabilities
                            = net acquisition of financial assets

If a sector has a financial surplus then it must be either acquiring additional financial assets, or repaying debt (reducing financial liabilities), or some combination of both adjustments, so that its net stock of financial assets increases. If a sector's investment conversely exceeds its savings then, formally, it has a negative financial surplus (i.e. a financial deficit) and, in this instance, the sector must be either selling financial assets or increasing its financial liabilities, or some combination thereof, so that its net stock of financial assets decreases.

In terms of the circular flow of income and expenditure, a financial surplus on the part of the household sector can be considered as a 'leakage' from the circular flow in that it does not directly result in expenditure on real goods and services and hence sales revenue for firms. Therefore, if the flow of income and expenditure is not to contract then it follows that this leakage must be matched by a corresponding 'injection' into the circular flow in the form of an excess of investment over savings, or a financial deficit, on the part of some other sector – in the economy being considered, of course, the firms sector. More precisely, if a planned financial surplus on the part of households exceeds a planned financial deficit on the part of firms (i.e. if for the economy as a whole planned savings exceed planned investment) then, by hydraulic analogy, the flow of income and expenditure will contract until at some point the planned financial surplus of households is brought into equality with the planned financial deficit of firms; when the flow of income around the circuit is constant and the economy can be considered to be in macroeconomic equilibrium, plans will be consistent and planned magnitudes will also be equal to realized, or ex-post, magnitudes. It therefore follows that, if the economy is to attain levels of income where the realized financial surplus of the household sector is consistently positive then there must exist matching financial deficits on the part of firms.

Firms, of course, contrary to our earlier unrealistic assumption, will invariably be final buyers of goods (from other firms), in that they make investment expenditures to replace and maintain existing real assets that have deteriorated with age or use, and, additionally, may be seeking to add to the stock of real assets under their control. Normally, also, most firms can be considered as saving, in that the residual profits earned in any period will not be fully distributed to households, but retained for use within the firm as a means of financing purchases of real assets. A financial deficit on the part of the firms sector implies that their gross investment expenditure exceeds their savings and that, in aggregate, they will be seeking to issue additional financial claims to finance part of their investment expenditure. In follows, therefore, that the orderly functioning of the economy requires some financial mechanisms which permit households to accumulate financial assets, while simultaneously providing firms with external finance to enable them to incur matching financial deficits; these financial mechanisms permit the non-spending on goods by households to be converted into spending on capital goods by firms, thus enabling the flow of current income and expenditure to be maintained in a manner consistent with wealth accumulation on the part of the household sector.

In the simplest case the intermediation between the household and firms sector might be carried out by a banking system. Households might choose to save simply by accumulating money balances (meaning of course notes and coin and bank deposits) while simultaneously the banking system (conditional on the necessary cash being provided by the public or the monetary authorities) might create additional bank deposits by acquiring the primary financial claims being issued by firms; firms are thereby able to finance their planned deficits, in effect, utilizing the claims on resources not being exercised by households while at the same time households are able to acquire the additional money balances they are seeking to accumulate. In more developed financial systems such a mechanism is likely to be complemented, however, by a more direct mechanism where there is a transmission of existing money from households to firms. Households may directly acquire primary financial claims being issued by firms, or they may acquire secondary financial claims issued by NBFIs who in turn acquire primary financial claims. Thus, given the sectoral specialization in the activities of saving and investment, the functioning of the economy will require a hypothetical financial circuit linking households and firms through which flows of money corresponding to exchanges of financial claims will pass and which, in reality, will require considerable organization in the form of markets and specialist institutions.

The structure of money-flows in our more realistic economy where households save and firms invest is illustrated in Figure 3.2. In the diagram we distinguish between income and expenditure flows (indicated by dashed lines) and financial flows (continuous lines) and we now introduce two additional sectors, non-bank financial intermediaries who issue non-monetary financial claims and the banking sector which issues claims used as money. We envisage household savings accruing in money form as flows initially into a 'reservoir' we have termed 'households' idle money balances' (the distinction between idle money balances and money balances that are 'active', in the sense that they are held purely to finance current transactions in the intervals between receipts of money income, is purely notional – we use the term to emphasize visually the fact that individuals can choose to build up their money balances by current saving). Depending on household port-folio decisions, there is then an outflow of funds from households' idle balances to the 'capital market', the term being used here as a generic term to describe all markets where primary financial claims issued by firms are exchanged; we thus encompass under this label both 'credit' markets where loans are made and 'secu-rities' markets where instruments such as bonds and shares are purchased. If during any period household savings exceed house-hold acquisitions of non-monetary financial claims then the stock of idle balances will increase and vice-versa. The flow of funds from the household sector to the capital market may be direct if households acquire the primary financial claims issued by firms or it may be indirect flowing through NBFIs. The inflow of funds to

Figure 3.2 The circular flow of income and expenditure and financial flows

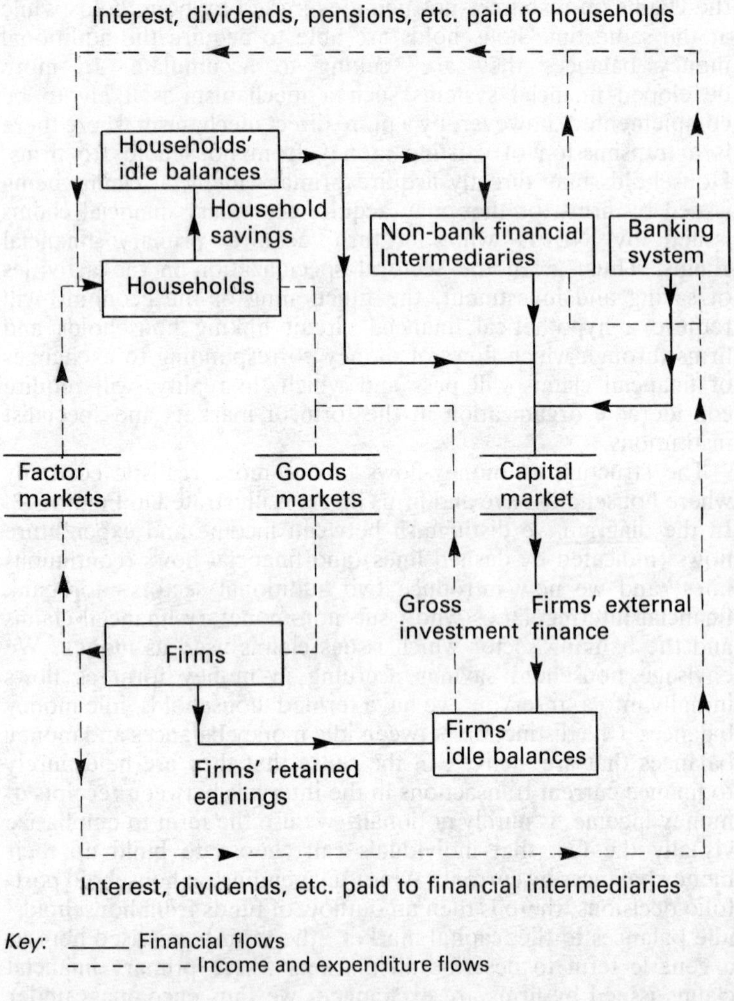

Interest, dividends, pensions, etc. paid to households

Interest, dividends, etc. paid to financial intermediaries

Key: ———— Financial flows
— — — — — Income and expenditure flows

the capital market from the household sector is combined with a separate inflow emanating from the banking sector, corresponding to the acquisition of primary financial claims via the creation of new bank deposits. From the capital market there is an outflow of funds into what we have termed 'firms' idle money balances' which is combined with an inflow of funds corresponding to the undistributed income diverted from the flows of profits being paid to households. Out of firms' idle money balances there is then an outflow of funds constituting investment expenditure by firms into the income and expenditure circuit.

Thus, if we assume that both households and firms maintain their idle money balances constant and new bank lending in net terms is zero, money leaks out of the income and expenditure circuit via savings into the financial circuit but eventually returns to the income and expenditure circuit via investment expenditure. The passage of money through the financial circuit is marked on each occasion by the issue of financial claims and thus over time as the stock of real assets increases there is an accumulation of stocks of financial assets held as wealth by the household sector. If the deficit spending of firms is primarily financed by the transmission of money balances from households rather than by new money creation on the part of the banking sector, one would expect to observe the stock of non-monetary financial assets to be growing at a faster rate than the stock of money.

We should note with reference to the diagram that once we explicitly identify the existence of NBFIs and banks in the economy then the income flows from firms to households can be visualized as being partially rerouted to pass through such institutions. Financial institutions will hold primary financial claims issued by firms and will be receiving annual flows of dividends and interest payments; most of these flows of income will be transmitted onwards to the household sector as interest on secondary financial claims and distributions of profits, but some may be retained as reserves constituting an additional source of saving in the economy.

The significance of the financial system

Given the existence of a sector within which economic units have a desire to save (accumulate wealth) without an equivalent desire to invest directly in real assets, the role of the financial system and the efficiency with which it is performed may be significant for the functioning of the economy under consideration in two primary contexts.

1. In the long run the rate of economic growth of an economy, while dependent on a number of factors, is plausibly related to the growth in the stock of the economy's real assets. Savings made by households in excess of their own investment in real assets make possible potential capital accumulation, but the utilization of such savings for actual capital accumulation depends on the ability of firms to obtain external finance, which enables them to

absorb the real resources which the household sector is releasing for use by its own net savings.

2. In the shorter run, the fact that savings and investment decisions are made largely independently by two groups of decision-takers poses problems for the macroeconomic stability of the economy. The economy will move to short-run equilibrium positions where, in the aggregate, households' and firms' plans are consistent and, whatever the level of income that is established, if households are observed to have an actual financial surplus then the financial system is performing the role of making funds available to firms to enable them to incur financial deficits. A key question, however, is whether the financial system can go further and successfully co-ordinate the plans of households and firms in a manner which results in short-run equilibrium positions for the economy at or near the 'full employment' level of income.

In principle, the financial system can play such a co-ordinating role via the mechanism of the interest rates that are established in the capital market. The planned financial surplus of households constitutes a supply of loanable funds to the capital market, while a planned financial deficit of firms constitutes a demand for loanable funds, and, just as changes in prices are conceived of as equilibrating the quantities demanded and supplied in the various 'micro' markets, so interest rates have the theoretical role of equilibrating the quantities of loanable funds being demanded and supplied in the capital market, thus bringing into consistency the plans of households and firms in a fashion which avoids fluctuations in aggregate monetary expenditure and consequent business cycles.

The ability of the financial system to co-ordinate plans in this way is, however, a matter of some considerable disagreement amongst economists. The critical assumption underlying 'Keynesian economics', for example, is that the interest rate mechanism cannot be guaranteed to co-ordinate savings and investment plans. Without delving into the intricacies of interest rate theory, the reasons for the postulated failure of the interest rate mechanism can be gauged in a simple fashion by consideration of Figure 3.2. From the diagram it can be deduced that the volume of loanable funds being supplied to the capital market by households may diverge from household net savings in any period if households are building up (or hoarding) idle money balances, or running down idle money balances. Equally, the volume of loanable funds supplied to the capital market can be influenced by the funds supplied by the banking system which are not necessarily related to planned household net savings. Thus the interest rate which equilibrates the quantity of loanable funds demanded and supplied in the capital market in the short run can be influenced by monetary factors which cause market interest rates to diverge from the rate at which planned savings and investment would be rendered consistent.

The alternative view could be said to be associated with those economists who are nowadays described loosely as 'monetarists'.[4] Such economists believe that, in practice, households (and firms) have a fairly stable and predictable demand for money balances in relation to their money incomes and thus the supply of funds to the capital market will not be affected markedly by the hoarding or dishoarding of money. Therefore, if the creation of money via the volume of bank lending is constrained by monetary policy to be consistent with the predictable changes in the community's demand for money, then it is asserted that the interest rates established in the capital market can co-ordinate savings and investment plans sufficiently well to avoid major fluctuations in aggregate monetary expenditure.

Some qualifications to the two-sector 'model'

Figure 3.2 emphasizes the role of the financial system in transmitting funds between the household and firms sectors but the degree of aggregation involved conceals a considerable amount of the gross financial activity that occurs in practice in private enterprise economies.

In reality not all households will have financial surpluses in any period. Some may be investing in real assets such as houses, cars, or consumer durables in excess of their own savings; equally some households may be dis-saving, i.e. spending amounts on consumption goods in excess of their current money incomes. Thus some households will have financial deficits in any period and will be either borrowing or running down their financial assets. Thus along the hypothetical financial channel linking the household sector to the capital market there will be gross flows of funds in both directions and Figure 3.2 only portrays the net flow on the assumption that the household sector in aggregate has a financial surplus. A considerable fraction of the actual gross flows of funds emanating to and from the household sector and the capital market will in effect, therefore, constitute transfers of funds between individual units within the aggregated household sector. In practice in the UK, for example, building societies acquire a considerable proportion of their funds directly from households and then transmit funds to other households in the form of mortgage loans. Additionally, we should recognize that individual households may be engaging in financial activity even though in particular periods they may have a zero financial surplus; households are not locked into particular portfolios but at particular times may change the composition of their portfolios by simultaneously buying certain financial claims and selling others.

A similar diversity of financial behaviour will be found within the aggregate firms sector; individual firms in particular periods have financial surpluses as well as financial deficits and again in practice there will be gross flows of funds in both directions along the hypothetical financial channel linking firms to the capital market.

We should note, additionally, that Figure 3.2 ignores the financial flows that occur in practice between different financial institutions – in the UK there are important financial markets in which the borrowers and lenders involved are primarily banks and other financial intermediaries.

The economy with a public sector

Up to this point we have been considering the structure of income and expenditure flows and financial flows in an economy which is essentially free enterprise. In reality, however, the UK economy, like all other economies, is a 'mixed economy' in that to an important extent decisions regarding the use of resources and the final distribution of income are taken collectively through the institutions of government. From the viewpoint of income and expenditure flows in the economy, the various forms of state intervention imply that we can identify an additional major sector – the public sector – comprising the institutions of central government, the local authorities, and the public corporations which will be making payments to and receiving payments from the household and firms sectors.

In their relations with the rest of the economy, public corporations (some of whom are termed 'nationalized industries') are for the most part similar to privately owned firms in that their final output is sold to households and firms via the normal market mechanisms, while their payments for hired resources are largely financed from sales revenue. The main contrast to privately owned firms lies in the fact that the real assets of public corporations are formally owned by the state, and the central government has a claim to any residual profits, net of interest payments on debt held by other sectors of the economy.

The real goods and services provided by the central government and local authorities on the other hand are generally not marketed but are provided at zero or nominal user charge. None the less, in their capacity as providers of such services, central and local governments are substantial buyers of goods and services produced by private sector firms (such as drugs used in the National Health Service) and also directly hire labour services from households. Additionally, payments are made in the form of subsidies and grants to private firms and a large variety of transfer payments, such as old age pensions, child benefits, and social security benefits to households. From the viewpoint of the circular flow of income between households and firms, these various expenditures can be regarded as injections into the circular flow but such injections are counterbalanced by corresponding leakages in the form of taxes formally paid by one or other of the private sectors of the economy to government.

The existence of the public sector, as well as resulting in a more complex structure of income and expenditure flows, has further implications for the financial system. In accounting terms, each of the elements of the public sector can be described as saving if its current receipts exceeds its current expenditure; the central government saves if its tax and other current revenues exceed its current expenditures on goods and services, subsidies, and transfer payments (if it has a current account budget surplus), local authority savings can be computed in the same way, while the public corporations' savings constitute their profits, net of interest payments on debt. If the amounts being spent on investment by each of the three elements are subtracted from their savings, then the result can be said to yield the financial surplus or deficit of the element concerned. The algebraic sum of the financial surpluses or deficits of the three elements can then be said to constitute the financial surplus or deficit of the public sector as a whole.[5] The emergence of a public sector financial surplus or deficit must involve financial flows between the public sector and other sectors of the economy. If the public sector has a financial deficit, then it must be issuing debt or selling assets which must be absorbed by other sectors and vice-versa if the public sector has a financial surplus.

The implications of a public sector financial deficit or surplus for the economy are, again, extremely controversial. The standard 'Keynesian' view is that variations in the financial position of the public sector can be used as an instrument to stabilize fluctuations in aggregate monetary expenditure. If, for example, the private sectors of the economy, taken together, have a planned financial surplus (i.e. planned private sector savings exceed planned private sector investment) at a level of income consistent will full employment, then it is asserted that a public sector financial deficit can maintain the level of aggregate monetary expenditure by absorbing excess private sector savings; savers can be provided with the financial assets they are demanding by the issue of public sector debt to augment the financial claims the private sector desires to issue and the non-spending of savers is thus translated into additional public spending. The alternative view is that, in the absence of monetary disturbance, the interest rate mechanism is capable of co-ordinating private sector savings and investment plans, so that at a full employment level of income there is no reason to expect the private sector as a whole to have a planned financial surplus of anything other than zero. In these circumstances the emergence of a public sector financial deficit sets in train mechanisms which eventually produce, as a consequence, a private sector financial surplus[6] – eventually some real private expenditure is 'crowded out' by the excess of public sector spending over its revenues.

However, whatever view is taken on this issue the immediate point to stress is that the emergence of a public sector financial surplus or deficit involves a further role for the financial system in facilitating the necessary transfers of funds between the public and other sectors of the economy. In practice in the UK the financial impact of the public sector is often summarized by an accounting concept termed the public sector borrowing requirement (PSBR). Technically, in the official statistics there are certain differences between the figures produced for the public sector financial deficit or surplus and the PSBR. These arise because:

1. The public sector financial deficit is computed in the official accounts on an accruals basis. Tax revenue, for example, is deemed to accrue within a given accounting period whenever the private sector earns income or makes expenditure on which a tax liability is incurred, but there is often some delay in practice before the actual payment of tax revenue to the government. Within any given accounting period the public sector may have to borrow additional amounts to cover the discrepancy between its actual spending and tax revenue which has accrued but not yet been paid; the additional amount it needs to borrow for this purpose is referred to as the 'accruals adjustment'.
2. The financial position of the public sector is complicated by the fact that central government also acts, in effect, as a financial

intermediary in that it makes loans to, or acquires securities issued by private firms. If the public sector acquires additional financial assets then the amount it needs to borrow is increased relative to its own financial deficit; correspondingly, if loans are being repaid to the public sector, or the public sector is disposing of assets, then the amount needing to be borrowed is reduced below its own financial deficit.

Financing the public sector borrowing requirement

In practice there are three distinct borrowing requirements for each of the constituent parts of the public sector: the central government, the local authorities, and the public corporations each raises funds via the financial system directly on its own account. However, particularly in recent years, a sizeable fraction of the borrowing requirement of the public corporations and local authorities is funded by loans and grants from the central government, which thus assumes the responsibility for funding most of the borrowing requirement of the whole public sector.

There are certain technical differences between the borrowing of the central government and other parts of the public sector. Payments made by the local authorities and public corporations to, or received from, the private sector are channelled through the commercial banking system rather than the Bank of England, i.e. the local authorities and public corporations hold accounts with the commercial banks. The local authorities and public corporations issue various sorts of financial claims to the capital market in the usual way and if these are purchased by individuals and institutions in the private sector outside the banking system, there is a flow of existing bank deposits to public sector accounts in the commercial banks. The financial claims issued may also be purchased by the banking system, in which case the banking system creates deposits for the public sectors in essentially the same way as loans to private sector borrowers. If the purchase of public sector financial claims results in a net increase in the total volume of bank loans then the stock of bank deposits increases and the counterpart acquisition of financial assets by the private sector takes the form of increased bank deposits. However, in the case where the banking system lends to the local authorities or the public corporations, the banking system has discretion regarding the volume of loans that it chooses to make.

The central government, as we stressed in Chapter 2, banks with the Bank of England. As such, any expenditure by the central government in excess of its current tax and other revenues, if necessary, will be financed automatically by the banking system which will create deposits for the recipients of cheques drawn on the Bank in exchange for cash balances at the Bank of England or other financial claims on the government. In this instance the corresponding acquisition of financial assets by the private sector again takes the form of increased bank deposits (or notes and coin). If the central government for monetary policy reasons does not wish to see the money supply increase then it must issue non-monetary financial claims to the non-bank private sector via the capital market in the usual way, so that, matching the automatic creation of bank deposits stemming from the borrowing require-ment per se, there is an offsetting extinction of bank deposits as the non-bank private sector makes payments for the non-monetary financial assets it is acquiring.

The domestic economy and the overseas sector

The structure of income and expenditure flows is further affected by the fact that the UK, like all economies to some extent, is an 'open economy' and, thus, in relation to the transactions being made by domestic residents, one can conceive of an addi-tional major sector – the overseas sector. Domestic sectors of the economy will be making current payments to the overseas sector with respect to goods and services imported from abroad, interest payments on financial claims on UK residents held by foreigners, transfer payments, etc. Likewise, there will be a corresponding flow of current payments to domestic UK sectors from abroad.

In relation to the circular flow of payments between domestic firms and households there is a further set of leakages and injec-tions and, as in particular periods current payment flows to and from abroad are not necessarily equal, there are further impli-cations for the financial system.

In a closed economy the realized financial surpluses and deficits of the various domestic sectors of the economy in any given period must sum to zero, but in an open economy this need no longer be the case. The difference between the aggregate current receipts of domestic sectors from the overseas sector and the aggregate current payments made by domestic sectors to the overseas sector constitutes the balance of payments surplus on current account (or if the difference is negative a balance of payments deficit on current account). As all payments by domestic sectors to other domestic sectors are simultaneously receipts of domestic sectors from other domestic sectors, it follows that, if during a particular period a country has a balance of payments surplus on current account, then the total current receipts of all domestic sectors exceeds the total current payments made by all domestic sectors. The summation of the financial surpluses and deficits of the individual domestic sectors must therefore yield a net financial surplus, which implies that the overseas sector in its dealings with the domestic economy must have a matching financial deficit. If the overseas sector has a financial deficit in relation to the UK this, in turn, implies an excess demand for sterling in the foreign exchange market with respect to payments on current account and, therefore, to obtain the sterling it requires to make current payments the overseas sector must be making net sales of financial assets to domestic sectors, i.e. UK residents must be lending to foreigners.

The precise way in which a financial deficit of the overseas sector is financed depends on the attitude taken by the government to the exchange rate. If the government decides on a policy of non-intervention in the foreign exchange market and allows the exchange rate to float freely, then an overseas sector financial deficit must be financed by net acquisitions of overseas financial assets by domestic sectors as a result of autonomous transactions, i.e. those which result from the voluntary choices of individual transactors within whatever constraints are imposed by economic variables or economic policy on their behaviour. If, however, the government has some implicit or explicit exchange rate target in mind, it may be the case that, at the chosen rate, the financial deficit of the overseas sector exceeds autonomous net acquisitions of overseas financial assets by domestic sectors. In this instance, in terms of the terminology used in the balance of payments accounts, there is a 'balance for official financing' and to prevent the sterling exchange rate from appreciating, as described in Chapter 2, the EEA has to intervene in the foreign exchange market, purchasing foreign currency for the official reserves. Thus the net acquisition of overseas financial assets by the domestic UK economy takes the form, in part, of additions to the official foreign currency reserves. At the same time, such intervention on the part of the EEA results in the creation of additional domestic bank deposits and therefore the net acquisition of financial assets corresponding to the net financial surplus of domestic sectors in part takes the form (unless the government attempts sterilization) of additional money balances.

The position, of course, is exactly symmetrical if the UK has a balance of payments deficit on current account so that the overseas sector has a financial surplus; in this instance there must be a net acquisition of sterling financial assets by the overseas sector corresponding to a collective financial deficit of UK domestic sectors.

The financial system therefore has an additional role to play in organizing the appropriate net financial flows which make current account balance of payments surpluses or deficits possible. This role is valuable in that it permits planned savings in the domestic economy to exceed planned investment and vice-versa, without there being necessarily any repercussions in the short run for the level of domestic income and expenditure.

Again, however, concentration on the 'net' position somewhat obscures the fact that in reality this position is arrived at as the difference between substantial gross flows of funds moving in both directions between domestic and overseas sectors: these are recorded as appropriate debit and credit items in the 'capital transfers' account in the official balance of payments statistics.

Consideration of the public and overseas sectors, therefore, adds to the complexity of the hypothetical financial circuit. The more complex nature of financial flows is illustrated in Figure 3.3, where to avoid clutter we omit the income and expenditure flows and where, for emphasis, we distinguish direct bank lending to other sectors from other financial flows.

Financial flows in the United Kingdom

The role of the financial system can be illustrated further by consideration of some of the main features of the actual financial flows in the UK economy in some recent years, as revealed in the official financial statistics. The sector financial accounts produced by the Central Statistical Office divide the economy into five main sectors: the personal sector, industrial and commercial companies, financial companies and institutions, the public sector, and the overseas sector, which, on occasion are further subdivided into various subsectors. We should note initially that the 'personal' sector and the 'industrial and commercial companies' sector identified do not correspond exactly to the conceptual households and firms sectors identified in our previous discussion. The personal sector in official statistics includes unincorporated business firms (i.e. partnerships and sole traders), as well as charities and other non-profit-making enterprises such as the universities, and is thus a hybrid sector containing both households and firms, although the individual household element does constitute the major fraction of the personal sector accounts. A further caveat concerns the reliability of the data; the figures for particular years have been

Figure 3.3 Financial flows in an economy with public and overseas sectors

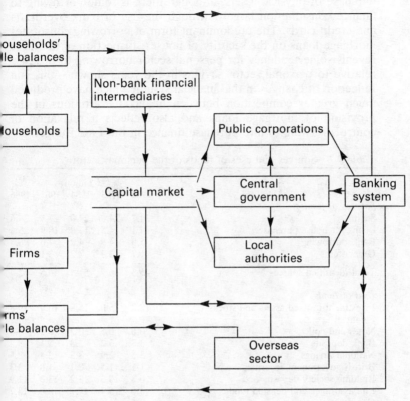

Key: > Direction of usual net flow

subject to substantial revision in successive official publications and there is a large residual error in the reconciliation of the individual sector accounts.

The personal sector

Some indication of the gross flows of funds between the personal sector and the capital market can be gauged by examining the sources and uses of funds account reproduced as Table 3.1. As can be seen from the table the amount of borrowing by the personal sector is substantial in relation to savings – indeed the amounts shown understate the gross amount borrowed as the recorded amount relates to net borrowing after repayments of existing loans. Most of the personal borrowing is related to the purchase of physical assets, although there is some borrowing to finance consumption largely through the use of bank overdrafts and credit cards. The predominant form of borrowing constitutes mortgage loans on the security of houses. Inspection of the table reveals some tendency for personal sector borrowing to increase relative to personal sector savings in the years shown – this is a reflection of changes in the financial system which have produced much greater competition between financial institutions in the provision of mortgage loans and also reflects a relaxation of controls relating to hire purchase finance in the 1982 Budget.

Table 3.1   Sources and uses of funds of the personal sector

	£ billion				
	1982	1983	1984	1985	1986
Sources of funds					
Saving	24.7	24.0	27.0	27.5	28.6
Loans for house purchase	14.1	14.5	17.0	18.9	25.4
Bank borrowing	5.0	4.9	4.2	7.0	6.3
Other items	1.7	3.3	3.2	3.1	2.1
Total identified sources	45.5	46.7	51.4	56.5	62.4
Uses of funds					
Investment in fixed assets and stocks	12.3	15.0	15.8	16.9	19.8
Financial assets					
Notes and coin	0.6	0.5	0.2	0.5	0.3
Bank deposits	3.8	3.2	3.3	5.1	8.4
National savings	3.5	2.9	3.3	2.5	2.5
British government securities	1.1	1.5	2.1	1.8	3.3
Building society deposits	10.3	10.3	13.2	13.3	11.9
Life assurance and pension funds	14.3	15.4	17.2	18.0	18.7
Company securities	−3.1	−1.6	−2.8	−1.6	−1.1
Other uses	1.3	0.9	1.4	1.1	0.9
Total identified uses	44.1	48.1	53.7	57.6	64.7

Source: *Financial Statistics*, April 1987, Table 9.2.

Turning to the uses of funds and the acquisition of financial assets, the dominance of secondary financial claims issued by financial intermediaries is clearly demonstrated. In 1986, of the gross financial assets acquired, 41.6 per cent took the form of contributions to life assurance pension funds, 26 per cent constituted building society deposits and a further 18.7 per cent consisted of bank deposits. Direct lending in the form of acquisitions of public sector debt, either in the form of national savings or marketable securities, amounted to only 12.9 per cent of acquisitions of financial assets, while the table reveals that the personal sector in aggregate was a net seller of company securities. This perpetuates a trend which has existed in the UK over many years and such disposals, over time, have constituted a major portfolio re-allocation on the part of the personal sector in favour of secondary financial claims, the primary claims released being absorbed by financial intermediaries, particularly life assurance and pension funds. Net disposals of company securities have been somewhat lower during the 1980s than previously, reflecting in recent years the privatization programme of the Conservative government, but there is no evidence to date of a reversal of this trend.

The dominance of secondary financial claims in the wealth portfolio of the personal sector can be illustrated further by examining the consolidated balance sheet at the end of the third quarter of 1986. At this date the gross financial assets held amounted to £698 billion and the proportions held in various forms are shown in Table 3.2.

Table 3.2 Financial assets held by the personal sector, end of third quarter 1986

	%
Money (M₃)	11.8
National savings	4.6
Public sector long-term debt	3.1
UK ordinary and preference shares	11.5
Building society shares and deposits	15.9
Equity in life assurance and pension funds	44.2
Unit trusts	2.0
Other	6.9

Source: derived from *Financial Statistics*, April 1987, Table 14.4.

The company sector

Table 3.3 depicts the sources and uses of funds account of the company sector. Examining the sources side it is clear that undistributed income constituted the most important source of company funds. The global figure, however, refers to gross profits (including net remittances of profits from subsidiaries abroad) after payment of corporate taxes, dividends and interest, but before providing for stock appreciation and depreciation of fixed assets. When provision is made for depreciation and stock appreciation, net company saving, i.e. the funds available to finance increases in the stock of real assets, is considerably reduced below the total figures for undistributed income.

Table 3.3 Sources and uses of funds of industrial and commercial companies

	1982	1983	£ billion 1984	1985	1986
Sources of funds					
Undistributed income	18.6	24.6	31.1	31.4	29.6
of which					
stock appreciation	3.5	4.1	4.5	2.6	n.a.
depreciation	14.0	14.9	15.8	18.7	n.a.
Bank borrowing	6.6	1.6	7.1	7.3	5.1
Ordinary shares	1.0	1.9	1.1	3.4	5.2
Debentures and preference shares	0.2	0.6	0.2	0.9	0.9
Other sources	1.2	3.5	−2.7	0.3	3.0
Total identified sources	27.6	32.2	36.8	43.3	43.8
Uses of funds					
Gross domestic capital formation	15.5	15.8	19.5	23.5	24.9
Increase in value of stocks	1.8	4.2	4.8	2.6	2.4
Investment in UK company securities	1.7	1.4	3.9	4.6	3.7
Liquid assets	1.4	4.9	1.4	4.5	12.0
Other uses	6.4	7.5	4.9	5.3	n.a.
Total identified uses	26.8	33.8	34.5	40.5	n.a.

Sources: *Financial Statistics*, April 1987, Table 8.2. *United Kingdom National Accounts*, 1986 edition (HMSO), Tables 5.1 and 11.5.

New issues of ordinary shares comprise a relatively minor source of total funds, although the sums raised increased considerably in 1985 and 1986. The global figures tend to understate, however, the significance of new share issues as a source of additional equity funds for companies. In 1985, for example, the additional equity funds derived from internal sources (i.e. undistributed income minus stock appreciation and depreciation) amounted to £10.1 billion so that new issues in that year of £3.4 billion amounted to around 25 per cent of total sources of equity funds.

In terms of loan finance the table reveals that a major source of funds for companies comprised borrowing from banks; in contrast, the issue of long-term debt in the form of debentures was much less significant. This situation represents a considerable change from the situation typical in the earlier post-war period when issues of debentures constituted broadly the same percentage of total sources of funds as bank borrowing. Given the long life of many company fixed assets, the issue of debentures with maturities of twenty to thirty years was a suitable means of financing investment in such assets, whereas bank borrowing constituted primarily short-term borrowing to finance investment in stocks and work in progress. This method of raising funds declined sharply in the 1970s with the incidence of high nominal interest rates on bonds associated with the increased rates of price inflation experienced in that decade.[7] A great deal of bank borrowing still comprises short-term loans made under overdraft arrangements, but increasingly bank borrowing has taken the form of fixed term loans or instalment loans with terms ranging up to ten years. Shorter term loans tend to be on fixed interest rate terms but most medium-term finance is at variable interest rates. 'Other sources of funds' refers mainly to capital transfers from the government and profits of UK subsidiaries of overseas companies retained within the UK.

On the user side of the account, the item 'investment in UK company securities' refers to shares of companies acquired by other companies for cash in the course of take-overs. As can be seen, the company sector also acquired financial assets and hence funds were flowing from the company sector to the capital market; 'liquid assets' refers to bank deposits, building society deposits, certificates of deposit, and government securities, while 'other financial assets' refers primarily to portfolio investment overseas. The main item in 'other uses' comprised direct investment in foreign subsidiary companies. It is worth noting that as an alternative to direct acquisitions of real assets, many companies in the 1980s leased assets from financial institutions (the growth in this practice was related to certain features of the tax treatment of investment by companies applicable up to 1985). In 1985, for example, expenditure on assets for leasing out to business users amounted to £5.6 billion.

The table also reveals that in the years shown, the company sector as a whole was a financial surplus sector in that its gross savings tended to exceed the amounts being spent domestically on capital formation, in contrast to the position in the 1970s when the company sector typically had a financial deficit.

The public sector

Table 3.4 shows the financial accounts of the public sector for the years 1981–5. The first row of the table indicates the financial deficit of the combined public sector and the four subsequent rows show the accounting adjustments made to arrive at the PSBR. Since 1983, net lending by the public sector has been negative; this reflects the accounting treatment of the government's privatization programme – sales of shares of public enterprises are regarded as reducing the PSBR rather than a method of financing the PSBR. 'Other financial transactions' are transactions relating to the operation of certain public sector pension schemes. In 1984 and 1985 the effect of these adjustments was to reduce the PSBR below the financial deficit.

Table 3.4 Public sector financial accounts 1981–5

	1981	1982	1983	1984	1985
			£ billion		
Financial deficit	8.2	7.3	11.2	13.1	9.7
Accruals adjustment	2.8	−1.7	0.6	0.6	0.6
Net lending and purchases of securities	0.9	0.8	−0.6	−2.5	−2.5
Other financial transactions	−0.9	−2.0	+1.3	−0.8	+0.5
Balancing item	−0.4	0.6	−0.9	−0.2	−0.7
PSBR	10.6	5.0	11.6	10.2	7.6
financed by					
non-bank private sector	9.3	6.4	12.2	8.3	8.6
monetary sector	−0.6	−2.8	−2.0	0.5	−2.4
overseas sector	1.9	1.4	1.4	1.4	1.4

Source: *UK National Accounts* 1986, Tables 13.13 and 13.14.

As can be seen, the bulk of the PSBR in the early 1980s was financed by the acquisition of public sector liabilities by the non-bank private sector. Typically, over the years shown, the non-bank private sector acquired additional amounts of notes and coin amounting on average to £0.5 billion per year, but the main acquisition of debt took the form of marketable government securities purchased directly by individuals or by financial intermediaries. Non-marketable debt in the form of various national savings instruments, however, was also important amounting on average to around 37 per cent of total debt issued to the non-bank private sector. In the early 1980s the contribution of the monetary sector (i.e. the banking system) to the financing of the PSBR was generally negative. This reflected the fact that the local authorities and public corporations made substantial net repayments of loans to the banks and also the fact that the central government in certain years 'overfunded' its borrowing requirement – sales of debt to the non-bank private sector exceeded the borrowing requirement with a negative impact on bank deposits. The overseas sector also made a significant contribution to public sector financing. The finance provided by the overseas sector is net of government transactions affecting the official reserves of foreign currency. If, for example, the government purchases foreign currency for the reserves, this transaction increases the amount of sterling finance the government requires (or the government's domestic borrowing requirement) and can thus be regarded as a negative overseas contribution to the financing of the PSBR. If, therefore, an American resident sells dollars for pounds on the foreign exchange market with a view to purchasing UK government securities, but the EEA buys the dollars for the official reserves, then on the one hand this increases the government's need for sterling, but the subsequent sale of the government security itself provides the sterling, so that there is a zero contribution to financing the PSBR.

The overseas sector

The overseas sector financial deficit or surplus is the inverse of the UK surplus deficit on the current account of the balance of payments, but as noted previously, the net position is the outcome of substantial gross financial flows to and from abroad. The magnitudes of these gross flows have increased substantially in the 1980s following the abolition of exchange controls on external financial transactions by UK residents in October 1979. The magnitudes of some of these gross flows are shown in Table 3.5. The scale of the flows indicated implies that since 1979 the UK domestic financial system is now integrated much more closely with that of the rest of the world. Prior to that year overseas portfolio investment had to be financed by foreign currency loans or by the purchase of foreign exchange from other UK residents who were selling

Table 3.5   UK financial transactions with overseas 1981–5

| | £ billion | | | | |
	1981	1982	1983	1984	1985
Investment overseas by UK residents					
Direct[1]	6.1	4.3	5.3	6.0	7.3
Portfolio investment[2]	4.3	6.7	6.5	9.5	18.2
of which					
UK banks	1.0	2.0	2.7	7.9	10.2
other UK financial institutions	3.1	4.3	3.5	1.5	4.9
other UK residents	0.2	0.4	0.3	0.1	3.1
Bank deposits and other short-term items	41.7	22.4	20.1	17.2	29.2
Investment in the UK by overseas residents					
Direct	2.9	3.0	3.4	0.4	3.4
Portfolio investment	0.3	0.2	1.9	1.4	7.0
Bank deposits and short-term items	39.8	25.3	20.8	23.1	32.3

Source: United Kingdom Balance of Payments, 1986 edition, London: HMSO, Tables 1.4, 8.1, and 8.3.

[1] Direct investment defines transactions between enterprises, usually, companies that are financially and organizationally related, i.e. subsidiaries, branches, and associate companies.
[2] Portfolio investment covers all investment in securities with an original maturity of more than one year as well as ordinary shares and bonds with no specified maturity.

overseas assets. In the ten years from 1970–9 the average annual portfolio investment of UK residents overseas only amounted to £0.17 billion. The magnitude of the entries for bank deposits and other short-term items reflects the position of the UK as an international banking centre and includes what are termed 'eurocurrency' transactions where UK banks obtain funds from overseas and re-lend the funds to other overseas borrowers.

Notes

1 The concept of a financial circuit was formalized originally by J. M. Keynes (1930) in *Treatise on Money*, London: Macmillan, pp. 47–8.
2 The separation between households and firms is real enough in the case of a joint-stock company, but obviously for a small owner-managed enterprise this separation may be purely notional.
3 In this identity 'financial assets' includes money balances.
4 The view that the essential differences between 'Keynesian' and 'monetarist' economists are traceable to different assessments of the ability of the interest rate mechanism to co-ordinate savings and investment plans is argued persuasively by Leijonhufvud, A. (1981) in *Information and Co-ordination*, Oxford: Oxford University Press, Chapter 7.
5 There is an essentially arbitrary element in the accounting definition of the financial surplus or deficit of each separate part of the public sector as, in practice, the central government makes current transfers to the local authorities and public corporations which are treated as current expenditure on the part of the central government and current revenue for local authorities and public corporations. For example, in 1985, 52 per cent of local authority current receipts of £39,773 million constituted current grants from central government.
6 The argument here essentially relates to a closed economy. In an open economy a public sector financial deficit may be matched by a financial surplus on the part of the overseas sector.
7 A clear explanation of the effects of uncertainty regarding future inflation rates on issues of company debentures can be found in Fleming, J. (1976) *Inflation*, Oxford: Oxford University Press, Chapter XI.

Further reading

Bain, A. D. (1981) *The Economics of the Financial System*, Oxford: Martin Robertson, Chapters 2, 6, 7, 8, and 9.
Newlyn, W. T. and Bootle, R. (1978) *The Theory of Money*, Oxford: Clarendon Press, Chapter IV.
Samuels, J. M. and Wilkes, F. M. (1980) *Management of Company Finance*, third edn, Walton on Thames: Nelson, Chapter 2.

Chapter four

The role of financial intermediaries and markets

In this chapter we consider how the various institutions and markets comprising the financial system facilitate the transmission of funds in the financial circuit linking financial surplus and deficit units. At various points we have emphasized that the relationship between ultimate lenders and borrowers is often an indirect one involving financial intermediaries. As financial intermediation involves the use of real resources, the costs of which are ultimately borne by the users of the services provided, there is therefore a presumption that, compared to the alternative of direct finance, such intermediation results in significant advantages for both lenders and borrowers, which are sufficient to outweigh the costs involved.

We have previously referred also to the 'capital market', using this term in a general way to encompass all transactions in primary financial claims. In reality, however, there are a variety of markets in which particular financial claims are exchanged with differing organizational characteristics. Some are what can be described as 'informal' markets where borrowers transact directly with lenders in a decentralized fashion, as in the case where an individual obtains a loan from a bank or a building society. Although, therefore, one frequently sees references in the financial press to the 'markets' for retail deposits or housing loans, the term 'market' in these contexts is being used in an abstract sense to indicate the fact that there is a continuous demand for, and supply of, the type of financial claim in question. However, many financial markets, particularly involving transactions in government or company securities, can be described as highly organized markets in that the majority of the buying and selling decisions of numerous final transactors involve the participation of small centralized groups of specialist institutions who arrange the actual exchanges that take place. In the case of organized markets, a fundamental distinction can be made again between primary and secondary markets. A primary market involves the issue of new financial claims which make a supply of additional funds available to the issuer, whereas secondary markets facilitate exchanges of existing financial claims. A central feature in the organization of both primary and secondary markets is the existence of specialist brokers who act in an agency capacity on behalf of ultimate buyers and sellers, in effect, bringing buyers and sellers together and arranging transactions between them. In many secondary markets there also exist specialist dealers or 'market-makers' who hold stocks of particular financial claims (or who have formalized arrangements for the short-term borrowing of financial claims) and who, unlike brokers, act as principals buying and selling on their own account.[1] As the operations of these market specialists again involve costs, ultimately borne by the users of their services, it is pertinent to consider the precise advantages which their existence provides.

Part of the explanation of the existence of financial intermediaries and markets could be said to arise for reasons common to the explanation of the existence of market intermediaries in other areas of the economy and which we have previously cited as an explanation of the existence of money itself. Financial institutions, like organized markets in commodities such as wheat, tea, copper, etc., or retail shops, serve to reduce the transaction costs involved in conducting exchanges in a world where spatially dispersed individuals have imperfect information regarding trading opportunities.

In addition, however, to the difficulties arising from imperfect information, financial transactions may be impeded if lenders and borrowers differ in their intrinsic preferences as to the characteristics of the financial claims which they desire to acquire on the one hand or issue on the other. All lenders, of course, do not have homogeneous preferences, but while some may be prepared to hold financial claims for long periods of time and subject themselves to considerable risks, it is reasonable to suppose that the average or 'representative' lender places a premium on the characteristics of exchange convenience and capital-certainty. Equally, borrowers' requirements are varied, but much borrowing takes place to finance the acquisition of durable real assets which yield streams of returns over lengthy future periods of time. Given the highly specialized nature of many real assets in form or location (many such assets cannot be switched easily into alternative uses or easily relocated), the value of the streams of future returns, and hence their future capital values, can be affected by myriad unpredictable events and is subject to considerable risk. These features of durable capital goods are likely to be reflected in the financial claims that borrowers prefer to issue. If borrowers, on average, are risk-averse they will seek to issue financial claims with a term to maturity related to the expected life of the real assets to be financed, so that there is a reasonable prospect of the investment project generating sufficient returns to repay the loan over the whole or a substantial part of the expected life of the assets in question. A borrower who borrows for short periods to finance the acquisition of long-life assets is incurring some risk, as he cannot be completely certain either of his ability to raise future loans or of the terms on which future loans might be made. Given the risks involved in holding real assets, investors may seek additionally to issue financial claims such as equity shares where the risk is borne by the provider of finance.

Thus the intrinsic preferences of many potential borrowers of funds may not match closely the preferences of many potential lenders. In these circumstances direct financial transactions may be possible only on terms which inhibit the volume of financial transactions actually conducted. To induce lenders to make long-term loans, for example, borrowers might have to offer them rates of interest sufficiently high to compensate for the loss of liquidity involved and, at the necessary interest rates, many potential investment projects, otherwise thought viable at lower interest rates, might not be undertaken. The existence of financial intermediaries and markets, however, can lead to a greater degree of reconciliation of the conflicting requirements of many borrowers and lenders. More precisely, the financial system can transform long-maturity and risky liabilities issued by borrowers into more liquid and less risky assets for lenders. By transforming the characteristics of financial claims in this way, the financial system can simultaneously provide lenders with their preferred sorts of financial assets while permitting borrowers to issue their preferred sorts of financial liabilities; thus the liquidity and risk premiums that might have to be offered lenders to supply a given volume of funds can be reduced and the consequentially lower interest rates might induce an increase in real capital formation compared to a situation where specialist financial institutions were absent.

Not all financial intermediaries and markets perform the joint functions of reducing transaction costs, maturity transformation, and risk transformation, but they invariably fulfil one or the other of these roles. Many financial intermediaries also provide other specialist services; banks provide a payments mechanism, insurance companies provide insurance for the dependents of individuals against the premature death of the individuals concerned, etc. While such specialist services are valuable on their own account, the central role of the financial system is concerned with the transmission of funds, and the remainder of this chapter is devoted to an elaboration of how the financial system is able to perform each of the general functions we have identified.

The reduction of transaction costs

Financial transactions involve costs of a sort similar to those involved in the exchange of any other good or service; given imperfect information, there are costs involved in searching out other individuals who may wish to borrow or lend funds, obtaining information regarding the quantities and terms on which transactions might be conducted, negotiating contractual agreements, etc. There are, however, certain additional costs involved in financial transactions that are not generally encountered in transactions in physical goods and services. In many exchanges of goods, once payment has been made particular, transactions are regarded as completed and one party has no further interest in the future behaviour of the other. Financial transactions, in contrast, involve contractual relationships whereby borrowers obtain present money on the strength of promises to be fulfilled in future periods of time so that potential lenders have a problem of assessing the likelihood of such promises being met. The financial claims issued by different borrowers cannot be regarded as homogeneous, but are more in the nature of 'branded' goods, the quality of which depends on the identity of the issuer. The assessment of quality in this instance involves lenders acquiring information about such things as the reputation of the borrower and his performance in past financial dealings, his financial standing or 'creditworthiness', or an assessment of the underlying prospects of a real investment project that a loan is to finance. Additionally, in financial transactions, lenders incur the continuing costs of monitoring the performance of the borrower during the period of the loan.

The existence of these various sorts of transaction costs incurred in financial transactions inserts a wedge between the net return received by a lender and the gross cost incurred by a borrower, despite the fact the explicit interest rate that may be transacted will be the same for both parties. Suppose that two individuals L (a lender) and B (a borrower) directly agree a loan transaction at a certain interest rate r. Denoting r_L as the net return to the lender and t_L as his total transaction costs expressed as a percentage of the loan, then symbolically:

$$r_L = r - t_L$$

i.e., the net return to the lender is equal to the interest rate minus percentage transactions costs incurred.

Similarly, denoting r_B as the gross cost to the borrower and t_B as total transaction costs expressed as a percentage of the loan, then:

$$r_B = r + t_B$$

i.e., the gross cost is equal to the interest rate plus the percentage transactions cost incurred. Therefore:

$$r_B - r_L = t_B + t_L$$

i.e., the differential between the gross cost to the borrower and the net return to the lender is equal to the sum of their respective transaction costs.

The existence of such a differential provides potential scope for the emergence of financial intermediaries and other specialist institutions. By dealing with a financial intermediary rather than directly with an ultimate borrower, the transaction cost incurred by a lender might be reduced below t_L to, say, t^i_L; likewise, the transaction cost for a borrower might be reduced below t_B to t^i_B. The operations of a financial intermediary will of course involve costs and suppose that the average cost, including a margin for profits, of intermediating in a similar loan transaction between the ultimate borrower and ultimate lender equals a certain amount C, again expressed as a percentage of the loan. The financial intermediary will receive remuneration for its services by interposing a margin equal to C between the interest rate it charges the borrower and the interest rate it offers the lender, so that the borrower may pay a higher explicit interest rate than r, while the lender correspondingly may receive a lower explicit interest rate. Nonetheless, despite this margin, if $(C + t^i_B + t^i_L)$ is less than $(t_B + t_L)$, then, compared to a situation where they transact with each other directly, an intermediary can simultaneously increase the net return to the lender while reducing the gross cost for the borrower, the magnitude of their gains depending on the size of the intermediary's margin, which in turn will depend on the degree of competition between individual intermediaries. If the transaction costs involved in direct finance are substantial it is possible that more than one intermediary may be interposed between an ultimate borrower and lender; certain intermediaries may specialize in collecting from funds from numerous lenders which are then transmitted in a wholesale fashion to other intermediaries who specialize in making loans to ultimate borrowers.

There are a number of reasons for supposing that financial intermediaries and markets can result in significant reductions in the total transactions costs involved in financial transactions.

1. Most obviously, the mere physical presence of financial intermediaries, such as the location of banks and building societies in the high streets of towns and cities, can economize on the costs involved for ultimate lenders and borrowers in searching out partners with whom financial transactions can be made. Likewise, search costs can be reduced by the use of brokers whose function rests in the specialized knowledge they possess regarding the identity of potential transactors.

2. Individual borrowers and lenders often differ substantially as regards the volume of funds they wish to transact in particular deals. Typically, given the 'lumpy' nature of many real assets, the average borrower seeks a size of loan in excess of that which the average lender has the ability or inclination to provide. Thus a borrower, to raise a given amount of funds in a direct fashion from lenders, might have to be involved in a number of separate transactions with different lenders. Financial intermediaries can eliminate this matching problem by collecting funds from numerous lenders in varying amounts and pooling them into a general fund, which can then be apportioned into loans of a size exactly tailored to meet a borrower's requirements; borrowing a given sum from a financial intermediary thus involves a single transaction compared with, possibly, several in the case of direct finance. Another way of describing this function would be to say that financial intermediaries 'split-bulk', as do wholesalers and retailers in the case of physical commodities, by breaking down large loans into smaller loans more suited to the particular circumstances of different individual lenders. A similar method of economizing on the transaction costs of arranging loans is exhibited by companies raising finance by the issue of securities which can be purchased in varying amounts by providers of funds, the whole issue being organized by a specialist institution which undertakes the tasks involved in contacting potential purchasers of securities.

3. Financial intermediaries provide standardized financial assets for lenders, thereby reducing the amount of information gathering and analysis which would be involved in the scrutiny of the heterogeneous primary financial claims being offered by borrowers – a lender may choose from a narrower range of secondary financial

assets rather than from a large range and variety of competing primary assets. Further, the use of financial intermediaries with an established 'reputation' reduces the problems for a lender in assessing the likelihood that the promises of a borrower will be fulfilled. The importance of reputation as a proxy for the quality of a promise is illustrated when a bank or similar institution 'accepts' a financial claim issued by a borrower (i.e. guarantees to meet the claim in the event of default) – the name of the accepting bank, in itself, increases the willingness of lenders to hold the financial claims in question. The acquisition of information for providers of funds is also simplified by the existence of organized markets for the trading of financial claims – such markets reduce the dispersion of prices at which particular financial claims are traded and the prices established in the market are widely disseminated through various information services and the financial press.

4. Financial intermediaries and other specialists reduce transaction costs for their users but do interpose margins between their borrowing and lending rates or charge commissions. What enables intermediaries to reduce total costs for lenders and borrowers are economies of scale and specialization in the acquisition of information about prospective borrowers, in monitoring the subsequent behaviour of borrowers after loans have been made, in routine record keeping, legal documentation, etc. Financial intermediaries plausibly possess considerable comparative advantages in the assessment of the creditworthiness of borrowers; banks and building societies, for example, can utilize information gained over time from managing the deposit accounts of particular customers to gauge their financial probity and their ability to service loans. Likewise, they may enjoy a comparative advantage in such areas as interpreting information provided in company accounts, in assessing the prospects for particular investment projects, or in assessing the wider prospects for particular industries or sectors of the economy.

Maturity transformation

Because of the existence of transaction costs some financial intermediaries, in principle, could operate with what are termed 'perfectly matched balance sheets', meaning that all their assets of particular terms to maturity would be exactly matched by a corresponding volume of liabilities of the same term. In practice, however, many financial intermediaries, particularly in the UK retail banks and building societies, have mismatched balance sheets, in that the average term to maturity of their assets exceeds that of their liabilities; in other words, they borrow 'short' and lend 'long'. By mismatching their balance sheets in this fashion, financial intermediaries do not therefore merely transmit funds from ultimate lenders to ultimate borrowers more efficiently, but also transform the longer maturity primary financial liabilities as seen by borrowers, into shorter maturity secondary financial assets as seen by lenders, thus permitting financial transactions which better suit the requirements of both groups of ultimate transactors. In a sense financial intermediaries could be said to be manufacturing 'liquidity services' for individuals in the form of the special characteristics possessed by the secondary financial claims they issue.

What enables financial intermediaries to operate profitably by mismatching their balance sheets are differentials in the term structure of interest rates. If lenders on average have a preference for shorter maturity loans while borrowers on average have a preference for longer maturity loans then, in the absence of financial intermediation and given neutral expectations of future changes in interest rates, the structure of interest rates as determined by the forces of demand and supply would exhibit a tendency for yields on longer dated securities to be above those on shorter dated securities, and certainly in excess of the zero nominal yield on notes and coin. Thus financial intermediaries can take advantage of these yield differentials by issuing their own short-term liabilities at low yields (but on terms sufficiently attractive to induce lenders to substitute them in their portfolios in place of other short-term assets) while simultaneously acquiring higher yielding assets. There are, of course, limits to the scale of financial intermediation of this type which can be profitable at any given time; such intermediation itself tends to augment the total demand for shorter maturity loans and the total supply of longer maturity loans, and therefore tends to narrow the yield differentials that might exist in the absence of intermediation. An expansion in scale, other things being equal, therefore leads to intermediaries incurring higher interest costs on their liabilities and a lower interest return on their assets and thus, as in any other industry, the profitable scale of operations is limited by diminishing marginal revenue and increasing marginal costs.

As we intimated in our previous discussion of the evolution of banking, institutions whose liabilities are of a very short-term nature in relation to their assets are subjecting themselves to liquidity risks, and what enables them to bear such risks is the law of large numbers effect, ensuring that net withdrawals of funds are small and highly predictable in relation to their total liabilities. There is still, however, a certain probability of some net withdrawal of funds from an individual bank in a particular period so banks, or similar institutions with mismatched balance sheets, need to hold a fraction of their assets as prudential reserves, to insure themselves against the risk of insolvency involved. From the viewpoint of the financial intermediaries concerned the interest foregone by holding liquid reserves is regarded as a cost of their operations which will be reflected in the margin between their borrowing and lending rates.

In addition to the role played by financial intermediaries, a substitute and complementary role in the process of maturity transformation is performed by organized secondary markets in which existing financial assets can be traded. Long-term bonds with maturity dates some distance in the future, and ordinary shares with no redemption dates, will be more willingly held by individuals who place a premium on liquidity, if they have prior knowledge that they can transform such securities easily into money at short notice. Essentially, long-term liquid securities from the point of view of an issuer are transformed into liquid assets from the point of view of the holder if they are easily marketable, although, compared to the deposits provided by banks or building societies whose redemption values are certain in money terms, there is still uncertainty regarding the exact price at which such securities can be sold. The existence of organized markets also enables financial intermediaries to hold earning assets other than cash as liquid assets and so reduces the costs of financial intermediation.

Although existing securities can be traded outside organized markets on an informal basis, the time delay involved in realizing an asset is reduced if there exist brokerage institutions who specialize as agents for large numbers of ultimate buyers and sellers in centralized trading of assets. The liquidity endowed on particular securities by organized secondary markets is further enhanced if, as in the UK Stock Exchange, there exist specialist middlemen, or dealing institutions, who hold inventories of securities and who are always prepared to buy and sell securities at firmly quoted prices as principals. In this instance, if offers to sell particular securities in any particular period exceed offers to buy, then within limits, dealers will absorb the excess supply and add to the inventories of such securities they are holding. Likewise, if offers to buy particular securities exceed offers to sell, then the excess demand can be absorbed by a run down of dealers' inventories. This commitment to continuous dealing means that, in any given trading day, the sale of a security by a holder can be completed with minimum time delay; a dealer will buy the security without the receipt of an exactly matching buying offer from someone else. In the absence of specialist dealers, even though offers might be channelled through centralized brokers, a prospective seller of a security would have to be matched with a prospective buyer (or buyers) and there is a possibility of some time delay before this can be achieved. In the very short run, by absorbing excess demand and supplies effectively, dealers also act as speculators helping to stabilize fluctuations in the market prices of particular securities, so that any individual investor can therefore feel more confident of his ability to buy or sell securities without unduly affecting the market price. The greater the capital resources of dealers the more able they are to act in this fashion.

There are obviously limits to the ability of dealers to absorb excess demands and supplies in relation to the securities they deal in. If the excess demand for securities in the market is large in relation to their inventories, to maintain their commitment to continuous trading, dealers will rapidly adjust their quoted prices upwards to encourage sellers and discourage buyers and vice-versa if there is substantial excess supply. Dealers may also adjust prices rapidly in anticipation of future excess demand or supply at current prices. If, for example, some piece of news or information is received which is anticipated to result in sales of a particular security (or securities in general), dealers may mark prices down immediately, in advance of actual selling pressure in the market, to avoid the anticipated losses which would arise through buying securities at higher prices than that at which they can subsequently be resold. Prices in organized security markets can fluctuate by the minute and substantial price changes can result within the course of a daily trading period.

None the less, although they are not directly involved with the raising of new funds for borrowers, organized secondary markets can influence the terms on which new funds can be raised in the primary markets by providing the holders of long-term or irredemable securities with a much greater degree of exchange convenience.

Risk transformation

Financial intermediation can not only transform the maturity of financial claims, it can also transform risk; risky primary financial claims issued by borrowers can be transformed into less risky secondary financial claims issued to lenders.

Whenever money is lent to borrowers to finance the acquisition of real assets, there is usually some degree of risk involved in the holding of primary financial claims, due to the underlying risk attached to the prospective earnings of the specialized assets which particular financial instruments might have financed – even secured loans involve some degree of risk for a lender, in that the value of the assets pledged as security by a borrower may themselves be subject to risk. In addition to this inherent risk arising from imperfect foresight, there is a further type of financial risk involved whenever the providers of finance are separated from those responsible for using the funds. There is a problem in this instance of what is termed 'moral hazard', i.e. the possibility that a person who would act in a certain way if he were using his own money, may act differently in a situation where he was using someone else's money. For example, in a public company with large numbers of ordinary shareholders the proximate control of the real assets involved is delegated to a small management group who, despite the formal provisions of company law, may choose to pursue policies that may be inimical in certain ways to the shareholders' interests; expenditures may be incurred on such items as lavish headquarters buildings, or excess office staff, which yield satisfaction for the managers concerned but do little to increase shareholders' dividends. Similarly in the case of loans, despite prior scrutiny of creditworthiness, etc., there is some possibility that borrowers may turn out to be fraudulent or incompetent and fail to fulfil their contractual obligations. Thus the holders of financial claims are incurring an additional risk which is sometimes termed 'lender's risk'.

The roles of different financial intermediaries in risk transformation are basically similar, but there are distinctions which can be made as to the type of risk involved in specific institutional circumstances. The asset portfolios of deposit-taking institutions, such as banks and building societies, are dominated by loans of various sorts and, generally speaking, organized markets for the secondary trading of such assets are not prevalent.[2] The relevant risk involved in this instance is default-risk, i.e. the risk that particular borrowers may fail to meet their contractual obligations to pay interest charges or redeem their loans at the due date. Prior vetting of potential borrowers can reduce such risks, but a residual degree of default risk is always present in a loan situation. The comparative advantage possessed by financial intermediaries with regard to assuming such risks is that the scale of their operations makes it possible for them to make a large number of independently risky loans and, in the same way as the law of large numbers enables deposit-taking institutions to predict with considerable accuracy the likelihood of net withdrawals of deposits, the pooling of independent risks enables them to predict very accurately the losses due to default that they will experience in any particular period. The expected losses can then be allowed for by the intermediary in the differential between its lending and borrowing rate, thereby considerably reducing the financial risks incurred by their depositors. The principles involved here can be illustrated by a simple example where, for emphasis, we use rather unrealistic numbers and, for simplicity, we ignore transaction costs and the need for an intermediary to hold reserves.

Suppose an individual lender is contemplating making a direct loan of £1,000 to a borrower for one year at an interest rate of 10 per cent. The lender, however, knows that there is a one in twenty chance of complete default on the part of the borrower, so that no interest is paid and there is complete loss of principal. Thus, if the lender made a continual series of such loans, 95 per cent of the time he would receive £1,100 after one year and 5 per cent of the time he would receive nothing. In making an individual loan, therefore, the expected future receipt for the lender is $(£1,100 \times 0.95) + (£0 \times 0.5) = £1,045$.

Suppose the individual lender, however, has the alternative of depositing £1,000 with a financial intermediary, which can then subsequently make a loan of £1,000 for a year at an interest rate of 10 per cent, with a similar one in twenty chance of complete default on the part of the borrower. Suppose, also, that this particular loan made by the financial intermediary is accompanied by 999 similar loans of £1,000 for one year, each of equivalent risk, the total sum of £1 million being lent corresponding to a total of £1 million received from depositors. The risks attached to each loan, however, are independent, in the sense that a default by a single borrower makes it neither more nor less likely that another borrower will also default. Given the chances of default on each individual loan, the financial intermediary can expect, with a high degree of probability, that out of a total of 1,000 borrowers, on average, 50 borrowers will default and that after a year it will receive repayments of principal plus interest from non-defaulting borrowers amounting to $(£950,000 \times 1.1) = £1,045,000$. Given its interest earnings, the financial intermediary could thus offer depositors after a year a near certain prospect of £1,045 for each £1,000 deposited – an interest rate of 4.5 per cent.

The expected return on a £1,000 deposit in the intermediary is thus equivalent to that on the direct lending option, but is one which many lenders might prefer if they are risk-averse. They would prefer to receive a lower explicit interest rate of 4.5 per cent and a more or less guaranteed return of their principal, rather than lending directly at a higher interest rate of 10 per cent and incurring the one in twenty chance of losing all of their funds; the expected return on both options is equivalent, but the direct lending option is more risky. The differential between the direct lending rate and the rate offered by the financial intermediary can be regarded, in effect, as a sort of insurance premium that lenders would have to pay for the reduction of the risk involved in lending.[3] By interposing a margin between the rates charged to borrowers and the rates offered to depositors to allow for expected losses, financial intermediaries can issue secondary financial claims with a high degree of (nominal) capital-certainty.

The greater the number of independently risky loans that a financial intermediary is able to make, the more predictable is the actual rate of default loss that it will experience. None the less, whatever the scale of a financial intermediary's operations, there is still some probability that actual losses may exceed the expected losses allowed for in its operating margins. The depositors in a financial intermediary, however, can be largely insulated from this residual risk if the intermediary itself has adequate capital and reserves in relation to the scale of its lending. If a financial intermediary is constituted as a company, then unexpected losses will be borne by the ordinary shareholders, and its depositors are at risk only in the event of unexpected losses greater in value than the institution's own equity capital.

A second distinguishable type of risk transformation is performed additionally by financial intermediaries such as, in the UK, investment and unit trusts. Individuals, as an alternative to direct acquisition of marketable securities, can acquire the secondary claims issued by these intermediaries who then use the funds to acquire asset portfolios consisting largely of marketable securities. The risk involved here arises from the fluctuation in the market value of securities so that the yield (except in the case of the nominal yield on a fixed-interest bond held to maturity) cannot be predicted with certainty. As previously intimated, ordinary shares are particularly risky assets, there is uncertainty both regarding current dividends and their capital value at particular future points in time. The explanation of risk transformation by financial intermediation in this instance lies in the principle of portfolio diversification – the inclusion of a larger number of different risky securities in a portfolio, as opposed to concentration on a smaller number of securities. More precisely, the inclusion in a portfolio of several securities with the same expected return and risk characteristics can result in a reduction in the risk of the whole portfolio, without the acceptance of a lower expected return. The principles involved can again be illustrated with reference to a simplified example.

Suppose an individual has £1,000 to invest and is contemplating purchasing the ordinary shares of two companies, a retailing company and an oil company, whose shares are both priced at £1 per share. The individual plans to hold his shares for a given period and conjectures that the purchase of shares in either company offers the possibility of two outcomes: a return of 10 pence per share, in the form of dividends and capital gains, if things go well, and a return of 2 pence per share if things go badly; he estimates that there is a 50 per cent chance of either a good or bad outcome occurring. Thus by purchasing 1,000 shares of either company he has a 0.5 chance of a return of £100 and a 0.5 chance of a return of £20. The expected return from investing £1,000 in the shares of either company is thus 0.5(£100) + 0.5(£20) = £60; the actual return will be either £100 or £20.

Suppose, however, the individual considers the alternative strategy of diversifying his portfolio of shares by investing £500 in the shares of both the retailing company and the oil company. Suppose, again, that the returns to be derived from the shares of both companies are independent – the chance of a good or bad outcome for the retailing company's shares is entirely unaffected by the actual outcome for the oil company's shares and vice-versa. The possible outcomes which can result from the diversified portfolio can be represented as follows:

| | | Retailing company | |
		Good	Bad
Oil company	Good	£100	£60
	Bad	£60	£20

Since the individual holds now 500 shares in both companies, a good outcome for his retailing company shares results in a return of £50; if at the same time there is a good outcome for the oil company shares then his shares in this company also yield £50 – making a return of £100 in total. There is now, however, only a 25 per cent chance of such an outcome occurring; there is a 50 per cent chance of the retailing company's shares doing well but since the returns on the shares of the two companies are independent, only on half of these occasions will the shares of the oil company do well simultaneously. Similarly, there is a 25 per cent chance of the shares of both companies doing badly at the same time, in which case both holdings yield £10, making £20 in total. There is also a 25 per cent chance that the shares of the retailing company will do well and those of the oil company will do badly (and vice-versa) and in this instance the return is £50 on one type of share and £10 on the other, yielding a total return of £60. Each of the four portfolio returns shown has thus a 25 per cent chance of occurring.

The expected return on the portfolio containing 500 shares of both companies is thus:

$$0.25(£100) + 0.25(£60) + 0.25 (£60) + 0.25(£20)$$

which sums to £60. This expected return is still the same as in the case where the individual purchased 1,000 shares in either company, but the important point to note is that the variability of the returns has been reduced. Instead of a 50 per cent chance of either £100 or £20, there is now only a 25 per cent chance of each of these extreme outcomes occurring and a 50 per cent chance that the diversified portfolio will yield the expected return of £60. Diversification has thus reduced risk without affecting the return which can be expected on average; the principle in homely terms is one of 'not putting all your eggs in one basket', so that there is a chance of possible losses being offset by possible gains elsewhere.

In general the risk of a portfolio declines as the number of independently risky assets is increased. However, this relationship is not a simple linear one – portfolio risk initially declines rapidly as the number of independent assets is increased from a position of complete specialization, but the rate of risk reduction declines as the portfolio is further diversified. It is thus possible for some individuals who have substantial funds to invest to derive most of the benefits from portfolio diversification by direct holdings of marketable securities. Indirect investment via financial intermediaries is most beneficial for individuals who have relatively small amounts of regular savings or who are substantially averse to risk. Because the transaction costs involved in handling a purchase or sale of securities are independent of the size of a particular transaction (the costs to brokers and dealers of handling a purchase of 200 shares are no different from one involving 20,000 shares) it is proportionately more expensive to transact small blocks of shares. Thus, by collecting relatively small amounts from a large number of individual savers and pooling them into a general fund, subsequently invested in large blocks of a large number of different securities, financial intermediaries can provide individual small savers with secondary financial claims which reflect the risk-return characteristics of a heavily diversified portfolio at much lower transaction costs.

Additionally, superior expertise in asset selection may enable financial intermediaries to reduce risk even further than in the way suggested by our simple example. In our example we assumed that asset returns were independently risky and, hence, uncorrelated. However, the returns on different assets may be correlated with each other – if they tend to move in the same direction over time they are positively correlated, whereas if they move in opposite directions they are negatively correlated. Positive and negative correlations have different implications for the effect of diversification on risk reduction. For example, suppose with reference to the example above that a good outcome for the shares of the retailing company could be expected only when there is a good outcome for the shares of the oil company, so that the returns on the shares were in fact positively correlated. In this instance there are only two outcomes on the diversified portfolio, a good outcome of £100 or a bad outcome of £20, each with a 50 per cent chance of occurring, so that the gains from diversification are zero. Conversely, suppose that the returns have negative correlation; the retailing company's shares do well only when the oil company's do badly and vice-versa. Here portfolio diversification eliminates risk completely – there is only one possible outcome, a certain return of £60. Thus, if a portfolio contains assets whose returns are negatively correlated, then the reduction in risk can be even greater than in the case where their returns are independent.

In practice the returns on different securities rarely, if ever, exhibit perfect negative correlation (indeed most individual share prices tend to move over time in the same general direction as share prices as a whole) so that the complete elimination of portfolio risk is not a practical possibility. None the less, systematic research may enable some assets to be identified which have some tendency for their returns to be negatively correlated with the returns on the shares traded in the market as a whole, and the inclusion of such assets in a portfolio can improve its risk-return characteristics. The specialized knowledge gained by the fund managers of financial intermediaries does give them some comparative advantages over the representative individual wealth-holder in the selection of different assets for inclusion in a diversified portfolio.

As in the case of liquidity transformation, organized markets may also play a significant role in reducing risks for the holders of financial assets. In recent years there have developed markets in the UK in financial futures and traded options and, like similar futures markets in commodities, such markets allow financial investors holding various assets to hedge against the risks of changes in market values. In essence, the existence of such markets enables financial investors to transfer risk to speculators who specialize in assuming risk.

Notes

1 Brokerage and dealing, as distinct activities, may be carried out in practice by a single institution.
2 The situation with regard to secondary markets in assets such as mortgage loans may be in a state of transition. In the USA a secondary market in mortgages already exists and there are indications of a similar development in the UK.
3 This example, in fact, exaggerates the likely insurance premium involved because of the comparative advantage which financial intermediaries possess in assessing creditworthiness and gauging the risks associated with individual loans.

Further reading

Bain, A. D. (1981) *The Economies of the Financial System*, Oxford: Martin Robertson, Chapter 4.
Coghlan, R. (1980) *The Theory of Money and Finance*, London: Macmillan, Chapters 7 and 8.

Part three

Institutions and Markets

Chapter five

The organization of the financial system

In the UK there has evolved a sophisticated financial system which comprises a large number of institutions of diverse size and legal form who perform a variety of specialized functions. In terms of overall employment or contribution to measured GDP the financial 'industry' can be considered as a significant element in the overall economy. It has been estimated that by 1982 around 1.7 million people constituting approximately 8 per cent of the employed population were engaged in the provision of financial services,[1] while the National Income accounts reveal that in 1985 the 'banking, finance, business services, and leasing sector' accounted for approximately 8.4 per cent of total GDP at factor cost. Over the last twenty-five years or so, the financial sector has constituted one of the fastest growing areas of the UK economy and along with this overall growth there has been considerable innovation and structural change. In this chapter we seek to describe in broad outline the main institutions and markets that comprise the financial system and to summarize some of the major changes that have occurred and which are still ongoing.

The financial system and the 'City'

In terms of geographical concentration, many financial institutions and the head offices of such institutions are physically located in the 'square mile' which constitutes the City of London and the 'City' can be thought of in a metaphorical sense as the nerve centre of the UK financial system. However, the whole financial system is by no means synonymous with the City. Most obviously, the financial system has a dispersed geographical presence in the form of the branch offices of the banks, building societies, and insurance companies which are spread throughout the country, while a number of important institutions have their head offices elsewhere in provincial cities. In fact, only about a fifth of those employed by financial institutions actually work in the City.

It should also be emphasized that the activities of those financial institutions located in the City are not limited purely or primarily to serving the needs of UK residents; the City has a long-established role as a major international financial centre. This role developed historically particularly during the late nineteenth century when sterling became widely used as an international means of payment and bills of exchange drawn on London and discounted in the London money market financed a large proportion of international trade transactions between residents of countries other than the UK. With the gradual decline in the use of sterling as an international currency in the fifty years after 1914 the City's external financial role diminished in importance, but in the 1960s and 1970s a major resurgence occurred with the rapid development of the so-called Euromarkets. In relation to banking, for example, what was termed the Eurocurrency market involved banks physically located in London accepting foreign currency deposits, mainly dollars, from foreign residents and then lending in the same currency to foreign borrowers. In effect, London became an 'offshore centre' for other countries through which financial transactions were routed often, initially, as a way of circumventing certain official regulations imposed on domestic financial transactions in these other countries. The development of the Eurocurrency market resulted in a substantial increase in the number of foreign banks with a physical presence in London (the number grew from around eighty in the late 1950s to over 300 by the end of 1979 and as far as the City banks were concerned, foreign currency deposits became far more significant than domestic sterling deposits. In recent years the significance of Eurocurrency business for the City has declined in relation to a growing Eurobond market which represents an internationalization of the issue and dealing in securities in fundamentally the same way as the internationalization of banking.

Thus grafted on to the role of the City institutions in the domestic financial system is an extensive offshore business in banking and securities. Prior to 1979 it was possible to conceive of fairly rigid demarcation lines between the international and domestic activities of the City in that exchange controls inhibited UK financial investors from fully participating in the Euromarket; since then, however, the demarcation lines have become much less distinct. It should also be appreciated that the City, as such, contains many institutions other than purely financial ones; it is a major international centre for non-life insurance business and it comprises various organized markets for spot and futures trading in a variety of physical commodities and also services such as international shipping.

The classification of financial institutions

In organizing the discussion of the structure of any complex system it is natural to seek some classification scheme which distinguishes between particular elements in the overall system and divides them into homogeneous subgroups. There are many possible criteria one could adopt for this purpose, but a typical approach is to attempt to classify institutions in terms of some common specialized functions they perform, as when, for example, economists group the population of manufacturing firms into particular 'industries' according to the type of physical commodity they produce. A simple clear-cut categorization of financial institutions along such lines at the present time, however, is much more difficult to devise than it would have been, for example, in 1959 when the Radcliffe Committee[2] reported on the workings of monetary and financial institutions. Although, even at that time, the Committee concluded that the various markets for credit functioned in the economic sense as a single unified market, note was made of the great differences in the activities of particular financial institutions and the fact that each type of institution had 'its special type of business and by tradition or commercial arrangement a preference for one form of lending rather than another'.[3]

The picture of a high degree of specialization in the activities of individual institutions has altered dramatically since the date of the Radcliffe Report. Not only have the boundaries between particular types of financial services become eroded, there has also been a substantial process of diversification in the range of functions carried out by individual institutions. In effect, both as a result of mergers and internal diversified growth, many financial institutions can now be described as multi-product rather than primarily single-product firms. Moreover many institutions, while formally constituted as separate companies, often are elements of much larger conglomerate groupings under unified ownership. The present structure of the financial system thus inhibits the use of any simple classification scheme where institutions, as distinct legal entities, can be grouped unambiguously according to certain specific functions they undertake. In the succeeding chapters, the discussion of the role of financial institutions is organized along the lines of the broad classification scheme adopted in the Wilson Committee Report on Financial Institutions,[4] which is primarily a

111

functional approach, but it should be appreciated that the 'institutions' referred to in specific instances may often span a variety of financial activities or they may be part of a much larger conglomerate grouping.

Apart from the Bank of England which, as the nation's central bank, stands as a distinct institution in its own right, one can make an initial broad distinction between those institutions which contribute to the workings of the organized financial markets and financial intermediaries in the sense defined earlier.

The organized financial markets

The institutions involved in these markets are those which carry out broking or agency functions on behalf of ultimate buyers and sellers and those which 'make' secondary markets in financial claims by acting as principals, buying and selling on their own account.

In the UK the organized financial markets are usually subdivided broadly according to the maturity of the financial claims being traded. The markets for short-term financial claims are generally termed the 'money markets' while the markets for longer-term financial claims are usually described collectively as the 'capital market'; the capital market is often explicitly further subdivided into the primary market – the new issue market – and the secondary market, which in the UK means primarily the Stock Exchange. Up to thirty years ago the distinction between the money and capital markets was fairly clear-cut in that it would have been safe to say that money market claims ranged from overnight money loans to bills of exchange with a maturity, typically of three months, and invariably less than a year. This distinction is now, however, somewhat blurred at the margin in that some of the claims traded in what are still conventionally termed the money markets, have maturities in some cases up to five years.

One can now distinguish a further broad category of organized financial markets. Such markets do not involve the purchase and sale of financial claims themselves, rather they involve the purchase and sale of options and futures contracts in particular financial claims.

Financial intermediaries

The Wilson Committee made a broad distinction between three types of financial intermediaries: deposit-taking institutions, investing institutions, and specialized financing agencies.

Deposit-taking institutions

The common feature ascribed to deposit-taking institutions is that they accept deposits which constitute generally liquid and nominally capital-certain financial claims and then make loans or acquire other assets with longer average maturities, i.e., they undertake maturity transformation.

We should note that this particular classification cuts across the distinction we made in Chapter 1 between banks and non-bank financial intermediaries. In the UK, as far as official statistics are concerned, all institutions deemed by the Bank of England to be engaged in banking activities are included in a subset of deposit-taking institutions termed the UK monetary sector. The classification of certain deposit-taking institutions as 'banks' is based primarily on the definition of a bank laid down in the Banking Act of 1979. For purposes of prudential control, the Banking Act defined a bank as an institution providing the following services:

1. current and deposit account facilities or the acceptance of funds in wholesale money markets;
2. finance in the form of overdraft or loan facilities, or the lending of funds in the wholesale money markets;
3. foreign exchange services;
4. financing through the medium of bills of exchange and promissory notes, together with finance for foreign trade;
5. financial advice or investment management services and facilities for arranging the purchase and sale of securities.

Under the terms of the 1979 Act, institutions performing these functions who had net assets of at least £5 million and who also 'enjoyed or should have enjoyed for a reasonable period of time a high reputation and standing in the financial community' were recognized by the Bank of England and allowed to call themselves 'banks'. The act also established a subsidiary category of 'licensed deposit-takers', which included institutions which met certain criteria as to financial standing, but which did not provide the range of services necessary to qualify for full bank status. Before November 1981 the Bank of England, for statistical purposes, included in the UK banking sector only recognized banks, but after this date recognized banks and licensed deposit-takers were grouped together as part of an extended sector – the UK monetary sector.

This particular definition of a bank again cuts across the distinction made earlier between banks and non-bank financial intermediaries. Previously, we defined banks as institutions whose liabilities for the most part serve as a means of payment, but the UK monetary sector includes a large number of institutions whose liabilities in large measure do not serve in this capacity. Within the UK monetary sector the institutions which correspond most closely to banks in the traditional sense are included in a subclassification termed 'retail banks'. Retail banks are defined for official statistical purposes as banks which either have extensive branch networks or which participate directly in a UK clearing system. Such banks are prepared to accept deposits, if necessary, in small amounts from a variety of personal and business clients at sight, or at short notice, and a large proportion of their sight deposits constitutes current accounts transferable by cheque – the provision of a money transfer mechanism is a major element in their operations.

Retail banks in this traditional sense are distinguished in the official statistics from other banks which are often described under the heading of 'wholesale banks'. In wholesale banks the depositors are primarily large industrial and commercial companies, governmental authorities, or other financial institutions and deposits are, for the most part, accepted only for large minimum amounts (of the order of £50,000), the bulk of deposits being time deposits for periods in excess of seven days. The deposits of wholesale banks are not generally transferable by cheque, any chequing facilities provided are operated through accounts they hold with retail banks and not by direct participation in the clearing house arrangements. Wholesale banks, as institutions, are like other non-bank financial intermediaries, in the sense that there is a tiered relationship between their liabilities and those of the retail banks.

We should note that the division between retail banking and wholesale banking based on the minimum size of deposit, etc., in institutional terms, is not particularly clear-cut. A significant fraction of the business of banks classified as retail banks now constitutes wholesale business, while many wholesale banks offer some traditional banking services. None the less, the weighting of retail and wholesale business does vary substantially among different institutions in an identifiable fashion. An alternative nomenclature commonly used to distinguish between the various institutions included in the UK monetary sector is to describe the retail banks as 'primary' banks, in contradistinction to other banks which are termed 'secondary banks'.

The main deposit-taking institutions classified as being outside the UK monetary sector are building societies – the main justification for classifying them separately from some institutions considered as banks being the specialized nature of the loans they make. Until very recently, their prime traditional function has been restricted by legislation to that of making mortgage loans largely to the personal sector for house purchase, their major sources of funds constituting retail savings deposits. In recent years, however, building societies have been evolving their activities in a way which again blurs the features distinguishing them sharply from banks – a trend which is likely to intensify following changes in the legislation controlling their activities operative from January 1987. Apart from the building societies, the other main deposit-taking institutions are the National Savings Bank (previously known as the Post Office Savings Bank), operated through post offices, and certain finance houses whose main business is the direct financing of instalment credit sales of motor vehicles and consumer durables to persons, and plant and equipment to businesses. Finance houses obtain most of their funds from institutions included in the UK monetary sector (some similar institutions are classified as being within the UK monetary sector).

Investing institutions

These are institutions which specialize in collecting funds from individuals mostly on a longer-term basis and investing the pooled funds largely in long-term securities or, to a lesser extent, directly in property – their main common feature is that of risk transformation. In the UK investment institutions can be further subdivided into (1) contractual savings institutions and (2) portfolio institutions.

Contractual savings institutions obtain funds from personal savers under long-term contractual arrangements, whereby savers make regular contributions over a period of years in return for a future terminal lump sum payment or a future annuity. The main media for long-term contractual savings in the UK are savings schemes linked to life assurance policies and pension funds.

Portfolio institutions are institutions which permit individuals to participate in pooled investment funds (which are used to acquire portfolios of marketable securities), thus giving them access to the reduced investment risks arising from portfolio diversification. The common feature of portfolio institutions is that the secondary claims they issue have essentially the same characteristics as the primary claims they hold as assets. In the UK the two major types of such institutions are unit trusts and investment trusts.

Specialized financing agencies

These are institutions created to fill perceived gaps in financial markets with respect to the requirements of certain specific groups of borrowers. Such institutions may be public sector agencies financed by the government, or private sector agencies set up with official support, raising funds from banks, other financial institutions, or by directly issuing securities. Their common feature is the provision of finance in situations where the risk involved, or the time lags before a monetary return accrues, may be unacceptable to other providers of finance. The main gaps which have been perceived in the operation of financial markets have been in the provision of long-term equity finance and loan capital to small firms and the funding of new enterprises based on the exploitation of new ideas and innovations.

In an effort to fill this small firm gap, two private sector institutions were established simultaneously in 1945 at the request of the government: the Industrial and Commercial Finance Corporation (ICFC), incorporated by the London and Scottish clearing banks and the Bank of England, and the Finance Corporation for Industry, incorporated under the ownership of the Bank of England and a range of insurance companies and investment trusts. These were grouped together in 1973 under a single holding company, Finance for Industry, which again was subsequently reorganized under a new name in 1983 known as Investors in Industry. The bulk of ICFC's finance for small firms consists largely of medium- and long-term loan capital, but in particular cases it may provide equity capital. Another example of a specialist financing institution is Equity Capital for Industry, established at the instigation of the Bank of England and by a consortium of financial institutions, 365 in all. It aims to provide equity capital and have a continuing involvement with the companies in which it invests.

The largest public sector institution is the British Technology Group, formed in 1981, whose function is the development or exploitation of innovations. In addition to these general institutions, finance is provided directly by the government for firms in certain regions under the terms of the 1971 Industry Act. The Scottish and Welsh Development Agencies also have the function of providing finance to firms operating in these geographical areas.

Innovation and structural change in the financial system

When viewed in a historical context, a marked feature of the financial system of the UK in the last two decades, and particularly in more recent years, has been the change which has occurred in the institutional framework. Indeed, such has been the pace of change, not only in the UK but in the USA and many other countries, that it is frequently referred to as constituting a 'revolution in financial services'. Whether this description is an appropriate one is a matter on which opinions differ, but, none the less, observers of the financial system have identified a number of major interlocking trends which have changed and are changing the institutional characteristics of the financial system.

Institutional diversification

In our discussion of the classification of financial institutions we have already alluded to the fact that institutions have diversified across previous demarcation lines, both by a process of internal expansion into areas outside their traditional lines of business and by mergers and take-overs. We can illustrate this feature by briefly examining the range of activities carried out by certain UK financial institutions under unified ownership.

In the mid-1950s the activities of the retail banks were largely confined to their traditional banking functions. The largest bank at this time – the Midland Bank – had five subsidiary companies, but two were banks in Scotland and N. Ireland doing exactly the same sort of business, while the remaining three were set up to undertake executor and trustee work for the bank's clients. Nowadays, all the major retail banks have evolved into diversified conglomerate organizations whereby, either directly or through subsidiary companies, they carry out a wide range of financial activities distinct from their traditional banking role. Since 1971, when certain controls on their activities were relaxed, they have diversified their banking business on both the deposit and lending side; they compete with secondary banks for wholesale deposits in both sterling and foreign currency and they now make medium-term loans to business borrowers and compete actively with the building societies in the provision of mortgage loans to homeowners. Mainly through subsidiary and associate companies, they are active in the areas of hire purchase finance, leasing, credit cards, accepting bills of exchange, unit trust and pension fund management, insurance, personal investment management, and in arranging and underwriting new issues of shares on the capital market. Most recently, following the relaxation of the membership rules of the Stock Exchange, they have either set up companies or acquired existing Stock Exchange firms to perform the new function of broker-dealer in securities in the secondary market.

A similar wide range of financial activities is encompassed in the City institutions generally known as merchant banks, of which there are probably around a hundred in number, most of which are included as banks in the UK monetary sector (since they vary individually in size and scope no precise categorization is possible). Amongst this group of institutions are a subset who for a long period were referred to as 'accepting houses' owing to their membership of a grouping formed in 1914 known as the 'Accepting Houses Committee' (but, at the time of writing, it has been announced in the financial press that there is some prospect of this grouping being formally disbanded). The accepting houses' original function was the accepting of bills of exchange for domestic and foreign borrowers. In the late nineteenth century they broadened their activities into arranging bond issues in London for foreign governments and, somewhat later, into arranging new issues of shares for domestic companies. In the 1960s they significantly expanded into wholesale banking, both in foreign currency and sterling, and they now do considerable business in unit trust, pension fund, and personal investment management. An important element in their activities now constitutes financial advisory services to non-financial companies, particularly regarding the handling of large take-over bids (and the provision of advice to companies contesting such bids). Like the retail banks, since 1986 many accepting houses have established an ownership interest in broker-dealer firms operating on the Stock Exchange.

The often expressed objective of diversification is that, by supplying a wide range of financial services for both corporate and individual clients, firms can increase their competitive edge in a wide range of markets because, like supermarkets in retail trade, they can offer one-stop financial shopping; by dealing with a single, well known supplier of established reputation customers can economize on search and information costs. Another reason is that there may exist economies of scope (i.e. cost savings whereby the total cost of producing two products jointly is lower than the combined cost of producing the same volume of each product separately), due to the existence of some common indivisible input. In the financial context it has been suggested, for example, that the widespread adoption of micro-electronic technology for routine operations has resulted in excess capacity in firms' existing facilities, which can be used for purposes other than an institution's traditional ones at little extra cost.

While the diversification of the activities of individual financial institutions across traditional boundary lines has usually resulted in increased competition in many areas, not all observers are agreed that the emergence of financial conglomerates is unambiguously in the wider public interest. A particular problem that has been identified with the newer financial groupings participating in the capital market concerns the possible conflicts of interest that can arise between the various agency relationships which institutions have with clients, when the activities of securities dealing, broking, corporate financial advice, and fund management are combined within a single organization. Most obviously, for example, a fund manager might transact with the securities dealing branch of his own organization, even though better prices might be available elsewhere in the market. The solution envisaged in the new legislative framework for investor protection, based on the Gower Report,[5] is that firms should create internal barriers, or demarcation arrangements, known colloquially as 'Chinese walls', which restrict the internal contacts between various parts of the business. Many have doubts, however, as to whether such artificial devices can be fully effective given the degree of self restraint on which they depend.

A further problem concerns the prudential supervision and regulation of financial conglomerates whether by statutory authorities or self-regulatory agencies. Although institutions may be legally free to move outside their existing boundaries, it may not be easy for the regulatory and supervisory authorities to follow, because in most countries prudential supervision of different types of activity is exercised by separate authorities. In the nature of things supervision must relate to institutions – their capital to liabilities ratios, their liquidity ratios, etc. – and there may be incompatability of regulation because different activities require different balance sheet requirements. The governor of the Bank of England has officially expressed concern regarding the possibility of what he called 'cross-infection', where, for example, the failure of a bank's Stock Exchange subsidiary might lead to difficulties for the parent company, putting at risk the interests of depositors.[6]

Internationalization

Advances in international communications have meant that as far as financial institutions are concerned, national frontiers are

119

becoming much less significant; it is possible for parent institutions to establish branches in other countries and manage them effectively as a single integrated operation. In the UK, foreign-owned institutions, having located initially in London primarily to participate in 'Euro' business, are playing an increasing role as competitors of domestic institutions in domestic markets, for example, in wholesale banking, mortgage lending to domestic residents, leasing, and securities trading. Likewise UK institutions are rapidly expanding their overseas network of branches and subsidiaries.

New financial instruments and markets

The pace of change in this area has been extremely rapid over the last twenty years and demonstrates the capacity of the financial system to adapt flexibly to changing circumstances. Many innovations developed in response to the increased volatility of interest rates and exchange rates experienced during the 1970s – a prime example being the development of markets in financial futures and traded options which facilitate the hedging of such risks. Other innovations, particularly in the USA, have developed as a way of avoiding restraints imposed by the regulatory authorities.

Many of these developments are blurring the conventional distinction often made between 'credit' and 'capital' markets. In credit markets, financial intermediaries originate loans for specified periods, hold the assets corresponding to the loans in their balance sheets until final repayment by the borrower, and monitor the performance of the borrower in making regular interest and amortization payments; in capital markets borrowers issue securities which can be transferred from the original lenders to subsequent holders. A traditional form of credit arrangement, for example, has been the mortgage loan, originated and held by a building society until maturity. In the USA during the 1970s, however, new forms of housing finance have emerged. Retail institutions originate mortgage loans in the usual way, but the assets corresponding to a number of individual loans are then pooled and used as collateral to issue mortgage-backed bonds in the primary capital market, the bonds being subsequently traded in the secondary market like other corporate and government securities. Retail institutions retain their functions of originating mortgage loans and, in many cases, receiving interest payments from the borrower, but the financing is subsequently hived off to the holders of the mortgage bonds, often pension funds and banks. This process of creating markets for certain debts previously considered unmarketable has been termed 'securitization' and an increasing percentage of new mortgages in the USA are securitized in this way. Such developments in housing finance are now being contemplated for the UK; one company, the National Home Loans Corporation, has been created specifically to develop this business using estate agents as retail outlets and other mortgage companies based on large American banks are reported as being potential participants.

The introduction of new technology

A primary factor underlying many other developments has been the introduction of microelectronic technology. The application of electronic data processing to clerical operations in banks, for example, has been going ahead for some twenty years, cheque handling by the banks is now largely automated, as is the clearing mechanism. As well as reducing the costs of routine transactions, new technology has also made possible the rapid dissemination of information to decision-takers in financial institutions, enabling them to deal with much larger volumes and ranges of business. Technology has made it possible to devise and manage more complicated financial instruments than would have been conceivable in the past. In financial markets brokers and dealers now use equipment giving them instant access on video screens to information on interest rates, exchange rates, quoted securities prices, company news, etc.; telephone contacts with other traders can be made in seconds and deals automatically recorded.

New technology is also increasingly affecting the contact relationships between retail deposit institutions and their depositors. The most obvious development to date has been the introduction of automated teller machines (ATMs), which permit customers to make cash withdrawals and, in some cases, cash deposits, or transfers between particular accounts, outside normal office hours. Certain institutions have begun to locate ATMs in petrol stations, supermarkets, places of work, or other locations away from their branch offices. The latest development in automation is a system known as 'electronic funds transfer at point of sale', a manifestation of which was the Barclays Bank 'Connect card' system introduced in June 1987, and which, it has been forecast, will replace many payments now being made by cash or cheque. This system involves retailers having specially designed electronic units at customer check-outs; the customer presents a card which is inserted into the unit and also registers a personal identification number; the unit then conveys a message to the computer of the issuing institution requesting a debit of the account of the card-holder and a credit of the account of the retailer involved. The development of this system requires considerable capital expenditure, but the advantage to deposit-taking institutions in the long run lies in a substantial reduction in the costs arising through the processing of cheques. Savings to retailers will accrue from a quicker transfer of funds to their accounts, less risk of bad debts arising from banks refusing to honour customers' cheques and, possibly, from lower administrative and security costs.

Another development concerns what is termed 'home' or 'office' banking, whereby personal or business clients can use their own computers to communicate directly with that of their bank to initiate money transfers or obtain immediate statements of account. The Nottingham Building Society, in conjunction with the Bank of Scotland, has already introduced such a system called 'Homelink' for personal customers with a minimum investment of £1,000.

Liberalization

By this term is meant a trend towards a breakdown of informal or formal cartel arrangements amongst financial institutions, together with a relaxation of many regulations imposed by the authorities constraining their freedom of action. A number of examples can serve to illustrate this trend: in 1971, in return for the relaxation of informal controls ('requests' from the Bank of England) restricting their lending, the clearing banks abandoned a long-standing cartel arrangement whereby their interest rates were set in a rigid relationship to Bank Rate (at this time the Bank's published discount rate). After 1981 further restraints on the banks, imposed by the supplementary special deposits arrangement, were ended, as were rigid reserve ratio requirements relating to the composition of banks' assets. For a long period the building societies operated an interest rate cartel, where individual societies set uniform rates recommended by the Building Societies Association; this, however, effectively broke down in 1983, while the rules governing the activities of building societies have been revised under the 1987 Building Societies Act, permitting them greater freedom to diversify away from their traditional activities. Again, in 1986, there took place a substantial revision of the rules of the Stock Exchange which had previously inhibited competition.

Notes

1 Rybczynski, T. M. (November 1984) 'The UK Financial System in Transition', *National Westminster Quarterly Bulletin*.
2 Committee on the Working of the Monetary System (1959) *Report*, Cmnd 827, London: HMSO.
3 Ibid., paragraph 25.
4 Committee to Review the Functioning of Financial Institutions (1980) *Report*, Cmnd 7937, London: HMSO.
5 Gower, L. C. B. (1982) *Review of Investor Protection: A Discussion Document*, London: HMSO.
6 Leigh-Pemberton, R. (March 1984) 'Changing boundaries in financial services', *Bank of England Quarterly Bulletin*.

Further reading

Carter, R. L., Chiplin, B. and Lewis, M. K. (eds) (1986) *Personal Financial Markets*, Deddington: Philip Allan.
Galletly, G. and Ritchie, N. (1986) *The Big Bang*, Plymouth: Northcote House.
Harrington, R. (1986) 'Money and finance: public expenditure and taxation' in Artis, M. J. (ed.) *The UK Economy*, London: Weidenfeld and Nicolson.
Maycock, J. (1986) *Financial Conglomerates: The New Phenomenon*, Aldershot: Gower Publishing Company.
Plender, J. and Wallace, P. (1985) *The Square Mile*, London: Century Publishing.

Chapter six

Organized financial markets

An initial point which should be noted in relation to the organized financial markets in the UK is that, unlike the organized markets for trading in physical commodities, in most instances there is no particular central location where participants meet to conduct transactions on a face to face basis; transactions are largely conducted by telex or telephone, or by personal visits to individual places of business. Until very recently the secondary market for trading in long-term bonds and ordinary shares did involve face to face trading on the floor of the Stock Exchange building. The traditional way of conducting business involved jobbers (dealers) in particular securities being located in booths on the trading floor and brokers (acting as agents for clients) conducted their deals with jobbers in this centralized location. The radical changes in the organization of the Stock Exchange introduced from 27 October 1986 (termed by the financial media as the 'Big Bang'), however, resulted in the traditional methods becoming obsolete, although prior to the event there was some uncertainty as to whether taking on the Stock Exchange floor would none the less continue. In the months following 'Big Bang' it became apparent that the vast majority of business was being transacted by telephone dealing from member firms' premises and, accordingly, the Stock Exchange Council announced on 2 March 1987 that trading of securities on the Stock Exchange floor would cease. At the time of writing, the market in traded options in securities is still conducted physically on the Stock Exchange floor.

Although it is conventional for descriptive purposes to classify the organized financial markets into 'money' markets and 'capital' markets according to the maturity of the financial claims being traded (and in this chapter we follow this convention) it should be emphasized that the boundary lines drawn on the basis of such a distinction are blurred – at the margin the money markets shade into the capital markets. Moreover since 'Big Bang' it is becoming less easy to identify particular institutions narrowly with either the money markets or capital markets; financial conglomerate organizations are tending to span all areas of the organized financial markets.

The money markets

The most important economic function of the organized money markets is to provide a means whereby various economic units can quickly adjust their cash positions. For all economic units, whether they be households, business enterprises, financial institutions, or governmental bodies, the timing of cash inflows or outflows is rarely perfectly synchronized or predictable in the very short run. An individual bank, for example, may experience at particular times an increase in its deposits and cash reserves in excess of the volume of loans being requested by customers, while at other times its situation may be reversed. For business enterprises the timing of receipts from sales of goods and services may differ markedly from the timing of expenditures on payrolls, inventory purchases, and other services. Similarly, for governments, tax receipts are often bunched at particular times of the year whereas expenditures are made on a fairly continuous basis.

Because of this lack of synchronization the cash holdings of economic units will vary over time, but on average a certain stock of cash will be held as a buffer stock to accommodate these ebbs and flows in cash inflows and outflows – a retail bank, for example, will hold an average stock of cash reserves in the form of notes and coin or bankers' deposits at the Bank of England, while business enterprises will hold a certain average current account deposit in a retail bank. However, the holding of buffer stocks in these forms ties up an economic unit's resources in a relatively unprofitable form, in that a higher interest rate may be available on alternative assets. If, however, a unit has access to facilities for short-term lending and borrowing at low transaction costs then, given the same general pattern of cash inflows and outflows, it can operate with a lower average stock of cash. In times when its cash balance is temporarily high it can reduce it by short-term lending, acquiring assets that are still relatively liquid; at times when it has a shortage of cash to meet immediate commitments, it can borrow short term in anticipation of future cash inflows which will enable its debt to be redeemed.

The importance of an organized market lies in the fact that, for many units such as banks and large companies, the sums involved are of a substantial magnitude and, as an alternative to attempting to contact matching partners directly in an informal way, there are obvious advantages in transacting via specialized brokers and dealers, who are in more or less continuous contact with other major potential borrowers and lenders and who can place or raise funds almost immediately. Given the sums involved, brokers' commissions are often only a tiny percentage of the value of loans they arrange. The money markets are thus exclusively 'wholesale' markets involving sums typically for a minimum of around £500,000 in individual transactions. Given this economic role of the money markets, the financial claims traded are characterized by low default risk (so that the institutions issuing claims are likely to be those with the highest credit standing, or alternatively, the claims will be accepted by institutions of similar standing) and short term to maturity (long-term securities may be highly market-able and, thus, almost equivalent to short-term securities in the exchange convenience sense, but there is much greater price risk). Thus the main institutions lending and borrowing money in the money markets are institutions within the UK monetary sector, other financial institutions, the Bank of England operating as agent for the central government, local authorities, public corpor-ations, and large industrial and commercial companies – most acting on occasion as both lenders and borrowers.

The traditional money market

Until around the middle 1950s there was essentially only one distinguishable money market referred to as the 'discount market', nowadays often called the 'traditional market'. This market revolved around uniquely British institutions called discount houses whose history can be traced back to the early nineteenth century. The ultimate lenders to the discount market were primarily the clearing banks and the ultimate borrowers commer-cial firms and later the central government. Essentially, the clearing banks lent money at very short term (on call or on an overnight basis) to the discount houses who then used these funds, together with a certain volume of funds raised from non-bank sources, to discount longer maturity Treasury bills or commercial bills that had been accepted by an established accepting house. The discount houses in a sense, therefore, acted as bankers to the banks and stood as an intermediary between the banks and the ultimate lenders. They thus enabled the banks to economize on their cash reserves by providing them with interest-bearing assets which were almost as liquid as cash – the default risks and interest rate risks involved being borne by the accepting and discount houses. The funds the discount houses obtained from the banks were secured – the discount houses pledged assets against their borrowing with a margin of security in excess of the actual amount borrowed. As far as the banks were concerned, the liquidity of call loans to the discount houses was underpinned by the fact that the Bank of England assumed the role of lender of last resort to the discount houses; the discount houses could, if necessary, obtain cash to repay the banks if loans were called, by rediscounting bills or borrowing on the security of bills from the Bank. The discount houses held bills to maturity but also made a secondary market in bills, the banks acquired bills nearing maturity from the discount houses for holding in their own portfolios.

The broadened money markets

The discount market is still of considerable importance, particularly to the workings of the monetary system, but over the last three decades the scope of the financial claims traded in the London money market has broadened significantly and trading in these newer claims now considerably exceeds that in commercial and Treasury bills. When organized trading in other short-term financial claims began to develop, such markets were often referred to as the 'parallel markets' – this particular term implying a separation of these markets from the traditional discount market. In the initial stages of the appearance of these newer markets in the late 1950s and during the 1960s, the notion of separate markets made some descriptive sense as the institutions borrowing and lending funds did not significantly overlap; the retail banks and the discount houses largely confined their participation to the traditional market (at this juncture the retail banks operated in the newer markets through their subsidiaries). This separation, however, began to break down in the late 1960s when the discount houses started to participate more actively in the newer markets, while after 1971 the retail banks likewise entered directly as significant borrowers and lenders. In the reverse direction the greater participation of wholesale banks in the discount market was induced by the liquidity ratio requirements imposed in 1971 on all banks, which required them to hold reserve assets in the form of discount market assets. Thus by the early 1970s the discount market had become much more closely related to the newer markets as one branch of a highly integrated set of markets.

Similar remarks apply to the newer markets themselves. Although it is often customary for descriptive purposes to distinguish between various submarkets on the basis of the

127

particular institutional borrowers involved, or on some other characteristic of the financial claims being traded, there is a high degree of overlap in the institutions lending funds in the various submarkets and the assets involved are in reality very close substitutes. Moreover, funds are frequently borrowed in one part of the overall market and lent in another. Thus, although there do exist systematic differentials between interest rates on financial assets of the same maturity traded in different submarkets, due to perceived differences in lenders' risk, funds are switched rapidly from one market to another in response to changes in interest rate differentials, and by this process of arbitrage, interest rate movements due to changes in the demand for funds in one submarket will be transmitted very quickly to other markets. The main submarkets usually separately identified are briefly described below.

The local authority market

Local authorities need to raise short-term finance due to differences in the timing of their receipts from local taxes and government grants in relation to their spending commitments. The primary forms in which local authorities borrow short term (apart from very short-term borrowing via bank overdrafts) are by way of the issue of short-term negotiable bonds, bills, and local authority deposits. Bonds are issued for periods of not less than a year and may be fixed interest or variable interest rate bonds. The title 'yearling bonds' is often used to describe such bonds, although some bonds are issued with maturities longer than a year. Since 1972, local authorities have been permitted to issue bills in anticipation of the receipt of future rate payments of value equal to one-fifth of the anticipated amount; bills are issued by tender, usually with a maximum life of six months, owing to the fact that bills with maturities of less than this period are eligible bills for rediscounting at the Bank of England. The main form of short-term borrowing for periods less than a year comprises local authority deposits for varying terms, but the majority have a maturity of less than seven days. Deposits are generally in units of £100,000 upwards, the instrument of borrowing being a non-negotiable deposit receipt.

The inter-bank market

As the name implies, this market is essentially a market where one bank places deposits with another, although many non-bank lenders with surplus funds could be said to be involved in that deposits are often placed in banks via market intermediaries. In the eighteenth and nineteenth centuries it was common practice for banks to place deposits in other banks, but with the growth of branch banking the practice ceased – indeed a tradition was firmly established in the UK that banks did not borrow from or lend directly to each other (rather transfers of funds took place indirectly via loans made to the discount houses). The origins of the modern market can be traced back to the 1950s, but the significant growth occurred after 1962 when the newly emerging wholesale banks located in London engaging in foreign currency lending began to make inter-bank loans of foreign currency; in 1964 these banks increasingly began to make inter-bank loans in sterling on an unsecured basis. The scope of the inter-bank market broadened considerably after 1971 when the retail banks entered as significant borrowers and lenders in the market both in sterling and foreign currency – on balance the retail banks as a group tend to be net lenders to the market, channelling funds to the wholesale banks. The size of the sterling inter-bank market can be gauged by the fact that gross inter-bank deposits in March 1987 amounted to some £59.5 billion, this total constituting around 22 per cent of the gross deposits of the banks included in the UK monetary sector.[1] Similarly, inter-bank deposits in foreign currency amounted to £99.9 billion. Inter-bank deposits are made for varying terms ranging from overnight to over three years, although the majority have terms of three months or less. The sums involved in individual transactions are very large, usually a minimum of £500,000.

The certificate of deposit market

Certificates of deposit (CDs) first emerged as a financial instrument in New York in 1961, and in 1966 dollar CDs were first issued in London by certain American banks. The market in sterling CDs originated in 1968 when the Bank of England gave permission to around forty wholesale banks to make such issues.

A sterling CD is a document certifying that a deposit has been made with the UK office of a UK or foreign bank; it states the rate of interest, the date of repayments, is fully negotiable and is in bearer form. It may be issued in multiples of £10,000 with a minimum of £50,000 and a maximum of £500,000 for any one certificate. Certificates may be issued in maturities of three months to five years and are issued at their par values. The issue of certificates is closely regulated by the Bank and at present around 300 banks are permitted to issue CDs. Since 1983 some of the large building societies have also been permitted to issue certificates.

The advantage of CDs is that from the issuing bank's point of view they are fixed-term deposits which cannot be withdrawn until the redemption date, but from the point of view of the depositor the negotiability of the certificate means that it is a highly liquid asset – the original depositor is not locked in to holding the certificate to maturity but can resell his certificate to a subsequent holder. There is, of course, some risk for the holder of the certificate in that if short-term interest rates generally rise this will be reflected, as with any fixed coupon bond, in a fall in the market price. CDs were originally conceived of as a way in which an individual bank could attract deposits from non-bank entities, but from the inception of the sterling market banks have held a significant fraction of the stock of CDs and the market has developed as an extension of the sterling inter-bank market for longer-term deposits. In March 1987, of the total outstanding CDs issued by banks operating in the UK, 43 per cent were held by other banks (including the discount houses)[2], the remainder being held by overseas holders and large commercial companies. In March 1987 institutions in the UK monetary sector had gross CD liabilities amounting to some £23.0 billion in sterling and £76.7 billion in foreign currency.

Finance house deposits

This market relates to the raising of wholesale deposits by institutions specializing in consumer finance, leasing, factoring, etc. Many such institutions are now formally classified as banks within the UK monetary sector, thus blurring the formal distinction between this market and the inter-bank market, but a significant number of finance houses are not so classified.

The commercial paper market

This market is the most recent UK market initiated in March 1986. Commercial paper comprises short-term unsecured promissory notes issued by large companies in bearer form and on a discount basis. Commercial paper differs from other money market instruments such as commercial bills in that it is an obligation of the issuer only, whereas bills are an obligation of both the drawer and an accepting bank. A further difference is that issuers of commercial paper do not have to be tied to specific trade transactions which, in many circumstances, is the case with bills. To be eligible an issuer must be listed on the London Stock Exchange and have net assets of at least £50 million (or the issuer must be a subsidiary of such a company). Maturities must be between 7 and 364 days and must be in minimum denominations of £500,000. The management of commercial paper programmes on behalf of the issuers at present is restricted to recognized banks.

Market institutions

Apart from the institutions borrowing and lending funds in money markets, the highly organized nature of the markets stems from the existence of various market intermediaries. Since 1986 the particular institutions involved have been subject to increasing change due to the growth of financial conglomerates (involving the loss of autonomy of many specialized institutions) and increasing competition across previously fairly well defined demarcation lines – many of the newer conglomerate institutions formed for trading in long-term securities are extending their activities into the money markets. One can, however, distinguish three primary functional roles which such intermediaries perform:

1. While certain transactions take place directly between ultimate borrowers and lenders, a key co-ordinating role is performed by institutions acting as deposit brokers, alternatively termed 'money' brokers, through which a substantial volume of transactions are channelled; the role of brokers is one of matching up potential borrowers and lenders. Brokers are in continual telephone contact with each other, the money market divisions of the banks, and with other regular clients, and their existence ensures that information is swiftly transmitted between various parts of the market and hence that the overall market is highly competitive.
2. Certain institutions combine the role of borrowing and lending funds with a role of secondary market makers in the negotiable instruments traded such as bills and CDs. Until recently, the primary institutions performing this role were the long-established discount houses of which in January 1987 eight remained in existence as distinct entities, but they are now subject to increasing competition in this role from other conglomerate institutions.
3. The traditional role originally performed by the accepting houses, but now performed by many other institutions, of accepting bills issued by commercial borrowers thereby reducing the default risks attached to such bills.

The capital market

The institutions involved in the workings of the capital market can be distinguished essentially on the basis of their functions in the primary market, where new securities are offered to the public, and in the secondary market where existing securities are traded.

The new issue market

In the case of ordinary shares, new issues can be made by companies with shares already traded on the Stock Exchange or by companies seeking a listing on the Stock Exchange for the first time. Every issue will involve a stockbroking institution, as they alone can fulfil certain requirements of the Stock Exchange authorities, and usually an issuing house (these days the stockbroking institution and the issuing house may be part of the same conglomerate institution). The main issuing houses are members of the Issuing Houses Association and comprise the accepting houses and other merchant banks included in the UK monetary sector as well as non-bank issuing houses. The function of the issuing house is to manage the issue, rendering advice on the timing of the issue, the terms on which it is offered and carrying out the associated legal, administrative and publicity tasks involved. In certain cases the issue house itself acts as a principal, buying the securities from the company and then offering the securities to the public. In other cases it acts primarily as an agent, but even in this case the issuing house accepts some risk in that it guarantees that a certain sum will be raised. To cover itself, the issuing house will arrange for the issue to be underwritten by a number of other financial institutions which, in return for some commission (often around 1½ per cent of the value of the issue) guarantee to buy a stated number of securities at an agreed price. If the whole issue is taken up by the general public the underwriters will not be called on; if some of the securities are unsold the underwriters are obligated to purchase them. The main institutions involved in the business of underwriting are investing institutions such as insurance companies, pension funds and investment trusts.

In the case of new issues of government bonds the procedures are rather simpler. The Bank of England manages the issue and, in the case where securities are sold by tender, itself acts as the underwriting institution; unsold stock is taken up by the Bank and then sold in the secondary market subsequently. The methods of issuing government stocks are described more fully in Chapter 7.

Initial flotations of shares

A company wishing to raise capital for the first time by the issue of shares subsequently to be traded on the Stock Exchange has to fulfil certain requirements as to its past trading record and financial standing laid down by the Exchange. Until 1980 there was a single set of requirements needed for a Stock Exchange listing, but in that year a second tier was introduced in response to criticism that the dominant UK secondary market was inaccessible to growing small and medium-sized companies. As an alternative to seeking a full Stock Exchange listing a company, by satisfying a less stringent set of requirements, could obtain a quotation on the Unlisted Securities Market (USM). In January 1987 access to the Stock Exchange was broadened still further by the introduction of a 'third market' which permits the entry of small untested companies. Many of the companies suitable for entry to the third market previously had access to an informal 'over the counter market' where certain institutions were prepared to make secondary markets in particular shares outside the Stock Exchange.

A company seeking admission to the first tier of the market may simply wish to obtain a quotation for its existing shares – in this case it can enter the market by 'introduction'. If a company wishes to use its listing to raise extra capital by the issue of new shares it has several choices of method:

1. *Placings*: with this method the company sells the shares to an issuing house which will have preplaced the majority of its shares with investors, predominantly investing institutions. One quarter of the issue must be made available to the general public. As from 27 October 1986 this method can be used for issues up to £15 million.
2. *Offers for sale*: here the issuing house or broker purchases the shares at a fixed price and the shares are then offered to the public at this price with the issuing house arranging the subunderwriting of the issue.
3. *Offers for sale by subscription*: the technical difference between this and the second method is that the company rather than an issuing house offers the shares directly to the public.
4. *Offers for sale by tender*: in this case the public is invited to tender for the shares at any price over a stated minimum. In a true tender the minimum price accepted would be that price which ensured that all the shares were sold but the method used in London is a common price tender. A single striking price is set at which it is believed that the issue will be fully taken up and anyone tendering for shares at a higher or equal price receives an allotment at the striking price. Offers for sale by tender are underwritten in the usual way.

The choice of issue method depends on the transaction costs for issuers in relation to the sums being raised. A placing is the preferred method for small issues because costs are usually lower; subunderwriting is not involved and advertising expense is avoided. The tender method is used when, for some reason, there is particular uncertainty regarding the price at which the shares might be taken up. In the USM the main method of raising funds has been via placings, while in the third market the responsibility for issuing shares falls on some sponsoring institution (which has to be a Stock Exchange member), which, again, places the shares with investors.

Additional issues of shares by companies

Companies already listed on the Stock Exchange wishing to raise additional capital have traditionally made 'rights issues'. Rights issues are similar to offers for sale except that new shares are offered for sale to existing shareholders in proportion to the shares they already own. Suppose, for example, a company has issued two million shares previously and seeks to issue 400,000 additional shares; it will then make a 'one for five' rights offer to its existing shareholders, each shareholder having the right to buy one new share for each five existing shares that he holds. A shareholder does not necessarily have to exercise his rights, he can sell his rights to another individual or institution and, as new shares are typically issued at a discount below the price of existing shares on the secondary market, the rights to buy shares have a value in themselves. The rationale of issuing shares at a discount is to ensure that the subscription price does not turn out to be higher than the market price of existing shares, due to possible falls in share prices between the announcement of the issue and the final date for subscription – new shares will obviously not be subscribed for if existing shares can be purchased at a lower price. Such issues are usually underwritten, but some companies avoid the costs of underwriting by making deep discount rights issues.

Generally speaking, companies issuing additional shares are largely restricted, under both the terms of the 1985 Companies Act and the rules of the Stock Exchange, to making rights issues in order to safeguard existing shareholders from the earnings dilution which would follow if new shareholders could obtain shares at a discount to the existing market price. Under amended Stock Exchange rules operative from October 1987, however, companies are allowed to make non-rights issues for periods up to a year, providing a majority of at least 75 per cent of the shareholders approves such a policy at a shareholders' meeting.

This amendment is designed to allow domestic companies to raise capital more freely in foreign capital markets.

Future changes in new issue methods

The changing institutional structure of the capital market has prompted speculation regarding possible changes in the techniques of issuing new shares. One possibility being mooted is that issuing houses in future will bear the entire underwriting risks of an issue rather than spread the risk by subunderwriting. A further possibility is that some issuing houses will adopt techniques common in the USA known as the 'bought deal'. In a bought deal a single institution purchases the whole issue of shares from the company and then subsequently places it with investors – the company gets its money at low transaction cost leaving the financial institution to bear the risk of disposing the shares on the market. The difference between a bought deal and a traditional UK placing lies in the timing and exposure of the institution involved. In a placing, although the issuing house technically purchases the whole of an issue and then places it with investors, it does not generally bear the risks of the whole issue because it has time to preplace the issue. In the USA the issuing house does not preplace securities, the whole issue is taken on to the institution's books and then resold on the market without knowledge of any firm commitments by financial investors to purchase the shares. Such activities can only be carried out by institutions with substantial capital resources because the risks involved are much greater. For companies seeking to issue additional shares, the bought deal technique, however, is in conflict with the principle of 'rights issues'.

The Stock Exchange

The dominant market for the secondary trading of long-term securities in the UK is now formally called the 'International Stock Exchange of the United Kingdom and the Republic of Ireland Limited' which in legal terms is now constituted as a company comprising individual members of the participating firms and also corporate members. Recent years have witnessed sweeping and fundamental changes in the organization of secondary trading in securities and in the institutions involved.

Under the traditional methods of trading developed in the nineteenth century, and later formalized in the rules of the Stock Exchange in 1908, a rigid distinction was made between members who traded as principals for their own profit or loss (stockjobbers) and those who traded as agents of others (stockbrokers). Brokers were the point of contact between the outside public and the Exchange; individuals or institutions wishing to buy or sell securities contacted a broker who, in return for a commission, executed the client's order with a jobber. Jobbers held portfolios of securities and stood ready to deal continuously with brokers who, by obtaining quotations from competing jobbers physically located on the trading floor of the Exchange, could obtain the most favourable prices on their clients' behalf. Under the rules each firm was allowed to act in a single capacity only – either as a jobber or broker. Jobbers undertook not to deal with non-members, while brokers undertook not to deal direct with other brokers nor execute matching buying and selling orders from clients – all orders were channelled through a jobber. Also, under rules originally introduced in 1912, competition between brokers was restricted in that they were not allowed to provide broking services below specified minimum rates of commission.

The single-capacity system of dealing was also accompanied by restrictions as to the permitted forms of institutions in which the functions of broking and jobbing could be pursued, and by various restrictions on the entry of new members. Until 1969 the only permitted form of organization was that of a private partnership and firms ranged in size from a single partner to a legal maximum of twenty. In that year brokers and jobbers were allowed the freedom to form limited companies and a further relaxation of the rules occurred in 1971 when 100 per cent of the capital of a corporate member firm was allowed to be owned by outside interests. The participation of outside financial interests in member firms was, however, limited by a proviso that no single shareholder could hold more than 10 per cent of the capital of an individual firm.

Until 1976, Restrictive Trade Practices legislation in the UK applied only to manufactured goods, but in that year the scope of the legislation was broadened to include services. Thus, under the terms of the new legislation the Stock Exchange had to register its Rule Book with the Office of Fair Trading and subsequently, in 1979, the practices of the Stock Exchange were referred for scrutiny by the Restrictive Trade Practices Court. In the event the case was never heard by the Court; in July 1983 the Secretary of State for Industry and Trade and the Chairman of the Stock Exchange reached an 'accord', whereby the government agreed to suspend the action in the Court providing the Stock Exchange abolished minimum commissions and relaxed the rules of entry. Following the accord a series of decisions were taken which have transformed the institutional structure of the Stock Exchange. Most fundamentally, from October 1986 the single-capacity system (which was unique to the UK) has ended and institutions can now combine the previously separated roles of jobbers and brokers, acting in a dual capacity.

The abandonment of minimum commissions and single capacity set in train substantial changes in the ownership of a number of member firms. With the prospect of lower commissions many broking firms concluded that to remain viable they would have to diversify into securities dealing, but dealing is a high-risk activity which requires substantial amounts of equity capital. As a result of the traditional dealing methods many broking firms were inadequately capitalized for a dual role and to expand into dealing they needed additional capital. Generally speaking, however, large sums of equity capital can only be raised if the contributors are given formal control over the firms concerned and, accordingly, the Stock Exchange Council relaxed their rules on the ownership of participating firms; from 1 March 1986 single outside interests were permitted to own 100 per cent of member firms[3] and limited liability corporate membership was allowed at the same time. Additionally, certain restrictions were lifted on the creation of new member firms by outside interests. The requirement for additional capital on the part of existing firms was matched by a desire on the part of other financial institutions to diversify into UK security dealing and broking and, in anticipation of the changes in ownership rules, throughout 1984 and 1985 practically all the jobbing firms and many of the major broking firms formed alliances with outside interests. After March 1986 these alliances hardened into formal mergers and take-overs.

By October 1986 out of 200 original member firms, most of whom were partnerships, more than half had become part of larger financial conglomerate groupings. A total of sixty-five outside entities had participations in original member firms, more than half such entities being primarily engaged in banking; thirty-six outside interests were UK companies, seven were American and the remainder were largely from the rest of Europe. In the restructuring process many traditional Stock Exchange firms lost their identity, others remain in existence as distinct entities although owned by outside interests. Roughly half remain independent of outside interests although many have switched from partnership to corporate status. Not all new entrants to the market pursued the method of acquiring existing firms; Lloyds Bank, for example chose to build up its own operation, a route chosen by some American and Japanese banks who created new subsidiary companies specifically for UK securities operations. By January 1987 membership of the Exchange had expanded to 360 firms, although some of these were separately constituted firms under unified ownership. (The Bank of England required that firms dealing in gilt-edged securities had to be separately capitalized entities.)

The new dealing arrangements

The new system that has replaced single capacity is termed the 'competing market maker system'. There is now only one type of member firm – the broker/dealer. A subset of such members is registered as market makers, or primary dealers, and they undertake to deal on a continuous basis in particular securities, in effect, performing the previous jobbing function. All members, whether or not they are market makers, can now act as principals buying and selling securities in direct deals with members of the public, or they can act in a purely agency capacity conveying clients' orders to other broker/dealers. Under the Stock Exchange rules, member firms do not have complete freedom to act at their discretion in either capacity; if a broker/dealer receives an order from a client in a security in which he is not a registered market maker then he can only deal as a principal, or match the order against another client's order, if he can produce a superior transaction price for the client than by going to a market maker. Similarly, if the firm receiving the client's order is a market maker in the security in question, it has to deal at a price as good as could be obtained by an agency transaction with another market maker. In transactions with the public a broker/dealer is obligated to inform the client of the capacity (either agent or principal) in which he is acting in any deal. Although within such restrictions all firms are free to act in a dual-capacity role, the majority of firms still continue to act primarily as old-style agency brokers.

In October 1986 there were twenty-seven firms registered as market makers in government securities (the gilt-edged market) and thirty-six firms registered as market makers in ordinary shares. It has been widely predicted, however, that the volume of business will not be sufficient to support this number of firms and that competition will cause the exit of many of the present participants. The present conventional wisdom seems to be that there is a high probability that market making in UK securities will come to be dominated by large foreign-owned multi-national institutions. At the time of writing (July 1987) the subsidiaries of two major UK banks, Midland and Lloyds, have retrenched on market-making activities.

Two other types of firm, again for the most part subsidiaries of conglomerates, have an important role in the structure of the secondary market:

1. In the gilt-edged market there are six 'inter-dealer brokers'; their function is to provide a mechanism through which market makers can trade anonymously with each other to unwind the positions they may incur by dealing with clients. If, for example, a large selling order is received from an institutional customer, a market maker might find itself holding more of a particular stock than it desires and rather than wait for a matching buying order it can dispose of its unwanted stock to other market makers via the broker mechanism. This mechanism enables the impact of large individual deals to be dispersed over several market makers and facilitates the ability of individual firms to deal continuously, thus enhancing the market's role in the provision of liquidity.
2. There are ten firms of Stock Exchange money brokers; their function again is to facilitate continuous dealing by arranging loans of securities from financial institutions or money from the banking system for market makers, who are thus enabled to settle transactions when they are temporarily short of securities to deliver or short of money to make payments for securities received.

Along with the change from single to dual capacity have come radical changes in the technical methods by which the market operates. The old face to face system has been replaced by a new computer-based price information system, the Stock Exchange automated quotations (SEAQ) system, modelled on the system by which shares were traded in the USA outside the physical trading floors of the existing Exchanges. Under this system market makers enter their quotes for certain sizes of deals from terminals located in individual dealing rooms into a central computer and the information is then relayed electronically via TOPIC (the Stock Exchange video screen information system) to other broker/dealers or to other investors subscribing to the system. Price quotations can be updated very quickly. Market makers also have to input details of every trade executed in the market within five minutes of its completion and, for certain securities, information on the prices of last trades completed is also displayed on the video network (all trading information is also stored in database records for purposes of market surveillance). Armed with this visually-displayed price information broker/dealers or other investors can then execute transactions with market makers by telephone. At present SEAQ is only a price-display system, but it has the capability of being upgraded to an all-electronic dealing system where orders up to a certain size can be automatically executed at the best price displayed by the market makers in a particular stock. Obviously, this system makes geographical location irrelevant as far as transacting is concerned.

To take account of different levels of trading activity in different ordinary shares for SEAQ purposes four categories of shares have been established:

1. *Alpha-stocks*: these are the most actively traded UK equities. Market makers are obliged to maintain continuous firm two-way prices for a minimum size of 1,000 shares during SEAG trading hours. Market makers have the option of posting firm quotes for deals of larger size.
2. *Beta-stocks*: these are less actively traded equities with fewer market makers. Market makers display continuous firm quotes for a minimum of 1,000 shares but details of last trades executed are not displayed.
3. *Gamma-stocks*: in this instance market makers are required to display only indicative two-way prices.
4. *Delta-stocks*: these are the least actively traded shares. In this case the video screen only gives information on market makers who are committed to quoting a price on enquiry, or information on accredited dealers. An accredited dealer, if approached by a seller, is obliged to seek a matching buyer or vice-versa, but is not required to quote firm two-way prices.

Gilt-edged and other fixed-interest securities for SEAQ purposes form a separate category. Market makers are obliged to display mid-prices only although many market makers quote two-way prices on a subsidiary closed user group network. The prices of last trades executed are not displayed.

The reasons for the changed trading system

As mentioned previously, the changes in the institutional structure were set in train by the threat of a Restrictive Practices Court action, but immediately following the accord both the government and the Stock Exchange Council announced that the single-capacity system was to be maintained. The single-capacity system did have the great advantage that it avoided conflicts of interest in the relationship between brokers and their clients; the jobbers acted as principals while brokers had no incentive to act in anything other than a disinterested fashion in obtaining the best available deal on their clients' behalf.

However, when the special committee set up by the Stock Exchange Council in November 1983 came to examine the problems associated with the ending of fixed commissions, it came to the conclusion that single capacity could not be maintained. Several sorts of pressures, it was contended, would lead to the effective breakdown of single capacity. For example, brokers faced with falling commission income would resort to certain strategies such as arranging matched deals between clients, thus getting two commissions and by-passing the jobbers. In fact, the original introduction of fixed commissions in 1912 had been a response to competitive pressures of this sort which were placing strains on the traditional single-capacity system. Given the incompatability between the abolition of minimum commissions and the continuation of single capacity, it was then concluded that the protection of investors' interests would best be served by a dealing system which simultaneously permitted the details of all deals made in the market to be stored in a central database.

Apart from doubts regarding the feasibility of continuing with single capacity while abandoning fixed commissions, other pressures for change had been building up. The main bulk of trading activity in securities was becoming increasingly dominated by the transactions of large institutions rather than individuals and the changing nature of the clientele using the market was placing increasing strains on the jobbing system. Institutional investors bought and sold securities in large blocks in relation to the inventories that jobbing firms were able to hold and, consequently, jobbers reacted to institutional buying or selling by moving prices more frequently and in larger steps; thus the market's role in the provision of liquidity was becoming less effective.

Further, the single-capacity system, while in principle providing protection for investors, led to transaction costs for users that were high in relation to securities exchanges in other countries (although transaction costs in the UK were also raised by the levy of stamp duty on transactions in securities) and there were indications that trading in UK securities was taking place to an increasing extent outside the ambit of the Stock Exchange. During the early 1970s some competition for the Exchange had emerged when a number of accepting houses instigated a computer-based communications link known as ARIEL (Automated Real-Time Investments Limited), whereby members could input bids for and offers of securities. A more significant development was the growth of trading in American deposit receipts (ADRs). Under this system American financial institutions bought blocks of shares in UK companies, registering them in the name of their UK

141

subsidiaries and paying stamp duty on the transaction. They then issued certificates, or titles, to the underlying shares (known as deposit receipts) which were then traded in New York in the usual way. After the removal of exchange controls in 1979, ADRs provided an alternative method for UK investing institutions of, in effect, trading in UK shares at the lower transaction costs offered in New York.

The growing trend towards internationalization of dealing in shares issued by companies based in other countries in the way represented by the ADR system was a major factor underlying the structural changes in the Stock Exchange. As mentioned previously, during the 1970s there had developed a vast international market in Eurobonds,[4] but London had emerged as the most important centre. The secondary market in Eurobonds was, however, conducted outside the Stock Exchange. An initial issue of Eurobonds involved a syndicate of investment banks who subscribed for the issue in a bought deal arrangement and then resold the bonds to investors; the secondary market was then made, usually by the original syndicate members in a dual-capacity role. The Eurobond market functioned effectively without the rigidities of the single-capacity system and the position of London as a centre for Eurobond trading depended on the ability of the institutions located there to compete on an equal footing with institutions located elsewhere. If London was to emerge as a major centre for global trading in shares the same principles applied – the dealing mechanisms needed to be reconciled with those used in other competing financial centres to remove any competitive disadvantage. London had certain natural advantages as an international centre in that it was located mid-way in the time zone between Tokyo and New York, but European centres such as Frankfurt and Paris were similarly situated and securities institutions located there traded on a dual-capacity basis offering lower transaction costs. Thus, international considerations reinforced the other considerations prompting a change in the system.

Parallel to the domestic SEAQ system is thus the SEAQ international system, whereby competing market makers in London quote two-way prices for a range of some 500 securities from seventeen different countries. This display is transmitted to international locations, permitting foreign investment institutions to transact via telephone in the London market.

The immediate effects of the 1986 changes

In February 1987 the Bank of England published the findings of a survey of some of the immediate changes following 'Big Bang'.[5]

As predicted, the indications were that transaction costs for large transactions had been substantially reduced. Commission rates for large bargains in the range between £100,000 and £1 million had fallen by around 50 per cent and, for very large deals in excess of £2 to 3 million, by even more. In many cases, large institutional investors were able to achieve greater reductions by dealing on a net of commission basis directly with market makers or with other broker/dealers acting as principals. For investors dealing in small bargains of less than £1,000, however, commissions had remained broadly unchanged.

The increased number of market makers also had some effect in narrowing margins between buying and selling prices, particularly in beta and gamma shares. Another effect has been that, compared to pre-1986, the spread between buying and selling prices does not widen as rapidly as the size of a deal increases and dealers are prepared to quote firm prices for deals of substantial sizes. This indicates greater 'depth' to the market, i.e. the capacity of individual market makers to absorb large orders without changing the price at which they are prepared to deal.

The markets in traded options and financial futures

One consequence of the greatly increased volatility in interest rates and prices of financial assets which occurred during the 1970s has been the emergence of markets in financial instruments which enable investors to hedge against the risks of future changes in asset prices.

In the UK one of the most important organized markets is the market in traded options, which began operations on the floor of the Stock Exchange in April 1978. As the name implies, the commodity traded on the market is an option to buy or sell a certain quantity of securities at a specified price at some future point in time. An option to buy a particular security is known as a 'call' option whereas an option to sell is known as a 'put' option. The price at which the purchase or sale is to be completed is known as the 'exercise' price or, sometimes, the 'striking' price. The arrangements regarding the future dates on which options can be exercised vary; with some types called European options the option must be exercised on a specific date, but the options traded in London are American options which can be exercised at any time during a specific period. Options are traded with a life of nine months and there are expiry dates every three months so that traders always have options with three different dates to choose from.

The working of traded options can be illustrated by considering an actual example of call options in a particular share. Table 6.1 shows the prices at which call options in the computer firm Amstrad were being traded on 11 May 1987.

Table 6.1   Call options on Amstrad shares on 11 May 1987

Exercise price	Prices		
	June	*September*	*December*
180	34	41	48
200	20	28	36
220	9	19	25

Source: Financial Times, 12 May 1987.

Suppose a certain individual A was considering buying call options on Amstrad shares on this date; he could have bought options expiring in June, September or December and he could choose three different exercise prices of 180p, 200p or 220p respectively, compared to the current market price of an Amstrad share, which on 11 May 1987 stood at 206p. Options with exercise prices at any particular time below the current market price are referred to as 'in the money options' and conversely as 'out of the money options' if the opposite case applies. The price of a traded option is known as the 'premium' and it is a measure of the risk involved in guaranteeing the delivery of the underlying shares during the period – as can be seen from the table, the premium for the longer periods to the expiry date (December options) invariably exceeds those for the shorter periods. Option prices refer to pence per share and options are traded in contracts of 1,000 shares.

Suppose individual A decides to buy September call options. He contacts a broker and instructs him to buy a contract giving him the right to buy 1,000 shares at an exercise price of 220p; the premium for this option is 19p, thus the total cost of the contract is £190. Matching individual A there must be another individual B who has sold, or 'written', a corresponding contract to deliver 1,000 shares if called upon to do so, at an exercise price of 220 pence. Individual B then receives £190 from the broker who arranged the sale of the option. The writing of a call option should not be confused with buying a put option. If individual B bought a put option he would have bought the option to sell shares at a certain exercise price but could decline to exercise the option; by writing a call option B is obligated to sell shares if called upon to do so. Because both parties must be free to close their positions at any time, ultimate buyers and sellers do not have obligations directly to each other but to a clearing house.

Whether A will exercise his option as September approaches depends on what happens to the underlying price of Amstrad shares. If the price of the shares remained at 206p, A will decline to exercise his option – why buy something at 220p which is available at 206p? Suppose, however the market price of the shares increases to 250p. Individual A may now exercise his option and buy the shares for 220p, or he can sell the option to somebody else at a price reflecting the fact that the underlying share price has risen (most individuals in fact buy call options with no ultimate intention of receiving any shares). Either way, A makes a profit on his transaction; by buying shares at 220p and reselling at 250p he makes 30p per share which, less his premium of 19p per share, yields him a net gain of $1000 \times 11p = £110$ (less transaction costs, interest foregone, and a possible capital gains tax liability).

As far as the writer of the option is concerned, if the share price remains below 220p then B is unlikely to be called upon to deliver and a gain is made of 19p per share. If, however, the share price rises above 220p B may be forced to sell shares at a price lower than the market price and thus makes a loss corresponding to A's gain. If the share price rises above 220p B has thus an incentive to renege on the agreement and in recognition of this problem there are rules which require the writers of options to lodge some collateral or 'margin' with the Exchange.

It should be emphasized that the buyer of a call option need not want to buy particular shares and the writer of the option need not own them. Both buying and selling parties may trade with the knowledge that if the share price subsequently moves, the market price of the relevant option will be greater or less than the price at which the option was initially transacted; either party prior to the exercise data can wind up a position by an opposite selling or buying transaction making a gain or loss on any difference between the appropriate option prices at two points in time.

Who trades in such options? As in all such markets there are two groups of traders: speculators and hedgers. Options permit speculators to bet on their beliefs that particular share prices are going to move. In the example above A was able to make a capital gain of £110 on an outlay of £190 which is less than he has to outlay if he wanted to speculate by holding the underlying shares themselves (to buy 1,000 Amstrad shares on 11 May 1987 would have required £2,060). By transacting in options, speculators expose themselves to risk. Hedgers, on the other hand, might use options to reduce risk. Suppose, for example, a market maker on the Stock Exchange at a particular time had a short position in a particular share – he has contracted to sell shares which he has not yet got at a particular price for delivery at the end of the account period. If share prices subsequently move upwards before the date of delivery the market maker stands to incur a loss on this particular deal. By buying appropriate call options the market maker, for the cost of the premium, can hedge against this risk – any losses due to the rise in share prices can be offset by gains in the option market as option prices move in concert with the underlying share price.

At the time of writing there are forty-nine individual shares on which options can be written in the London market. Options can also be written on gilt-edged stocks and on a general index of share prices (the FT–SE 100 index) which enables hedging against general movements in share prices. In a call option relating to the FT–SE index, if the actual value of the index is above the exercise value the buyer of the option receives money from the writer of the option.

The Stock Exchange has a competitor in the London International Financial Futures Exchange (LIFFE) established in 1982.[6] Most of LIFFE's contracts are futures contracts. Futures and options are similar in that they both constitute claims on assets to be implemented at a future date but there is one major difference which affects the risk-return characteristics of the contract. Whereas at delivery on a futures contract both buyer and seller are obliged, if necessary, to take and make delivery of an underlying asset at a certain price, in the case of an option the obligation to make or take delivery is restricted to the seller, or writer, of the option. For a buyer an option is a right not an obligation and may not be exercised; thus the maximum loss for the buyer of an option is restricted to the price at which the option was bought. With futures contracts neither party has a limit to his potential loss, buyers and sellers of futures gain and lose symmetrically.

Notes

1 Source: *Bank of England Quarterly Bulletin*, June 1987, Table 5.2.
2 Source: ibid., Table 5.2.
3 The 10 per cent limit imposed in 1971 had been raised to 29.9 per cent in 1982.
4 Technically, Eurobonds are bonds denominated entirely in one currency but issued in a number of capital markets of currency

denomination different to that of the issue. The main borrowers are international organizations, public sector institutions and large multi-national companies.

5 *Bank of England Quarterly Bulletin*, February 1987.
6 At the time of writing there is a prospect of LIFFE and the Stock Exchange forming a single exchange for options and futures trading.

Further reading

Hamilton, J. Dundas (1986) *Stockbroking Tomorrow*, London: Macmillan.
Higson, C. J. (1986) *Business Finance*, London: Butterworths, Chapter 11.
Kidwell, D. S. and Peterson, R. L. (1984) *Financial Institutions, Markets and Money*, New York: Dryden Press, Chapter 21.
Shaw, E. R. (1981) *The London Money Market*, third edn, London: Heinemann.
Stonham, P. (1987) *Global Stock Market Reforms*, Aldershot: Gower Publishing, Chapters 1 and 4.
Thomas, W. A. (1986) *The Big Bang*, Deddington: Philip Allan.

Chapter seven

The Bank of England

We have already discussed briefly in Chapter 1 how many of the Bank of England's functions evolved historically by unconscious rather than conscious design when it was operating as a profit-making private concern. The continuation of the Bank as a private institution for a long period after its role as a central bank was recognized could be said to have been somewhat anomalous, although in practice, as the Governor of the Bank from 1922 to 1944 (Montague Norman) made clear, the Bank's role in policy making was subject always 'to the supreme authority of the government'. The formal recognition of the Bank's role as a central bank eventually came in 1946 when the Bank was nationalized.

Constitutionally the Bank is not a Department of State administered by a Minister and civil servants, rather, it is a public corporation with the right to manage its internal affairs independently. The subordinate status of the Bank to the Treasury, however, is established in statutory terms in Clause 4 of the 1946 Bank of England Act: 'The Treasury may from time to time give such directions to the Bank as, after consultation with the Governor of the Bank, they think necessary in the public interest'.

Significantly, though Clause 4 is constitutionally operative, formal directives from the Treasury to the Bank have never been used; policy is arrived at by a process of joint consultation, discussion and persuasion. The Bank, of course, is closely involved with the participants in the financial system and in this sense it is a means of channelling the views and opinions of the financial community to the government, as well as offering its own independent policy advice. As far as the organization of the Bank is concerned, the controlling body is the Court of Directors which comprises six full-time or executive directors and twelve part-time directors. Technically, directors are appointed by the Crown which means in reality they are made by the Prime Minister on the advice of the Chancellor of the Exchequer.

The Bank of England balance sheet

An appreciation of the structure of the Bank's balance sheet is useful as an aid to the understanding of certain facets of its operations. The balance sheet is illustrated in Table 7.1. It is still presented in the form laid down in the 1844 Bank Charter Act. As the Bank is no longer required to receive gold before issuing notes, the division between the Issue Department and the Banking Department has lost much of its previous significance. In administrative terms and for purposes of national income accounting, however, the Issue Department is treated as being part of the central government sector while the Banking Department alone is treated as a public corporation. Any income earned by the Issue Department accrues automatically to the Exchequer while the Bank, as a separate institution, receives its income from the interest on the assets it holds in the Banking Department.

Table 7.1 The Bank of England balance sheet as at 29 October 1986

		£ million		
Issue department				
Liabilities			*Assets*	
Notes in circulation	12,623		Government securities	3,469
Notes in banking department	7		Other securities	9,161
	12,630			12,630
Banking department				
Liabilities			*Assets*	
Public deposits	92		Government securities	688
Banker's deposits	962		Advances and other accounts	833
Special deposits			Premises, equipment, and	
	0		other securities	1,526
Reserves and other accounts	1,985		Notes and coin	7
Capital	15			
	3,054			3,054

Source: *Bank of England Quarterly Bulletin*, December 1986, Table 1.

Examining the Issue Department account, the liabilities side of the balance sheet needs little explanation, the only liabilities being notes issued either in circulation or held in the Banking Department. At one time, as discussed previously, notes issued constituted genuine liabilities in that the Bank could be called upon to redeem them for gold; since 1931 this has not been the case and notes are therefore liabilities in a book-keeping sense only. On the assets side, most of the gold reserves previously held by the Issue Department were transferred to the EEA in 1939 and the remainder in 1970. The note issue is thus entirely a fiduciary one nominally 'backed' by securities. Until fairly recently the majority of the securities held in the Issue Department were government securities which, since the Issue Department is treated as part of the government sector, were simply technical book-keeping assets. In the early 1980s, however, as a consequence of the Bank's operations in the discount market the item 'other securities' grew rapidly – these consist largely of commercial bills issued by private borrowers (in the financial press this large stock of commercial bills was often referred to as the 'bill mountain').

Turning to the Banking Department account, 'public deposits' refers to the consolidated accounts of the various revenue collecting and spending departments of the central government. 'Bankers' deposits' refers to the accounts held by institutions in the UK monetary sector. There are two elements in the total:

1. It includes the mandatory cash ratio which institutions above a certain size in the UK monetary sector are required to hold at the Bank, set in 1981 at 0.5 per cent of each institution's eligible liabilities, but amended in September 1986 to 0.45 per cent. This is not an 'operational' cash ratio for monetary control purposes – its primary objective is to provide revenue for the Bank to finance its operations; as a counterpart to these deposits, which are non-interest bearing, the Banking Department holds interest-bearing securities as assets. The mandatory cash ratio can be regarded as an implicit tax specifically imposed on monetary sector institutions.
2. The remainder comprises balances held by the retail banks and forms part of their effective cash reserves in that, unlike mandatory cash ratio deposits, they are redeemable for notes and coin on demand.

The item 'special deposits' refers to additional interest-bearing deposits which the Bank reserves the right to call from monetary sector institutions. Such deposits constitute an additional technical instrument in the Bank's armoury for monetary control purposes but they have not been used since the early 1980s – hence the zero entry in the balance sheet for October 1986.

The item 'other accounts' refers mainly to accounts held by

overseas governments and central banks and a small number of private accounts mainly dating from prenationalization days. The remaining items on the liabilities' side are book-keeping items designed to ensure the equality of total assets and liabilities in the double-entry balance sheet. 'Capital' refers to the amounts subscribed by the original shareholders and 'reserves' represents the undistributed profits of the Bank, which if the Bank were a private concern would be legally due to the shareholders in the event of its winding up.

On the assets side 'government securities' refers to the debt owed by the government to the Bank as a separate institution – such debt comprises government bonds, Treasury bills and loans made to the government in the form of ways and means advances. 'Advances and other accounts' include short-term loans to the discount houses, holdings of commercial bills and funds contributed to special financing agencies. The item 'notes and coin' corresponds with the item 'notes in Banking Department' in the Issue Department balance sheet (both totals are rounded up to £7 million although coins held in the Banking Department constitute a slight difference between the two totals) and indicates the reserve held by the Bank to meet withdrawals of deposits. Since the note issue became wholly fiduciary and the fiduciary issue is varied in practice at the Bank's request, the size of this reserve is nowadays of little significance.

The functions of the Bank of England

Although the Bank performs a diverse range of specialized activities, the key functions that account for the significance of the Bank in the workings of the monetary and financial system are traditionally summarized under a number of distinct headings.

Bankers' bank

As we referred to in our previous discussion of the evolution of banking in Chapter 1, the holding of balances at the Bank serves as a convenient method for settling inter-bank indebtedness arising from the ebbs and flows of payments between customers of different banks. The clearing mechanism works in essentially the same way today as when it was formally instigated in 1773, except that of course the mechanisms are now computerized. We should note here that not all the institutions in the UK monetary sector maintain deposits at the Bank as a means of effecting inter-bank settlements; secondary banks maintain balances for this purpose with the clearing banks.

It is through its position as a bankers' bank that the Bank performs its role as the central note-issuing authority for the UK, which is nowadays an administrative and not a policy matter. If the general public increase their demand for notes vis-à-vis bank deposits this will be reflected in a decrease in the stock of notes held in the tills of the banks. To replenish their stocks the banks would then draw down Bankers' deposits in exchange for notes and the stock of notes held as a reserve in the Banking Department declines. If the Banking Department wishes to replenish its own reserve of notes, a change in the fiduciary issue is authorized and the Issue Department provides more notes to the Banking Department (the Issue Department holds a store of unissued notes for this purpose and the transfer is made simply by an entry in the Bank's ledgers). The Banking Department then 'pays' for the additional notes by transferring securities of equivalent value to the Issue Department, providing it with additional assets to match the increase in its liabilities. As the Issue Department for accounting purposes is part of the central government sector and its liabilities are book-keeping liabilities only, any increase in its assets through a take up of interest-bearing securities improves the financial position of the central government in relation to the rest of the economy. If the securities taken up are the government's own securities then its net liabilities are reduced – if the securities taken up are issued by other sectors its claims on other sectors are increased. Thus, in effect, an increase in the note issue provides the central government with additional finance, providing, of course, that the purchasing power of the notes exceeds the real cost of printing them.

Essentially the same mechanism operates when the banking system demands coins in redemption for bankers' deposits, but the accounting procedures are slightly different. Coins are produced by the Royal Mint, a separate government department, and in this instance when the Banking Department replenishes its reserve of coins it pays for the coins by directly crediting public deposits.

Lender of last resort to the banking system

The stability of a fractional reserve banking system ultimately rests on the 'confidence' held by the general public as to their ability to redeem bank deposits for notes and coin on demand. As we noted previously in Chapter 1 the Bank, as a pragmatic response to periodic crises of confidence which occurred in the nineteenth century, evolved the role of supplying its notes freely to other banks to maintain the general convertibility of bank deposits. Since around 1870 the Bank has consistently under-pinned the stability of the system by acting as the last resort provider of cash to the banking system.

In modern day to day terms the Bank exercises this function primarily through its operations in the discount market. In practice the daily cash position of the banking system as a whole can be affected by a variety of unpredictable factors which can be quantitatively significant in relation to the cash reserves being held; these can stem from changes in the general public's demand for notes and coin, but more usually from transactions between the central government and the non-bank public (including the Exchange Equalisation Account). For example, companies pay corporation taxes at discrete half-yearly intervals of time and the coincidence of a number of large companies choosing to make corporation tax payments on one particular day can result in a substantial net flow from Bankers' deposits into public deposits. A collective drain on the banks' cash reserves of this sort will be reflected in the calling of loans from the discount market by the banks and the discount houses in turn must find cash from somewhere to repay the banks. In the short run the only effective source of cash is the Bank and the Bank consequently stands ready on a daily basis to offset such cash shortages by open market purchases of bills from or lending to the discount market. The terms on which the Bank is prepared to deal have implications for the level of short-term interest rates, but in the immediate context the main point to note is that the Bank's support oper-ations in the discount market result in offsetting flow into bankers' deposits thus restoring the cash position of the banking system. The Bank therefore, in its contact with the rest of the banking system, operates primarily via the discount market, although in the case of particularly large cash shortages it has placed funds directly into the local authority short-term deposit market. The Bank has also on occasion dealt directly with the banks via purchases of gilt-edged securities for resale to them at a later date.

For a long period after the late nineteenth century the problem of bank failures in the UK seemed to have been relegated to past history, but the continuing potential for instability was demon-strated in the 1970s when a number of secondary banks got into difficulties. Many secondary banks expanded their deposits rapidly in this period and a considerable fraction of the assets of some banks constituted loans to property development companies secured by the value of land and property, which, at the time, was appreciating rapidly. In 1973, however, following some tightening in monetary policy, net withdrawals of deposits were made from a number of secondary banks and in November of that year the London and Country Securities bank experienced liquidity difficulties; this was followed in December by the threatened collapse of another secondary bank – Cedar Holdings. What began as a liquidity crisis for certain banks broadened in 1974 into a solvency problem as property values started to decline rapidly; certain property companies defaulted on loans and the banks found that the value of the underlying security for such loans was considerably less than the amounts lent. The Bank of England became concerned because some major banks had made interbank loans to the secondary banks experiencing difficulties and accordingly it organized a support operation which became known as the 'Lifeboat', whereby the Bank co-operated with the major clearing banks enabling them to redeem their deposit liabilities. In all around twenty-six secondary banks called on the Lifeboat for assistance and the Bank on its own account helped a number of other banks after 1975 outside the main Lifeboat operation.

Opinion on the necessity of the Lifeboat operation tends to vary. The Bank, by acting in the way it did, prevented the collapse of a number of secondary banks, but there is some doubt as to whether the failure of these banks would have resulted in a crisis of confidence sufficient to threaten the wider banking system. None the less, this episode and a later incident in 1984, when the Bank took control of the failed Johnson Matthey bank, demonstrated that the Bank itself regards its responsibility for ensuring the stability of the banking system as one of its primary functions.

Regulation of the monetary sector

The existence of an institution prepared to act as a lender of last resort may be crucial in guaranteeing the stability of the banking system, but at the same time the existence of such an institution creates a problem of 'moral hazard'. The business of banking necessarily involves taking risks, but if individual bankers know that there is an institution prepared to bail them out in the 'public interest' if they get into difficulties they may be tempted to take undue risks in the pursuit of profits. As a 'quid pro quo', therefore, for the provision of lender of last resort support, some prudential regulation of banking institutions is justified, to ensure that the public at large, via the Bank of England, are not assuming risks which should properly be assumed by the shareholders of individual banks.

The Bank's general powers to regulate the banking system were enshrined in the 1946 Nationalisation Act, but for a long period supervision was restricted largely to the large clearing banks on an informal basis. Given the structure of the banking system in the UK as it existed up until the 1960s, when the system was dominated by the clearing banks with a long conservative tradition of cautious lending practices, such informal methods may have been sufficient, but during this decade the number of institutions operating in the UK who described themselves as banks expanded considerably. At this juncture there was no comprehensive statutory definition of a bank and a number of the institutions who found themselves in difficulty during the secondary banking crisis were in fact not regarded as banks by the Bank and hence were not subject in practice to close regulation.

The experience of the secondary banking crisis and the need to comply with certain requirements of the European Economic Community resulted in steps being taken to strengthen the legal basis of the Bank's regulatory powers and these culminated in the Banking Act of 1979. In broad terms the Act sought to establish a comprehensive system of chartering deposit-taking institutions and to establish machinery to monitor and control the risks being assumed. Under the terms of the legislation no new deposit-taking business could be established without prior authorization from the Bank and existing firms had to apply for authorization in order to continue in business. The Act initially defined two categories – a recognized bank or a licensed deposit-taker, depending on the longevity of the applying institution and the range of banking functions pursued. The Act required all banks to provide the Bank with information on a regular basis for the monitoring of their risks and exposures. The Bank has developed general criteria for assessing the capital adequacy and liquidity risks of banks and how these should apply in detail to each bank is discussed on a case by case basis by meetings between officials of the Bank and the management of the bank concerned. The Bank, if it is dissatisfied with a bank, can as a last resort revoke its authorization. In the five years following 1979 twelve institutions had their authorization revoked on various grounds, including inadequate capital to absorb potential losses, insufficient liquidity, evidence of imprudent lending and failure to provide the Bank with adequate information.

Recently, in view of the growing internalization of banking, the Bank has sought to harmonize its criteria for the assessment of banks with the criteria adopted by the authorities in other countries. More specifically, in 1987 the Bank reached an accord with the USA authorities on definitions of a bank's capital, measures of capital adequacy in relation to the size and riskiness of a bank's assets and on the need for all banks to have a certain minimum ratio of capital to total assets. It is hoped that this agreement will be extended to European nations and Japan.

Following the failure of Johnson Matthey Bankers in 1984 the supervisory arrangements of the Bank as conducted since 1979 were the subject of further criticism and in 1985 a government White Paper envisaged some further strengthening of the Bank's powers.[1] A new Banking Act implemented in 1987 retains the same fundamental objectives as its predecessor, but gives the Bank greater powers in obtaining information from the auditors of a bank as well as its management and provides the Bank with powers to make formal directives to ensure compliance. The Act also removes the previous distinction between recognized banks and licensed deposit-takers.

In addition to the authorization and monitoring procedures, the Banking Act also established a Deposit Protection Fund which the Bank is responsible for administering. The Fund is aimed at providing depositors with some explicit insurance against the failure of an authorized bank and is financed by a levy on banks in relation to their deposits. In the event of failure depositors would receive compensation from the fund amounting to 75 per cent of the first £10,000 of sterling deposits with any one institution, i.e. a maximum of £7,500 per depositor per institution. The protection applies to corporate deposits as well as those of private individuals, but it does not apply to inter-bank deposits. The Deposit Protection Fund has been used in fourteen cases in the period from 1979 to 1987.

Banker to the government

The Bank, from its inception, has acted as the primary banker to the central government and performs the technical function of managing the vast majority of payments being made between the government and the rest of the economy. The government does not hold balances, other than very small working accounts, with other banks.

Apart from this technical function a further aspect of the Bank's role as a government bank is to ensure that the government always has funds at its disposal to implement its current spending commitments and to meet its obligations to redeem maturing debt. The government, of course, through its taxation policy can determine to a large extent the long-run inflows into the Exchequer account, but tax revenue flows over shorter-run periods of time are uneven and often unpredictable and are not perfectly synchronized with the short-run flows of government expenditure; even if the government has a zero budget deficit over the fiscal year as a whole there may be periods when the government is short of funds. Moreover, the government frequently incurs a financial deficit over the fiscal year.

In a purely technical sense the Bank has little difficulty in ensuring that finance for the government is always available. As we described earlier in Chapter 2 all the Bank has to do is to make a ways and means advance to the government – as the government overdraws on its account there is an increase in the item 'government securities' in the assets of the Banking Department and a corresponding increase in Bankers' deposits on the liabilities' side of the account. Ways and means advances, therefore, not only directly increase bank deposits but provide the banking system with cash and thus have implications regarding the level of short-term interest rates and the level of bank lending. If the monetary consequences of ways and means advances are to be avoided then other methods of obtaining finance for the government must be used and this involves the Bank in the function of managing the National Debt on the government's behalf; this in turn is subsumed in the wider function of implementing the government's monetary and/or interest rate policy.

The monetary policy role

A more detailed discussion of the methods the Bank uses to implement monetary policy is relegated to Chapter 13; at this juncture we seek primarily to describe the institutional framework within which the Bank operates. Since 1980 the primary instruments the Bank has used have been operations in the gilt-edged market and operations in the discount market.

The gilt-edged market

The sales of any form of government debt to the non-bank private sector can neutralize the monetary effects of central government financial deficits and can be used further to influence monetary growth arising from other causes. Some sales of debt to the non-bank private sector take the form of non-marketable instruments such as National Savings certificates and deposits in the National Savings Bank and in some years this method of government borrowing has constituted as much as 30 per cent of all funds raised. The main bulk of debt sales, however, constitutes new issues of gilt-edged securities on the capital market. The main methods the Bank uses to make new issues of stocks are:

1. Offers of new stocks, or large new tranches of existing stock for sale by tender. Tenders for conventional fixed-interest stocks normally have a minimum price set in line with market prices at the time new stock is announced. Tenders are allotted on a common prices basis, all successful bidders pay a common price which is the lowest price at which tenders are accepted, but higher bidders have priority in the allotment of stock. The tender is effectively underwritten by the Bank – any stock not taken up is taken into the Issue Department and is then subsequently available for sale on 'tap' to the market makers in the secondary market. Tenders offer sizeable amounts of stock usually in the range from £750 to £1,000 million and to facilitate the take up of stock are often offered on a partly paid basis, i.e. an investor contributes only part of the subscription price at the date of issue and pays the remainder at a future date.

2. Issues of what are called 'tranchettes' of existing stocks – the Bank takes directly into the Issue Department additional supplies of several different stocks which are then available for sale to the market makers in the secondary market. In the new Stock Exchange structure the Bank now deals directly with market makers by telephone.

3. Given the new institutional structure of the Stock Exchange, in 1987 the Bank supplemented its existing tender and tap methods of issuing stock by adopting on an experimental basis the US Treasury method of auctions of gilt-edged stock in blocks of at least £1 billion; the first such auction took place on 15 May 1987. With an auction no minimum price is set for the stock auctioned (i.e. there is no underwriting): the price at which the stock is sold depends entirely on the market (although the Bank announced that it would retain the right not to allot all stock in what it considered to be exceptional circumstances). Stock is allocated on a bid-price basis, where successful bidders pay the price which they bid, rather than on a common price basis as is the case with tenders. As part of the arrangements, all market makers in gilt-edged stocks were required to participate actively in the auctions.

With an auction system the Bank loses some of the influence it can exert on day to day interest rates in the gilt-edged market as, if it requires to sell a given block of stock, it cannot be completely certain as to the price at which it will be absorbed by the market.

The auction system is also more risky for dealers and other holders of gilt-edged securities as the market price of securities can fall in an unpredictable way. In the auction conducted in January 1988, for example, the Bank, in order to dispose of the volume of stock offered, had to accept bids at £1.50 below the price at which similar stock was trading prior to the auction, and the market price of gilt-edged securities fell sharply on this announcement. At the time of writing, it is uncertain whether this experiment will be continued.

In relation to its funding objectives there is always some residual uncertainty as far as the Bank is concerned regarding the extent to which sales of gilt-edged stock on the open market will in fact constitute net sales to the non-bank private sector, as some of the gilt-edged securities may be acquired by the banking system.

The discount market

The Bank's operations in the discount market are intertwined with its previously discussed function of lender of last resort to the banking system. The Bank's declared objective since 1981 is to 'offset daily cash flows between the Bank and the money market' and simultaneously to 'keep very short-term interest rates within an unpublished band which would be determined by the authorities with a view to the achievement of their monetary objectives'.[2]

As noted previously, the cash position of the banking system fluctuates from day to day, depending on the public's demand for notes and coin and the balance of transactions between the central government and the private sector. Some of these flows, such as the volume of maturing Treasury bills or, in the reverse direction, the volume of maturing commercial bills held by the Bank, are predictable in advance but there is inevitably considerable uncertainty as to the exact position at the start of each day. Each morning at around 9.45 a.m. the Bank publishes an initial estimate of the likely change in the cash position of the banking system and hence of the expected cash shortage or surplus in the discount market; this estimate is then amended in the light of the actual withdrawals of funds by the banks from the discount market which usually occurs during the morning. At around noon, if necessary, the Bank publishes a revised estimate and decides whether or not it is to operate in the market on that particular day.

If there is expected to be a cash shortage in the money market the usual method of intervention is that the Bank will offer to buy eligible bills (i.e. Treasury bills, local authority bills, or commercial bills accepted by an eligible bank) in some or all of four specified maturity bands within an overall range from one to ninety-one days, with two rounds of assistance normally taking place at noon and 2 p.m. In comparison with the operating method used before 1981 the Bank does not deal on pre-announced terms, rather the discount houses compete to sell bills to the Bank at offer prices of their own choice which the Bank may accept or not at its discretion.

The second method used by the Bank is to offer the discount houses sale and repurchase agreements which, in effect, are secured loans for a certain period. This method involves the same types of bills as in outright purchases but the Bank specifies a terminal date for repurchase and the discount rate at which the proceeds of the sale of bills to the Bank will be calculated. The discount houses then offer a rate of interest on the proceeds for the specified period, which again the Bank may accept or not. This technique is sometimes employed when the Bank estimates that there will be cash surplus in the market on certain future days, but more usually when there is a shortage of bills nearing maturity and the discount houses are reluctant to make outright sales of longer-dated bills because they have firm expectations that interest rates are about to fall (if interest rates fall the capital value of such bills rises and the houses are reluctant to forego this potential profit).

The final method of intervention is lending at an interest rate set by the Bank. This is used in situations where there is an unexpected cash shortage on a large scale or if the Bank wishes to see short-term interest rates increase, but believes, or discovers after the event, that the houses will not offer, or have not offered, sufficient bills at rates acceptable to the Bank for the shortage to be absorbed. The Bank may then limit its open market operations in bills and force the discount houses to borrow at a lending rate which is indicative of the higher level of short-term interest rates it is seeking to establish. Such lending normally takes place in the afternoons of particular days in late assistance to the market.

In the opposite case of a cash surplus in the market on a particular day the Bank usually operates in the afternoon by inviting the discount houses and the retail banks to bid for Treasury bills in one or more maturity bands. Even though in the 1980s the typical daily situation has been one of cash shortages rather than surpluses, the Bank is still concerned to preserve the market in Treasury bills and continues to offer them in a weekly tender. A number of institutions bid for Treasury bills, but the discount houses underwrite the tender, i.e. take up bills not subscribed for by other bidders.

The terms on which the Bank will operate by open market operations in bills, or by lending, constitute the prime source of the Bank's ability to influence short-term interest rates. Given that the authorities now view the appropriate level of interest rates as being within a band there is scope for other market forces to establish the exact level and pattern of interest rates. None the less, whenever the Bank intervenes in the market its policy has a direct effect on very short-term interest rates as it influences the immediate demand and supply situation for very short-term money and bills. Beyond this immediate impact, however, the Bank's actions are likely to be interpreted as having policy intentions with respect to the future level of short-term interest rates and, as such, will be one of the major influences affecting the expectations of borrowers and lenders in the money markets. If the Bank raises the unpublished interest rate band and responds to cash shortages in the discount market by reducing the price at which it will accept offers of bills from the discount houses, the houses are likely to suffer running losses because, unless they had anticipated the change, they would have originally discounted the bills at higher prices than they receive from the Bank. Unless the discount houses have some other grounds for firmly believing that future short-term interest rates are likely to fall, they are thus likely to respond to this signal from the Bank by raising their own discount rates on bills to avoid the risk of future losses and, given the interdependence of the money markets, interest rate changes will be transmitted to other claims of similar maturity and along the term structure.

The degree to which the Bank can determine short-term interest rates in a mechanical way contrary to the expectations held in the money markets in the very short run should not be exaggerated and it is possible to cite examples where the Bank has seemed to follow rather than lead the markets. Very often, however, official and unofficial interpretations of financial developments coincide and the Bank's operations in the discount market and market expectations can be complementary in effect.

The Exchange Equalisation Account

The final key function of the Bank is to manage on behalf of the government the EEA, which is a Treasury account and does not form part of the Bank's own balance sheet. This account, originally established in 1932, is the official repository of the nation's gold and foreign currency reserves. The function of the account is to implement any chosen official policy with regard to the sterling exchange rate – to sell foreign currency for sterling whenever the volume of foreign currency demanded exceeds the volume supplied at a chosen rate and vice-versa. The significance of EEA operations, of course, was far greater under the Bretton Woods system which operated from 1945 to 1972, whereby governments were committed to maintaining the value of their currencies in a pegged relationship to the US dollar. The EEA would be again vitally significant if the UK were to join the exchange rate mechanism of the European monetary system. Many economists, though, have doubts as to whether the EEA could be as successful as previously in maintaining a particular chosen rate in anything other than the very short run, because the volume of potential capital flows between the UK and abroad has become so much larger than the size of the official reserves. This consideration implies that if the authorities wished to implement a policy of stabilizing fluctuations in the foreign exchange rate they might have to rely primarily on variations in short-term interest rates as their main instrument (so that they could not then use short-term interest rates as a separate instrument for influencing the stock of domestic money).

None the less, in recent years the UK authorities have entered into collaborative agreements with the authorities of other major countries – the Plaza and Louvre Agreements – to attempt to influence the movements of exchange rates, and at various junctures active intervention in the foreign exchange markets has taken place, mainly designed to affect the value of the US dollar.

Notes

1 Committee set up to consider Banking Supervision (1985) *Report*, Cmnd 9550, London: HMSO.
2 Stated in 'Methods of monetary control', *Bank of England Quarterly Bulletin*, December 1980.

Further reading

Carter, H. and Partington, I. (1984) *Applied Economics in Banking and Finance*, Oxford: Oxford University Press, Chapter 7.
Lomax, D. F. (August 1987) 'Risk asset ratios – a new departure in supervisory policy', *National Westminster Bank Quarterly Review*.
'The Bank's operational procedures for meeting monetary objections', *Bank of England Quarterly Bulletin*, June 1983.
'The role of the Bank of England in the money market', *Bank of England Quarterly Bulletin*, March 1982.

Chapter eight

Retail banking

The structure of retail banking in the UK

On 8 January 1987 there were nineteen institutions in the UK monetary sector separately identified for official statistical purposes as retail banks. As has been emphasized previously, most of the banks identified as retail banks are nowadays not exclusively or even primarily so, but are extensively engaged in wholesale banking, not only in sterling but also in foreign currency.

Of the banks identified there are six banks which have extensive nationwide branch outlets; these comprise National Westminster, Lloyds, Barclays, Midland, the Trustee Savings Banks,[1] and the Girobank (operated through post offices). There are three banks, the Bank of Scotland, the Clydesdale, and the Royal Bank of Scotland, whose operations are mainly confined to Scotland (although the latter has a considerable presence elsewhere) and similarly four banks, the Allied Irish, the Bank of Ireland, the Northern, and the Ulster, whose operations are concentrated in Northern Ireland (some of the Scottish and Irish banks are partially or wholly owned subsidiaries of the main nationwide banks).[2] Also included are Coutts, a bank largely confined to the City of London, the Co-operative, the Yorkshire, and finally, because it participates in the clearing house arrangements, the Bank of England Banking Department.

Retail banking in the UK exhibits a high degree of concentration – the nationwide system is dominated by the previous 'big four' high street banks, together with the recently transformed Trustee Savings Bank. Each of these five groups has an extensive nationwide branch network, which at the end of 1985 comprised in total 12,241 branches.

The explanation of this highly concentrated structure lies primarily in the fact that there are important economies of scale involved in retail banking. The larger an individual bank, the

163

more stable become net withdrawals of notes and coin in relation to its deposits, thus a bank can economize on the fraction of its assets it needs to hold in low yielding form as liquid reserves. Moreover, there are often systematic regional differences in the seasonal flows of funds between banks and their customers; in these circumstances a large branch network, by permitting internal transfers of cash between one branch and another, can again result in economies in the amount of liquid assets a bank needs to hold. Another advantage of a nationwide branch network is that it provides for a better geographical spread of risks over different industries and regions, while large banks are better able to accommodate the borrowing requirements of all types of personal and corporate borrowers without exposing themselves to undue risk. Finally, there are significant economies of scale in electronic data processing; economies in the use of computing facilities were, for example, key arguments used to justify the merger in 1968 of the National Provincial and Westminster Banks and the proposed merger in the same year between Barclays and Lloyds.[3]

Retail bank operations

The classic problem facing a retail bank is how to structure its asset portfolio in such a way as to reconcile the objective of profit maximization in the interests of its shareholders with that of maintaining the bank in business as a going concern. As a bank has to pay interest on its deposits and incurs various operating expenses, the greater the fraction of its assets it can hold in higher yielding forms, the greater will be the bank's profits. The safety of the bank as an institution, however, means that the process of profit maximization is subject to certain constraints, the most important being those of liquidity and solvency.

Liquidity

Because a large fraction of a retail bank's deposits constitute either sight deposits or deposits at short notice it can expect periodic demands for cash, either because depositors are making net withdrawals of notes and coins or because they are making net payments by way of cheques to customers of other banks or the central government. While net withdrawals of cash are highly predictable, they are not entirely so, and to avoid failure a bank must ensure that a sufficient fraction of its assets are held either in cash or in forms that are quickly convertible into cash in order to enable it to redeem its deposit liabilities when called upon to do so.

Solvency

Solvency is concerned with the longer-term viability of a bank and its ability to withstand losses that may arise in the course of its business – a firm legally becomes insolvent when the value of its liabilities exceeds the value of its assets. Solvency is a major concern for banks because typically their capital to total assets ratios (capital meaning here the equity or ownership funds of a bank – the funds contributed by the bank's shareholders plus its accumulated undistributed profits) are low compared to other types of business, most of a bank's total assets being acquired with funds provided by the bank's depositors, i.e. creditors. The lower a bank's capital to total asset ratio, the more susceptible does it become to insolvency due to depreciation in the value of its assets in relation to its nominal deposit liabilities. The value of a bank's assets is subject to risks of depreciation in value on three main counts:

1. *Default risk* The risk involved here is that the loans made by a bank may not be redeemable at their nominal value recorded in the bank's accounts (their 'book value') due to default on the part of borrowers. To illustrate, suppose that a bank has deposit liabilities equal to £95 million and capital equal to £5 million and holds its assets in the form of cash equal to £10 million and advances equal to £90 million. In these circumstances, if for simplicity we ignore the interest being paid to the bank on its advances, a complete default on the part of certain borrowers which led to 6 per cent of its loans becoming worthless would reduce the actual realizable value of its advances to £84.6 million and its total assets to £94.6 million – below the value of its deposit liabilities.

2. *Investment risk* The risk in this instance is that marketable financial claims being held by a bank may be subject to a decline in market value below their nominal book value. Suppose a bank had capital of 5 per cent in relation to its deposits, but for the sake of argument invested all of its funds in 2½ per cent consols. In these circumstances, if interest rates subsequently increased, resulting in a fall in the market price of consols of greater than 5 per cent, then the bank again would become insolvent.

3. *Forced sale risk* This refers to the risk that the actual realizable value of certain assets may lie below their nominal book value if the assets have to be sold quickly. This might be the case, for example, if a bank holds real property for which organized markets do not exist.

Thus a bank's strategy in relation to the proportion of risky assets it holds in its asset portfolio is constrained by the adequacy of its capital in relation to its deposit liabilities. What matters also as well as total capital is a bank's 'free capital' resources; some of a bank's capital may be tied up in premises and equipment which may be subject to considerable forced sale risk. Free capital resources are defined as the difference between a bank's total capital and the value of its physical assets.

In practice, these considerations of a bank's liquidity and a bank's solvency are inter-related. Historically speaking, many bank runs leading to liquidity difficulties for banks have often been triggered by depositors' expectations of extraordinary losses on a bank's loan or investment portfolio. In 1984, for example, depositors in Continental Illinois, the seventh largest bank in the USA, expected losses on its loans portfolio to result in substantial operating losses and a reduction in the bank's capital – the result was a run on the bank by large depositors and it was only after a massive injection of funds by the Federal Reserve System and an infusion of additional capital from shareholders that confidence in the bank was restored.

The goals of profitability on the one hand and those of liquidity and solvency on the other, are invariably in conflict because there is typically a positive relationship between the yield on financial assets and the degree of risk or illiquidity associated with them. A cloakroom bank which held only cash as assets would be a perfectly safe bank, but it is unlikely to be particularly profitable as it could not pay interest on its deposits to attract customers; indeed, it would have to cover its costs by levying charges for its services. In practice, banks resolve this conflict by holding a mix of different assets, each with a varying degree of liquidity and risk; there is no such thing as a 'proper' asset mix, the trade-off between the objectives of bank profitability and bank safety essentially involves a subjective judgement on the part of a bank's management.

For a long period retail banks in the UK tended to adopt highly cautious attitudes in their asset portfolio decisions which were reflected in the type of advances they were prepared to make to borrowers; generally speaking, advances consisted primarily of short-term loans to business firms for the purposes of financing working capital. The underlying argument justifying such loans as 'sound banking assets' has a long ancestry traceable back to Adam Smith's *Wealth of Nations* (published in 1776) and was generally termed the 'self-liquidating principle'. Basically it was held that banks should make only short-term, 'productive' and 'self-liquidating' loans. Short-term loans were considered appropriate because of the short-term nature of a bank's liabilities and because the redemption dates of the loans could be staggered so as to result in a steady stream of repayments to the bank. A 'productive' loan was a loan for the purchase of real goods providing tangible realizable security and evidence of genuine commercial operations, while a 'self-liquidating' loan was one in which the funds to repay the loan were generated by the subsequent sale of the goods which the loan had originally financed. Thus the classic example of this type of loan was a short-term loan to finance the acquisition of inventories, such as shelf goods in a retail shop or new materials used in a manufacturing process. The loan used to acquire the inventory could be repaid from the sale of the inventory or from the sale of some corresponding finished goods into which raw materials had been transformed after a short period and, as such, the loan was deemed to be self-liquidating.

Whether such loans, in contrast to longer-term loans, are invariably as liquid as the self-liquidating principle implied, however, is debatable. A bank, for example, might make a short-term loan to a manufacturer for the acquisition of raw materials and the ability of the manufacturer to repay his loan promptly might depend on the sale of the finished goods to, say, a wholesaler. The purchase of the finished goods from the manufacturer might depend in turn, however, on the ability of the wholesaler to obtain short-term bank credit, thus the particular loan to the manufacturer may be only self-liquidating in practice if credit for wholesalers is readily available from other lenders; given the interdependencies existing in the economy, loans are only self-liquidating if most of them are not being liquidated. If at a particular time in the face of heavy net withdrawals of cash, the banking system as a whole was attempting to improve its cash position by restricting its lending, then a failure of wholesalers to obtain credit might result in the manufacturer being unable to sell his finished goods quickly at his anticipated price, thus causing him to default on this apparently safe loan (from the individual bank's viewpoint). Thus the safety attached to so-called self-liquidating loans is largely illusory in times when the banking system as a whole is experiencing a cash drain; in such circumstances the liquidity of bank assets depends not so much on the type of loan being made but on the existence of a lender of last resort prepared to supply cash to the banking system. During the 1970s and 1980s in particular, retail banks in the UK have moved away from their narrow concentration on short-term lending and now engage in a much wider range of lending activity – the exact nature of the assets that loans are being used to finance is becoming a less important criterion and more emphasis is being placed on assessing whether borrowers have a capacity to repay loans from their anticipated future income streams.

A fundamental change in the retail banks' traditional approach to balance sheet management in the UK followed the package of reforms known as competition and credit control (CCC) introduced in 1971. Previously, with the tacit approval of the Bank of England, the banks had for a long period operated a cartel agreement, whereby the interest rates of individual banks were administratively fixed in adherence to fairly rigid conventions. On current account deposits the banks paid zero interest and levied bank charges for the use of money transmission services, while interest rates on seven-day deposit accounts were fixed at 2 per cent below Bank Rate (the announced rate at which the Bank of England was prepared to lend to the discount market). Similarly the banks fixed interest rates on advances in a range from 1 to 5 per cent above Bank Rate depending on such factors as the nature of the borrower, the use of the funds and the size of the loan. Given this situation retail banks typically treated their deposits as being more or less given in the short run by the demand of the public to hold deposits at those interest rates and on the monetary policy being pursued by the Bank, and adjusted their assets in line with these predetermined deposit inflows – liquidity was derived largely from the management of the assets side of their balance sheets.

Following CCC the banks were encouraged to compete in a situation, not only where direct controls previously applied to their lending were dropped, but also where expansionary macro-economic policies were adopted by the authorities and the banks increased their lending aggressively. In order to fund additional lending the banks adopted the techniques employed in wholesale banking which have come to be termed liability management. This approach is based on the assumption that, as far as an individual bank is concerned, wholesale deposits are very sensitive to the interest rates offered. Thus by raising interest rates offered on wholesale deposits fractionally above the going market rate, a bank can immediately attract additional funds via the issue of CDs, borrowing on the inter-bank market, etc. This ability to attract wholesale deposits quickly provides a bank with much greater flexibility in its operations.

1. It can be used to counteract retail deposit inflows and outflows, thus reducing the liquid reserves they need to hold; sudden or

unexpected deposit outflows can be offset immediately by bidding for additional wholesale funds.

2. Potential borrowers need not be denied loans due to an immediate shortage of funds; a bank can agree to make additional loans even though it may not have funds immediately available, on the knowledge that it can subsequently bid for the necessary funds in wholesale markets. In other words, an individual bank can adjust its liabilities to the prior growth of its assets rather than the converse.

While liability management thus provides individual banks with much greater flexibility in adjusting their balance sheets, it does not mean, of course, that they have the ability to expand their advances and deposits at will. Expansion via the use of wholesale funds is only profitable if the expected marginal return on additional loans exceeds the expected marginal cost of funds and a collective expansion on the part of the banking system will, ultimately, at some point reduce the marginal return below the marginal cost of funds.

Following CCC the proportion of wholesale deposits as a proportion of banks' total deposits increased markedly, although in the late 1970s this tendency was dampened by further controls designed to limit the expansion of a bank's interest-bearing liabilities (more precisely, by the supplementary special deposits scheme). Following a second wave of deregulation at the start of the Conservative Government's term of office in 1979/80 the extent of usage of wholesale deposits by the retail banks increased sharply again.

The retail banks' balance sheet

The operating decisions made by the retail banks in practice can be illustrated by an examination of their combined balance sheet which is reproduced in Table 8.1.

As can be seen from the table the retail banks in the UK are no longer purely confined to accepting sterling deposits; foreign currency liabilities amounted, on the date indicated, to around 28 per cent of their total deposit liabilities or 40 per cent of their sterling deposits (almost all such foreign currency deposits constituted wholesale deposits).

If we consider sterling deposits Table 8.1 does not break down the total into retail and wholesale deposits respectively, but the growth in the wholesale deposit component can be gauged in an approximate fashion from the figures shown in Table 8.2. These

Table 8.1 The combined balance sheet of UK retail banks as at 31 October 1986

Sterling liabilities		Sterling assets		(Percentage of total sterling assets)
		£ billion		
Notes issued	1.0	Notes and coin	2.1	1.5
Total sterling deposits	129.5	Balances with Bank of England (including		
(of which sight deposits)	62.2	cash ratio deposits)	0.7	0.5
UK monetary sector	10.8	Market loans		
		Secured money with		
UK public sector	2.9	LMDA	4.2	3.1
		Other UK monetary		
UK private sector	96.2	sector	19.5	14.2
		UK monetary sector		
Overseas	12.0	CDs	3.8	2.8
Certificates of deposit	7.6	UK local authorities	1.5	1.1
		Overseas	2.8	2.0
		Bills		
		Treasury bills	0.1	0.1
		Local authority bills	0.2	0.2
		Eligible bank bills	3.5	2.6
		Other bills	0.1	0.1
		Investments		
		British government		
		stocks	6.3	4.6
		Other	3.4	2.5
		Advances to		
		UK public sector	0.3	0.2
		UK private sector	84.3	61.4
		Overseas	4.3	3.1
Foreign currency liabilities	51.4	*Foreign currency assets*	80.1	
Items in suspense and transmission and capital funds	35.3			
Total liabilities	217.2	*Total assets*	217.2	
Eligible liabilities	98.5			

Source: *Bank of England Quarterly Bulletin*, December 1986, Table 3.2.

figures exaggerate the wholesale deposit component of the retail banks *per se* as they refer to clearing bank groups, i.e., they include subsidiary banks which are classified separately as wholesale banks.

Reverting to Table 8.1, the small item recorded under sterling liabilities as 'notes issued' relates to the private banknotes still issued by the Scottish and Northern Ireland banks which, apart from a small fiduciary element, are fully backed by reserves of Bank of England notes.

Table 8.2 Clearing bank group deposits at mid-November of selected years

	Percentage of total sterling deposits		
	1975	*1980*	*1985*
Retail deposits			
Current accounts	32.9	27.8	23.8
Deposit accounts (seven days)	28.1	28.1	12.7
Wholesale deposits	39.0	44.1	63.5

Source: Committee of London Clearing Banks (1975–85) *Abstract of Banking Statistics*.

Notes: 'Wholesale' deposits comprise large-value deposits raised from other banks, by the issue of CDs, deposits of commercial enterprises and overseas residents. Wholesale deposits are calculated as the difference between all sterling deposits and 'retail' deposits, where the latter consist of ordinary current accounts, high-interest chequing deposits, other interest-bearing sight deposits and seven-day deposit accounts.

Turning to the assets side of the balance sheet we should note initially that the main mandatory ratio requirement imposed on the banks is the 'cash ratio' requirement, whereby all banks with eligible liabilities in excess of £10 million are required to hold 0.45 per cent of their eligible liabilities in a non-interest-bearing account at the Bank of England (as stated previously in Chapter 7 this is not really a prudential ratio, but rather a specific tax imposed on all banks for purposes of financing the Bank's operation). Formally, a bank's eligible liabilities comprise sterling deposit liabilities to non-banks, excluding deposits with an original maturity of two years or more, plus net sterling inter-bank borrowing, plus sterling certificates of deposit issued less sterling certificates of deposit held, plus any sterling resources obtained by switching foreign currency into sterling, less 60 per cent of the net value of transit items. The banks at present, therefore, have considerably more freedom to choose their asset structures than previously when much stricter mandatory cash or liquidity ratios were imposed, but they are still subject, of course, to the general prudential supervision of the Bank which, as we have already described in Chapter 7, is exercised in a relatively informal way on an individual case by case basis.

Examination of Table 8.1 reveals that the retail banks now choose to operate with small ratios of cash to their total assets. Of their balances at the Bank of England around £0.5 billion constituted the compulsory cash ratio requirement so that net of

171

this the banks were holding cash in the ratio of 1.7 per cent to their total sterling assets or in a ratio of 2.3 per cent to their eligible liabilities. There are two main reasons why the retail banks deem it prudent to operate with such a low cash base:

1. The highly concentrated structure of retail banking in the UK means that periodic net withdrawals of cash from individual banks arising in the course of inter-bank settlements are much smaller than they would be if the structure comprised a greater number of smaller individual banks.
2. The existence in the UK of the highly organized money markets enables individual banks to economize on their cash reserves by investing in earning assets without incurring a significant loss of liquidity. Moreover, the existence of such markets provides a means whereby an individual bank can borrow cash at short notice.

Under the heading of market loans (the term being used to emphasize lending via an organized market as opposed to an informal market) we see, for example, that the banks made secured loans amounting to 3.2 per cent of their sterling assets with the discount houses. Such loans comprise call or overnight money and the substitutability of such assets for cash is rendered more or less perfect by the fact that they are made on the security of assets held by the discount houses which are eligible for redis-counting at the Bank. Traditionally, call loans made to the discount houses provided a means whereby individual banks could indirectly transfer cash from one to another to maintain their cash ratios at desired levels. Suppose that during a particular period Midland depositors were writing more cheques in favour of Lloyds depositors than vice-versa, in which case the clearing mechanism would result in a decrease in Midland's cash reserves and an increase in Lloyds' cash reserves. Midland would then supplement its cash reserves by a net withdrawal of call loans from the discount houses, but Lloyds would be simultaneously making additional call loans to adjust its cash position; thus effectively by this mech-anism cash would be transferred from Lloyds to Midland via the intermediation of the discount houses.

This traditional mechanism has largely been supplanted since 1971 by the retail banks' participation in the inter-bank market – reflected in the item 'market loans to other UK monetary sectors' and 'UK monetary sector CDs' – which enables cash to be lent directly from one bank to another. However, the inter-bank market is less useful as a means of adjusting an individual bank's cash position when the banking system as a whole is experiencing a cash drain, due to net withdrawals of notes and coin by the general public or, more importantly in practice, due to net payments being made by the non-bank private sector to central government. In these circumstances the banks generally will be seeking to borrow funds on the inter-bank market rather than lend and a shortage of inter-bank funds will induce the banks to call loans from the discount houses, the discount houses in turn obtaining the funds, if necessary, from the Bank of England.

In the event of a cash drain affecting the whole system further liquidity is provided by the assets recorded under the 'bills' entry, most of the bills held being eligible for rediscounting via the discount houses at the Bank. The low percentage of Treasury bills held in October 1986 is a reflection of the policy in the early 1980s of overfunding the PSBR, or more recently full funding of the PSBR, which resulted in a decrease in the amount of Treasury bills being issued. Until 1971 the banks had an agreement not to bid for Treasury bills directly in the weekly tender but they now on occasion do so; most of the Treasury bills held, however, are bills nearer to maturity which on redemption automatically result in a cash flow to the banks. Most of the bills held by the banks in 1986 constituted commercial bills eligible for rediscounting at the Bank by virtue of their acceptance by a recognized institution.

The item 'investments' refers to holdings of marketable securities that are quoted on the Stock Exchange. To minimize default risk most of the securities held are either British government stocks, public corporation stocks guaranteed by the government, local authority stocks or stocks issued by Commonwealth government. From a bank's viewpoint the ready marketability of such securities means that such assets have liquidity in this sense, although the holdings of such assets involves investment risk. To reduce such risks the banks primarily tend to hold securities with less than five years to maturity and arrange their portfolio to ensure that there is a steady stream of maturing securities which can be run off if necessary to provide additional cash.

The bulk of the retail banks' sterling assets, as is clearly demonstrated in Table 8.1, constitutes 'advances to the UK private sector'. The majority of advances by retail banks still tend to constitute loans to business borrowers by a traditional method not commonly used in other countries, i.e. the overdraft system. Under this system a potential borrower negotiates with a bank an overdraft facility which entitles him to write cheques on the bank up to a certain limit in excess of the funds he may have in a current account; the actual loan from the bank to a client is then only instigated when cheques are actually written and the client's account becomes overdrawn. The obvious advantage of this system to the borrower is its flexibility, the borrower is not tied to any fixed repayment schedule and is charged interest only to the extent to which his overdraft facility is used. Technically, overdrafts are repayable on demand through withdrawal of the facility on the part of the bank, but the whole system in practice is based on conventions, one of which is that bankers will not demand repayment without reasonable notice. Thus loans made by overdraft are not in practice as liquid from a bank's viewpoint as they seem to be in formal terms.

While the overdraft system has certain advantages to the banks in that the interest rates charged on outstanding loans can be varied contractually at a bank's discretion, it also has certain disadvantages as far as bank management is concerned. Overdraft facilities are granted in advance of the actual lending of funds and, at any one time, there is usually a sizeable amount of unused overdraft facilities outstanding which potentially could be utilized by borrowers; typically, in many years utilization of sanctioned overdraft limits has been of the order of 60 per cent. Although banks are legally entitled not to honour agreed limits, in the interests of client relationships such refusals are rare and, accordingly, the actual amount of funds they are committed to lend in the short run is effectively demand-determined.

During the 1970s the traditional overdraft system was increasingly complemented by the use of term loans, in particular for loans made to smaller-size companies. With a term loan arrangement the amount to be lent is agreed at the outset, the sum involved is credited to a customer's account in a single block and a fixed repayment schedule arranged. Loans are made for periods as long as twenty years and are often unrelated to the security of specific assets. Rates of interest may be fixed or floating by negotiation with a customer for the period of the loan and the exact repayment schedules are arranged to fit estimated future cash flows – it is fairly common for no repayments to be required until two years after the commencement of a loan. The average original maturity of term loans tends to be around seven years, although the actual average life of term loans is somewhat less than this because many are repaid in advance of the final maturity date. By the beginning of the 1980s term loans made by some of the retail banks accounted for 25 per cent of lending to manufacturing industry and around 15 per cent of lending to other borrowers.[4]

In the 1980s a major development has been the growth in bank lending to personal borrowers, particularly in the provision of long-term mortgage finance, a form of lending which in the UK was traditionally dominated by the building societies. In the 1970s the banks' share of new net mortgage loans averaged just over 5 per cent but in the period 1981–2 this share expanded to nearly 40 per cent.[5] This period of rapid growth in mortgage lending partly constituted a stock adjustment effect in the banks' loan portfolio following a period when they felt inhibited from entering the housing finance market and since this period of rapid expansion the banks' share of new mortgage loans has dropped back towards nearer 20 per cent.

Retail bank interest rates

Following 'Competition and Credit control', bank interest rates are now determined largely by competitive market forces, not only by competition between individual retail banks but by competition with other deposit-taking institutions, mainly the building societies. On the retail deposit side most banks at the present time offer 'free banking' on current accounts, i.e. no charges are levied for money transmission services as long as depositors maintain positive balances in their accounts and do not become 'overdrawn'. As money transmission services are costly for the banks to operate, free banking is tantamount to the payment of implicit interest on current accounts, the amount being received by each depositor being dependent on the use made of the bank's services. Most banks now also offer high-interest-bearing current accounts, usually with restrictions on the size of the minimum balance held and on the minimum amount for which cheques can be written, and have also introduced new savings accounts from which notes can be withdrawn on demand or transferred immediately to current accounts (such transfers can be effected outside normal office hours via ATMs), the interest rate varying in ranges according to the balance outstanding at a particular time. At the time of writing a new competitive innovation is the Midland 'Vector Account'; with this current account the depositor pays a fixed monthly charge, but is paid explicit interest with no restrictions as to the size of the minimum balance held and is additionally given an overdraft limit of £1,000 with zero interest being levied for overdrawn accounts up to £250. The decision of the banks to extend the range of interest-bearing retail deposits has been viewed by some commentators as a desire to limit the growth of wholesale deposits which have the disadvantage of being more immediately mobile in terms of stress, as well as a direct counter to competition from the building societies.[6]

On the lending side, for administrative purposes each bank now generally fixes a key interest rate termed 'base rate' and individual rates for advances to particular categories of borrower are often expressed in terms of some margin in relation to base rate. However base rates, although they are administered rates set by individual banks (and can vary slightly between different banks at any particular time), are altered frequently in line with the general trend of interest rates determined in the inter-bank market. Inter-bank interest rates are relevant because they, in effect, represent the marginal cost of funds for an individual bank. As an alternative to making an additional advance at the margin to a non-bank borrower, an individual bank has the option of lending funds in the inter-bank market, and considerations of profit maximization therefore dictate that the interest rate charged for advances should reflect this implicit opportunity cost. Equally, at the margin, advances are made with funds borrowed in the inter-bank market and the marginal cost in this case is explicit. Many of the term loans made by the banks in fact have interest rates explicitly related to the current London inter-bank offer rate, in particular the three-month rate, rather than to base rates, as such, since a substantial proportion of the term lending of the banks is financed by funds obtained through the inter-bank market.

Another reason in practice why the banks' advance rates tend to be closely related to interest rates in the money markets is that, if a divergence in rates emerges, this sets up arbitrage opportunities for large non-bank borrowers. At certain periods during the early 1970s bank interest rates tended to be set below money market interest rates and, in those circumstances, large companies with agreed overdraft limits borrowed from the banks, not for their own purposes, but for relending in the wholesale markets; in effect, such companies functioned as financial intermediaries making additional profits at the expense of the banks.

In the situation prior to 1971, given the conventions adopted by the retail banks, the Bank of England could directly change bank interest rates by an administrative change in Bank Rate. Now that bank interest rates are related to interest rate trends in the inter-bank market this direct mechanism no longer applies. None the less, as described in Chapter 7, the Bank, via its operations in the discount market, can exert an influence on money market interest rates and thus ultimately on retail bank interest rates.

Notes

1 The Trustee Savings Banks now formally constitute four separate companies established for England and Wales, Scotland, Northern Ireland, and the Channel Islands.
2 At the time of writing, the Clydesdale Bank and the Northern Bank were wholly-owned subsidiaries of the Midland Bank, but it has been announced that these subsidiary companies are to be sold to the National Australia Bank.
3 The proposed merger between Barclays and Lloyds was subsequently disallowed by the Monopolies Commission.
4 These figures were reported by the Midland Bank in the *Midland Bank Review*, Autumn/Winter 1981, p. 18.
5 The figures relating to mortgage lending by the banks are derived from the *Bank of England Quarterly Bulletin*, March 1985, pp. 80–1.
6 For example, Rose, H. (Winter 1986) 'Change in financial intermediation in the UK', *Oxford Review of Economic Policy*, vol. 2, no. 4, p. 33.

Further reading

Carter, H. and Partington, I. (1984) *Applied Economics in Banking and Finance*, Oxford: Oxford University Press, Chapter 5.
Committee to Review the Functioning of Financial Institutions (1980) *Appendices*, Cmnd 7937, London: HMSO, Appendix 3.I.
Committee of London Clearing Banks (1978) *The London Clearing Banks*, London: Longman.
Fforde, J. S. (September 1983) 'Competition, innovation and regulations in British banking', *Bank of England Quarterly Bulletin*.
Lewis, M. K. and Davis, K. T. (1987) *Domestic and International Banking*, Dedington: Philip Allen, Chapter 3.

Chapter nine

Wholesale banking

The structure of wholesale banking in the UK

In the UK there are a large number of individual institutions classified for official statistical purposes as non-retail banks which collectively comprise the remainder of the UK monetary sector.[1] In Bank of England statistics these institutions are further divided into various subgroups, the basis for subdivision being primarily one of ownership rather than differences in banking functions performed. The various groups of banks identified, together with the numbers of banks in each group in January 1987, are as follows:

1. *Accepting houses* (35) The institutions identified are members of the Accepting Houses Committee together with a number of their offshore subsidiaries in the Channel Islands and the Isle of Man. (As intimated previously there is a possibility that the Accepting Houses Committee will be formally disbanded.)

2. *Other British banks* (206) This category comprises a large number of institutions of considerable diversity in terms of size and financial activities, many of which were previously classified as licensed deposit-takers. Some are specialized subsidiaries of the large retail banks; others could be classified as merchant banks which, as well as being engaged in banking, compete with the accepting houses in arranging new issues, managing investment funds, etc. For many institutions the primary business is similar to that of some institutions not included in the UK monetary sector, i.e. the financing of consumer credit sales and instalment purchases and the leasing of capital equipment.

3. *American banks* (56)

4. *Japanese banks* (27)

5. *Other overseas banks* (254)

6. *Consortium banks* (22) Consortium banks are banks jointly

owned by other banks, no one bank having a direct shareholding of more than 50 per cent, while at least one of the parent banks is based overseas. One of the main reasons for the formation of such banks is that they serve as a vehicle whereby a number of small parent banks can establish a presence in London which they might not be able to afford individually.

The balance sheet structure of wholesale banks

The institutions classified as non-retail banks are considerably more heterogeneous than the retail banks, but none the less there are a number of general features which distinguish such banks as a group from the retail banks.

1. Compared to the retail banks, wholesale banks in the UK are involved to a much greater extent in foreign currency as opposed to domestic sterling business. The gross deposits of the various groups of banks in sterling and foreign currency are shown in Table 9.1.

Table 9.1 Gross deposits of various banking groups as at 31 October 1986

	Sterling	Other currencies
	£ billion	£ billion
Accepting houses	15.4	14.1
Other British banks	37.3	28.0
American banks	14.5	86.2
Japanese banks	13.4	217.9
Other overseas banks	39.5	176.4
Consortium banks	2.2	13.8

Source: Bank of England Quarterly Bulletin, December 1986, Tables 3.3, 3.4, 3.5, 3.6, 3.7, and 3.8.

As is evident from the table the overseas banks' main business is primarily in foreign currency but all of the groups have diversified to some extent into domestic sterling business.

2. The structure of sterling deposits is markedly different from those of the retail banks. In general, the bulk of their deposits constitute time deposits with maturities in excess of seven days. For all the non-retail banks the proportion of gross sterling deposits constituting sight deposits in October 1986 was 17 per cent and sight deposits were in the large majority interest-bearing money at call rather than current accounts on which cheques can be written. Many of the banks do offer current account facilities but there are usually limits as to the minimum initial deposit

(usually upwards of £1,000) and again cheques can be written often for certain minimum sums only; for the most part wholesale banks are involved to only a limited extent in money transmission services. For many banks the minimum acceptable size of deposit ranges from £50,000 to £100,000 and thus the majority of non-bank depositors tend to be business firms, other financial institutions or governmental bodies.

Another feature is that a large proportion of their gross sterling deposits is obtained through the sterling inter-bank market. Of the American and Japanese banks' combined sterling deposits of £27.9 billion, for example, £12.8 billion constituted liabilities to other institutions in the UK monetary sector and a further £2.8 billion consisted of certificates of deposit, of which a substantial fraction would have been held by other banks. Because of the nature of their deposits most wholesale banks have no particular need for widespread branch networks.

3. The structure of the wholesale banks' sterling assets is illustrated in Table 9.2 which shows the combined assets of all the banking groups listed in Table 9.1.

Table 9.2 Combined sterling assets of various banking groups as at 31 October 1986

	£ billion
Notes and coin	0.03
Balances at the Bank of England	0.4
Market loans	
Secured with LDMA	2.5
UK monetary sector	35.9
UK monetary sector CDs	4.9
UK local authorities	1.5
Overseas	12.3
Bills	0.9
Advances	65.5
Investments	9.0
Total assets	132.9 (approx.)

Source: *Bank of England Quarterly Bulletin*, December 1986, Tables 3.3, 3.4, 3.5, 3.6, 3.7, and 3.8.

This aggregated balance sheet conceals a number of differences between the individual groups of banks but does bring out certain general features of their activities. As can be seen, the wholesale banks keep a very small percentage of their assets (0.02 per cent) in the form of notes and coin. This illustrates the tiered relationship of the wholesale banks to the clearing banks. When a non-bank depositor makes a new deposit of, say, £1 million with a wholesale bank, it would be unusual, to say the least, for this to be in the form of notes and coin – rather the depositor writes a cheque on a clearing bank in favour of the wholesale bank. Similarly, a wholesale bank's deposit liability is essentially a promise to repay, not notes and coin, but a clearing bank deposit and the withdrawal of a deposit from a wholesale bank invariably takes the form of a cheque written on a clearing bank in favour of the depositor. Because some current accounts are operated for customers some notes and coin are held, but because of their tiered relationship with the clearing banks they have no particular need for large reserves in this form. Equally, although wholesale banks do keep balances at the Bank of England these are almost entirely the compulsory cash ratio deposits required of all banks; inter-bank settlements between wholesale banks take the form of exchanges of clearing bank deposits.

Compared to the retail banks, a larger fraction of gross assets constituted money market loans (43 per cent), largely loans on the inter-bank market and holdings of certificates of deposit. The wholesale banks held a similar fraction of their assets in the form of advances, but a fundamental difference is that the majority of such advances comprised term loans. The average size of loan tends to be very large, occasionally running into millions of pounds, so that the main non-bank borrowers are large companies and governmental organizations.

Wholesale bank operations

The main contrast between the operations of the wholesale banks and those of the retail banks stems from the fact that, in a typical wholesale bank, the average size of a deposit is much larger and consequently, for a given size of total deposits, the number of individual depositors tends to be much smaller. For example, although no published figures are available, one can make a crude estimate of the number of individual deposits held in sterling by non-bank depositors in the group of American banks in London. In January 1987 the sterling deposits of this group of banks, net of sterling deposits held by the UK monetary sector and sterling CDs issued (some of which would have been held by other banks) amounted to £7,697 million. The number of American banks amounted to fifty-six and if we assume that the minimum sum deposited was £½ million then the average number of individual deposits per bank could have been no greater than 275. This contrasts with the retail banks where the average number of accounts per bank, on the basis of information published in 1983, was of the order of 3.8 million. Wholesale banks therefore cannot rely on 'the law of large numbers effect' which makes net withdrawals from retail banks in normal circumstances relatively small and predictable in relation to their total deposits. Thus, to reduce the risk of failure, individual wholesale banks aim to structure their balance sheets in a different way to retail banks. More precisely, the wholesale banks' balance sheets exhibit a greater degree of matching of their liabilities and assets with respect to their terms of maturity.

As mentioned previously in Chapter 4, a perfectly matched balance sheet exhibits the property that the terms to maturity of an intermediary's various liabilities will exactly equal that of its various assets. If, for example, a bank has £500,000 of its deposit liabilities in time deposits due to mature in one month, on the assets side of its balance sheet it would have, say, £500,000 in term loans due for payment on exactly the same date.[2] In principle, an individual bank with a perfectly matched balance sheet and a negligible risk of default on its loans would be a perfectly safe bank and would have no particular need to hold liquid reserves as such. In practice, the balance sheets of wholesale banks are never perfectly matched, but the general principle of matching is evident in that the proportions of their deposits with various terms to maturity are correlated with the proportion of assets of similar terms to a much greater extent than is the case with the retail banks.

Given this general principle of matching, an essential element in wholesale bank operations is the existence of the inter-bank market. Suppose a wholesale bank receives a time deposit of £300,000 for three months; the bank, however, may be unable to contact immediately a non-bank customer, or customers, who wish to borrow precisely that amount for a three-month period. The bank, though, might receive an approach from a non-bank borrower requesting a loan of £200,000 for three months, in which case the bank makes this loan and then contacts a money broker offering to lend £100,000 on the inter-bank market. Equally, the existence of the inter-bank market facilitates liability management on the part of banks in a way consistent with the principle of matching. Suppose, again, that a bank is approached by a borrower requesting a loan of £1 million for three months. The bank might agree to make the loan even though, initially, it has not got the necessary funds available and despite the fact that it cannot rely on a non-bank depositor, or depositors, offering deposits immediately to the bank for the same amount and for a similar term. The bank in this instance can turn to the inter-bank market for the deposits it requires to finance the loan – the prospect being that somewhere in the wholesale banking system three-month deposits will have been placed with banks which have no immediate use for the funds. In this latter instance an alternative, more formal, arrangement is that of a syndicated loan, where a lead bank makes contact with a borrower and then invites other banks to participate in the provision of the overall loan. Because the inter-bank constitutes an integral element in wholesale bank operations it follows that, as with the retail banks, wholesale bank interest rates will reflect closely the trend of interest rates in the inter-bank market.

While the nature of their deposits means that some degree of matching is a typical element in an individual wholesale bank's operations, as mentioned above, this is rarely, if ever, perfect and various arguments can be cited as to why this mismatching is normal practice.

1. At the longer end of the maturity spectrum, at any given interest rate, the volume of funds demanded by borrowers might well exceed the volume of funds offered by depositors (i.e., there may be a 'constitutional weakness' regarding the demand and supply of funds). Therefore to induce depositors to lend 'long' in sufficient quantities to match the demand for loans of similar maturity, the banks might have to offer interest rates on deposits exceeding those obtainable on loans. Thus, if longer-term lending is to be profitable for the banks, some degree of mismatching may be inevitable.

2. Wholesale banking is very competitive and interest rate margins between deposits and loans of the same term tend to be very narrow. Given that longer-term interest rates often exceed shorter-term interest rates, a bank can widen the margin between its borrowing and lending rates by making loans of somewhat longer average terms to maturity then the average term of its deposits. In other words, a bank may trade off safety for profitability by deliberately choosing not to match its balance sheet as closely as is viably possible. The choices a bank makes in this respect at various times may possibly be influenced also by the view it takes regarding future short-term interest rates. Suppose a bank has firm expectations that future short-term rates are likely to fall, but that this expectation is not reflected generally in the current term structure of interest rates. In this instance a bank may deem it appropriate to lengthen temporarily the average term

of its lending at current interest rates relative to the average term of its borrowing.

3. In practice, not all of a bank's time deposit liabilities are withdrawn from the bank on maturity; to a certain extent it can rely on the 'rolling over' of some of its deposits for a further period. Additionally, a bank may feel confident in its ability to borrow short term on the inter-bank market to offset any net withdrawals of deposits by non-bank depositors.

Apart from mismatching by individual banks, an additional point about wholesale bank intermediation is that if one considers wholesale banks as a group and inter-bank deposits are netted out to reveal the banks' transactions with non-banks, then a much greater degree of mismatching is evident between the average term to maturity of assets and liabilities for the system as a whole, than is the case for an individual bank.[3] Transactions in the inter-bank market, therefore, tend to disguise the degree to which the wholesale banks collectively are borrowing short and lending long. The way this can happen might, for example, involve the following sequence of hypothetical transactions: bank A might engage in liability management making a six-month loan obtaining the funds by bidding in the inter-bank market for a three-month deposit which is provided by bank B; bank B in turn finances the inter-bank loan by receiving a twenty-eight-day inter-bank deposit from bank C, which in turn might have received a seven-day deposit from a non-bank depositor. Each individual bank in this sequence of transactions is mismatched, but to a much lesser extent than the system as a whole – in effect, when inter-bank transactions are netted out, a six-month loan has been made on the basis of a seven-day deposit. It can be argued, therefore, that the differences between retail banks and wholesale banks regarding the degree of maturity transformation undertaken can be overstated; the major contrast is that in retail banking maturity transformation is carried out fully by the bank which accepts the deposit from the non-bank public.

It also follows that the safety for each individual bank which the general principle of matching seems to provide is somewhat illusory. Because of the way in which the assets and liabilities of individual banks are intertwined via inter-bank transactions, as the Secondary Bank crisis in the UK in 1973–4 demonstrated, there is a much greater risk of systemic instability where the failure of one bank through a number of significant defaults on loans can generate a chain reaction causing difficulties for a number of other banks.

The relationship between the wholesale and retail banks

As we have emphasized previously, wholesale bank deposits stand in a tiered relationship to those of the retail banks. Thus each wholesale bank, as part of its operations, will have a bank account with a particular clearing bank and transactions between a non-bank customer and a wholesale bank, or transactions between two wholesale banks, or between a clearing bank and a wholesale bank in the inter-bank market may therefore affect the deposit and cash positions of individual clearing banks in the same way as transactions between any of their customers and customers of other clearing banks. To illustrate, suppose a non-bank customer of Midland holding a current account deposit switches this to a time deposit in the Chemical Bank which, say, banks with Lloyds. Deposits in Lloyds thus increase and deposits in Midland decrease and Midland transfers cash to Lloyds in the course of inter-bank settlement. If subsequently the Chemical Bank then lends part of the funds in the inter-bank market to the First National Boston which, say, banks with Barclays, then deposits rise in Barclays, fall in Lloyds, while cash is transferred from Lloyds to Barclays. Similarly, if Midland itself makes an inter-bank loan to the Chemical Bank the effect is the same as in the case where Midland lends to a non-bank customer who subsequently makes a transaction with a customer of Lloyds, i.e. deposits in Midland remain unchanged, deposits in Lloyds increase and cash is transferred from Midland to Lloyds.

Switches by non-bank depositors from clearing bank deposits into wholesale bank deposits can thus affect the position of individual clearing banks; the effect on total clearing bank deposits is, however, a more complex matter. In the 1960s, when wholesale banking developed rapidly in the UK, wholesale banks were not subject to the liquidity ratio requirements imposed by the authorities on the clearing banks and they kept a minimal amount of cash in the form of notes and coin or balances at the Bank of England (the exception being some accepting houses which, for historical reasons, held such balances). Thus if the wholesale banks attracted additional deposits from non-bank customers, they would have been unlikely to convert any of their additional clearning bank deposits into cash and therefore the clearing banks collectively would not have experienced a drain of cash or deposits. Apart from the working balances held with the clearing banks most of the funds obtained by wholesale banks were lent to other banks, local authorities, or private sector borrowers, so that the immediate consequences of an expansion of wholesale bank deposits was a reshuffling of the ownership of clearing bank deposits, but no diminution in their total (the process would have been that described in the example in Chapter 2 illustrating the effect of NBFIs in circulating bank deposits). It follows also that the immediate effect of a switch from a deposit in a clearing bank to a wholesale bank would have been a net increase in the total stock of bank deposits (i.e. the combined deposits of the clearing and wholesale banks).

It could be argued, therefore, that during this period the wholesale banks did not compete directly with the retail banks in the sense that wholesale banks could bid deposits away from the retail banks.[4] A counter argument, however, asserted that in the longer run an indirect mechanism might cause an expansion of wholesale bank deposits to restrict the growth of clearing bank deposits.[5] This counter-argument related to the effects of the policies being pursued by the monetary authorities. In the 1960s the monetary authorities did not set any explicit monetary objectives, but in response to a persistent problem of current account balance of payments deficits they frequently imposed informal controls on clearing bank lending, thus inhibiting the growth of clearing bank deposits. The wholesale banks, however, were uncontrolled and it was argued that the expansion of wholesale bank deposits, by expanding the supply of credit, might result in an expansion of aggregate monetary expenditure which would exacerbate the problem of external imbalance. This, it was argued, might lead the authorities to intensify their controls on clearing bank lending, thus further restricting their deposit growth; thus in the longer run, by this indirect mechanism, an expansion in wholesale bank deposits might take place at the expense of clearing bank deposits. (It can be adduced that a similar sort of indirect mechanism would have come into play after 1976 when the authorities started to set explicit targets for the growth of 'sterling M_3' a monetary aggregate which includes wholesale bank deposits as well as clearing bank deposits.)

However, since 1971 the nature of competition between the clearing banks and the wholesale banks as distinct groups of banks has been affected by the extension of the reserve requirements imposed by the authorities on the clearing banks to all banks; currently, as we have previously discussed, all banks are required to keep 0.45 per cent of their eligible liabilities in a compulsory cash ratio at the Bank of England. Thus in present circumstances, if non-bank depositors increase their deposits in wholesale banks in substitution for clearing bank deposits, then the total of clearing bank deposits (other things being equal) will now directly diminish to a certain extent. A deposit switch of this kind will increase the wholesale banks' eligible liabilities (assuming that the new deposits have an original maturity of two years or less – and that the bank on-lends most of the funds to non-bank borrowers) and hence they have to make additional cash ratio deposits at the Bank. They thus write cheques on their clearing bank accounts in favour of the Bank and hence clearing bank deposits decrease as do clearing bank balances at the Bank by an equivalent amount. Given the magnitudes involved, however, the direct effect on clearing bank deposits of wholesale bank cash ratio deposits is fairly small. For example, a switch of £100,000 to a wholesale bank from a clearing bank, which increases the eligible liabilities of the wholesale bank by this amount, results in an additional cash ratio deposit of £450 with an equivalent direct loss of clearing bank deposits.

Eurobanking

As we have previously intimated, the main banking business of many wholesale banks operating in the UK is concerned, not with domestic sterling borrowing and lending, but with transactions in the so-called Eurocurrency markets. Formally, a Eurocurrency deposit is defined as a bank deposit denominated in currencies other than that of the country in which the bank is physically located. Essentially the same institutional mechanisms are involved in Eurobanking as in domestic wholesale banking, the main difference being that the tiered relationship involved is with retail banks in other countries whose demand deposits serve as a means of payment in those countries.

To illustrate the institutional mechanisms of Eurobanking, let us consider a hypothetical sequence of transactions which might lead to the creation of an important Eurocurrency, i.e. Eurodollars. Suppose initially that a French company has exported goods to the USA worth $1 million and has received payment from a US resident in the form of a cheque written on a US bank. As an alternative to selling the dollars to a French bank in exchange for francs, the company might decide to retain the proceeds as a dollar balance and place $1 million in a time deposit with a wholesale bank in London, say, the Charterhouse Bank. What this involves is the transfer of a chequeable demand deposit in the US banking system from the ownership of the US resident concerned to the ownership of the Charterhouse Bank which will have an account with a US correspondent bank. (If the US resident's bank and the Charterhouse correspondent bank happened to be different banks, then this would require also an inter-bank settlement in the

187

form of a transfer of commercial bank balances held with the Federal Reserve System.) Thus the initial balance sheet changes are:

US combined banking system
$ million

Liabilities		Assets	
Demand deposits			
US resident	−1		
Charterhouse Bank	+1		
Net change	0	Net change	0

Charterhouse Bank
$ million

Liabilities		Assets	
Time deposits			
French company	+1	Demand deposit in US Bank	+1
Net change	+1	Net change	+1

Demand deposits in the US banking system remain unchanged in total, but a Eurodollar deposit has been created. The Charterhouse Bank, having received this time deposit on which it pays interest, will seek to convert its dollar demand deposit into a higher yielding asset. Suppose that Charterhouse, having no immediate non-bank borrower in prospect, contacts a money broker in the London inter-bank market and transacts an inter-bank loan of $1 million with the London branch of a Japanese bank, say, the Bank of Tokyo, at an interest rate higher than its time deposit rate. (In practice Charterhouse might keep a fraction of the $1 million as a liquid reserve but this does not affect the essential argument.) Charterhouse then instructs its correspondent bank in the USA to transfer $1 million to the demand deposit account of the Bank of Tokyo held in a similar correspondent bank. The subsequent balance sheet changes are:

USA combined banking system
$ million

Liabilities		Assets	
Demand deposits			
Charterhouse Bank	−1		
Bank of Tokyo	+1		
Net change	0	Net change	0

Charterhouse Bank

$ million

Liabilities		Assets	
		Demand deposit in US bank	−1
		Time deposit in Bank of Tokyo	+1
Net change	0	Net change	0

Bank of Tokyo

$ million

Liabilities		Assets	
Time deposits		Demand deposit in US bank	+1
Charterhouse Bank	+1		
Net change	+1	Net change	+1

Thus the Charterhouse Bank has converted a demand deposit in a US bank into an additional Eurodollar deposit bringing the total of gross Eurodollar deposits to $2 million. Neither Charterhouse nor the US correspondent bank involved puts restraints on what the Bank of Tokyo subsequently does with the funds. If inter-bank interest rates rise marginally, the Bank of Tokyo might decide to make another inter-bank loan in the London market, which would result in a further transfer of demand deposits in US correspondent banks and a further increase in gross Eurodollar deposits. Suppose, however, that at this stage the Bank of Tokyo is contacted by a British company seeking a dollar loan of $1 million to make a purchase of capital equipment from a US exporter. The Bank of Tokyo makes a Eurodollar loan and the subsequent balance sheet changes are:

US combined banking system

$ million

Liabilities		Assets	
Demand deposits			
a) Bank of Tokyo	−1		
British company	+1		
b) British company	−1		
US exporter	+1		
Net change	0	Net change	0

Bank of Tokyo

$ million

Liabilities		Assets	
		Demand deposit in US Bank	−1
		Loan to British company	+1
Net change	0	Net change	0

This is the end of the chain as far as the Eurodollar market is concerned. Conceptually speaking, therefore, the Eurodollar market constitutes a financial circuit through which US demand deposits may pass – transactions made between companies and Eurobanks, or between Eurobanks themselves, result in an underlying movement in dollar demand deposits in US banks. The proximate means of payment are US demand deposits, while at an even lower tier, the ultimate means of payment between USA correspondent banks are deposits with the Federal Reserve System. To state the obvious, the image of Eurodollars as US banknotes transferred to Europe in suitcases, which then circulate independently abroad, is not a correct description of reality.

While there are markets in London in different Eurocurrencies the most important currency is dollars and the reason for this is the importance of the dollar as a means of international payment; a significant fraction of world trade involving countries other than the USA is invoiced and settled in dollars (as was the case with sterling in the nineteenth century). Thus many large non-American companies making and receiving payments in dollars find it useful to hold dollar balances. The question is, however, why should such balances be held in banks outside the USA itself?

Various reasons have been cited as to why this should be the case, but the most generally accepted reason is that the USA domestic banking system in the past has been subject to various regulations which have made the holding of dollar balances in US banks a relatively unattractive prospect, not only for foreigners, but for US residents themselves. In particular, as well as being subject to mandatory cash ratio requirements, for a long period after the 1930s US banks were prohibited by law from paying interest on demand deposits, while during the 1960s interest ceilings were imposed on time and savings deposits; such ceilings became progressively more restrictive as nominal interest rates rose in more open markets consequent upon accelerating inflation in the USA. In contrast, in centres such as London, regulations imposed on the domestic clearing banks were not applied to wholesale banks transacting in Eurocurrency; banks were able to accept deposits and make loans denominated in dollars subject only to very informal monitoring of such transactions by the Bank of England. Thus the Eurobanks were able to offer more attractive interest rates on wholesale dollar deposits than banks located in the USA and as the US authorities imposed no restrictions on the holding of demand deposits by foreign located banks, or on the lending of dollars to, or the borrowing of dollars from such banks, many wholesale transactions in dollars were simply rerouted through offshore countries. London emerged as a major base for Eurobanks, not only because it had certain comparative advantages stemming from its previous historical role as an international financial centre, but also because, apart from small countries such as Singapore, the Cayman Islands, or Hong Kong, other major financial centres were not so free from regulations applying to foreign currency transactions by banks. Although controls on domestic US banks are now much less onerous, the difference in the regulatory environment undoubtedly did much to establish the Eurocurrency market during its period of rapid growth during the 1960s and 1970s.

Prior to 1979, exchange controls inhibited UK residents from freely transacting in the Eurocurrency markets but since then such barriers as existed have been removed. The Eurocurrency markets thus constitute an alternative source of funds for domestic borrowers. As an alternative to borrowing funds directly in sterling, for example, large corporate borrowers can borrow Eurodollars, selling such dollars for sterling on the 'spot' foreign exchange market while simultaneously covering the foreign exchange risk by buying forward dollars. Equally, for companies involved in international trade, transactions in Eurocurrency can provide a means of obtaining short-term credit and a means of hedging against exchange risk. Suppose that a UK exporter has sold goods to the USA on a three-month trade credit basis and expects to receive a certain sum of dollars in three months' time. To obtain short-term finance he can borrow an equivalent sum in Eurodollars for three months and sell the dollars immediately for sterling at the current spot rate. In this way he obtains sterling immediately for the sale of his goods and is fully hedged, in that when he eventually receives payment in dollars he can redeem his loan in the same currency.

We should note finally that there is no reason, in the absence of controls, why wholesale banking in sterling cannot be conducted from foreign centres offshore to the UK analogously to the Eurodollar market; in fact there exist at the present Euro-sterling markets abroad, the main centres being Paris, Amsterdam, and Luxembourg. These work in essentially the same way as the Eurodollar market; Eurosterling transactions have their counterpart in the shuffling of current account deposits in UK clearing banks and in Bankers' deposits at the Bank of England. It also follows that, in the absence of controls on sterling trans-actions with foreign located banks, the UK authorities are constrained in the regulations they can impose on UK wholesale banks, at least if they want to avoid the American experience of a migration of wholesale banking to offshore centres (which would mean that the regulations would simply be circumvented). In practice, the possibility of such a Eurocurrency loophole explains why certain instruments used by the Bank of England to control bank lending in the 1970s, such as the supplementary special deposits scheme (popularly known in City circles as the 'corset'), were considered by the authorities to be no longer tenable after 1979.

Notes

1 Also formally included in the UK monetary sector are the discount houses.
2 A simple analogy often used to illustrate a perfectly matched balance sheet is to make a comparison with a picture of a Christmas tree, on which branches on one side of the tree, the length of which symbolizes deposits of various terms to maturity, are matched by branches on the opposite side of the tree, symbolizing assets, of equal length.
3 See, for example, the evidence reviewed in Artis, M. J. and Lewis, M. K. (1981) *Monetary Control in the United Kingdom*, Oxford: Philip Allan, pp. 97–100.
4 Such an argument was advanced in Clark, R. J. (1970) 'The evolution of monetary and financial institutions' in Croome, D. R. and Johnson, H. G. (eds) *Money in Britain 1959–69*, Oxford: Oxford University Press, pp. 146–9.
5 See, for example, National Board for Prices and Incomes (1967) *Report No. 34, Bank Charges*, Cmnd 3292, London: HMSO.

Further reading

Artis, M. J. and Lewis, M. K. (1981) *Monetary Control in the United Kingdom*, Dedington: Philip Allan, Chapter 5.
Lewis, M. K. and Davis, K. T. (1987) *Domestic and International Banking*, Dedington: Philip Allan, Chapter 4.

McKinnon, R. I. (1979) *Money in International Exchange*, New York: Oxford University Press, Chapter 9.
Revell, J. (1973) *The British Financial System*, London: Macmillan, Chapters 9 and 11.

Chapter ten

Building societies

In the UK the traditional function of building societies has been that of retail deposit-taking institutions, providing an investment medium for small savers while specializing in making mortgage loans to personal borrowers.

The first recorded building society was founded in Birmingham in 1775, but they have expanded most rapidly in this century, particularly since 1960. The original societies were 'terminating societies' in which small groups of individuals joined together to contribute funds and often labour for the mutual acquisition of houses; the individuals in the group were provided with houses in turn, the allocation of finished houses often being decided by lotteries, and when each member had finally acquired a house the society was dissolved. Although the societies evolved in the nineteenth century into permanent financial intermediaries, where depositors and borrowers constituted separate groups of individuals, their origins are still reflected in the fact that they remain mutual non-profit organizations – there are no owners distinct from those placing funds in a society to whom any excess of receipts over outgoings can be distributed and any surplus is accumulated and retained as reserves.

Over the last thirty years the building societies have experienced dramatic growth as measured by the size of their liabilities, especially in relation to the growth of the deposits of the retail banks. In 1957, for example, building society liabilities amounted to £2.4 billion, roughly one-quarter of the size of retail bank deposits; by the end of 1985, building society retail deposits had expanded to approximately £104 billion, a total around 33 per cent greater than the total of sterling bank deposits held by the personal sector. In real terms, building society liabilities were nearly 500 per cent greater at the end of this period.

This growth is largely attributable to the underlying conditions in the markets in which the societies operated. The personal sector savings ratio increased substantially during the late 1960s and the 1970s and the societies had a competitive edge in the market for liquid deposits by virtue of certain favourable tax arrangements. More precisely, they benefited from an arrangement whereby the income tax payable by depositors on interest received was deducted at source – the societies paid interest net of tax. The tax deducted, however, did not correspond to the basic rate of income tax, but to a composite rate designed to reflect the average tax liability of all depositors, and as a proportion of building society depositors were low-income individuals with zero income tax liabilities, the composite rate was below the basic rate of income tax. Thus, for a given gross interest rate, building societies were able to offer higher net of tax interest rates to taxpayers subject to the basic rate of income tax.[1]

Equally, as far as the lending side of their business was concerned, the societies experienced growth in the demand for mortgage loans due to the underlying growth in home ownership. While much of this growth is attributable to rising real incomes, the demand for owner-occupied housing also reflected government policies in the housing market. Rent controls restricted the supply of private rental accommodation and, while rents of local authority houses were subsidized, there was almost permanent quantity rationing. At the same time the policies resulted in owner-occupied houses becoming privileged assets; in 1963 the income tax levied on the imputed income received by homeowners from ownership of their property was abolished, but homeowners with outstanding mortgages were still permitted to deduct interest payments from their incomes for tax purposes; further, when capital gains tax was introduced in the UK in 1965, houses which constituted the primary residence of the taxpayer concerned were made assets exempt from tax. Thus, for a given market price of houses, the real costs of housing services for owner-occupiers were substantially reduced by these tax concessions.

Taken together, all these factors ensured a growing demand for funds to finance the acquisition of owner-occupied housing, a demand which was largely concentrated on the building societies. Although at various times there were other providers of housing finance, such as insurance companies and local authorities, they were not a major presence and, until the banks entered the field in a major way in the early 1980s, the societies had a virtual monopoly on such lending.

195

The structure of building societies

Along with the rapid growth in overall building society liabilities there have occurred marked changes in the structure of the societies; most importantly, there has been a decline in the numbers of individual societies and consequently an increase in their average size. In 1957 there were in existence around 755 societies; by 1971 this had declined to around 460 and at the end of 1985 the number of societies operating had fallen further to approximately 200. As a result of the rules governing the formation of new societies, there has been comparatively little new entry – only eighteen new societies have been formed in the period since 1964.

The decline in numbers has occurred mainly through what are technically termed 'transfers of engagements' whereby smaller societies have transferred their membership and assets to larger ones. Unlike a formal union, transfers of engagements do not require a special resolution on the part of the membership of the transferring society. Formal mergers between larger societies have been rarer; where they have occurred the objective has often been to merge societies with different regional coverage. Within the total number of existing societies, there is a considerable diversity in the size of individual societies and a substantial degree of concentration of total assets in a small number of very large societies. At the end of 1985 the two largest societies held over 33 per cent of total assets, the largest five societies held over 50 per cent, the largest twenty held over 85 per cent and the largest thirty-six held 90 per cent. Thus there are still many very small societies who operate primarily in narrower geographical localities. The total number of branch offices grew from just over 1,500 in 1955 to over 6,000 in 1980.

Building society operations

The combined balance sheet of the building societies at the end of 1985 is shown in Table 10.1. As is evident, the vast bulk of building society liabilities constitute 'shares and deposits'. The technical difference between these two categories is that deposits constitute a loan to a society and in the event of a liquidation depositors rank as creditors with priority status as regards repayment. Shares, on the other hand, rank behind deposits in the event of liquidation, but carry voting rights at a society's AGM. The resemblance to shares in a public limited company is, however, slight; a building society does not have fixed share capital, does not make public issues of specific numbers of shares and shares are not marketable. An individual becomes a shareholder in a society simply by depositing funds in essentially the same way as if he were making a formal 'deposit' and he relinquishes his shareholding by withdrawing funds – the methods of investing and withdrawing funds are equivalent. For a long period deposits and shares were fairly homogeneous categories with deposits carrying a slightly lower rate of interest (often ½ to ¼ per cent) and being subject formally to a shorter period of notice of withdrawal. In practice, however, competition between individual building societies often took the form of an easing in withdrawal conditions, and both shares and deposits in normal circumstances become effectively withdrawable on demand or at very short notice (at any rate for moderate withdrawals), so that for most investors the technical difference between deposits and shares is now largely semantic. The vast majority of individuals now invest in shares rather than deposits.

Table 10.1 Building societies' combined balance sheet as at 31 December 1985

Liabilities		Assets	
	£ billion		£ billion
Shares and deposits	104.9	Short-term assets	9.5
Interest accrued but not credited	1.6	British government securities	10.9
Time deposits and CDs	3.4	Other marketable securities	1.5
Bank borrowing and bonds	2.9	Other assets	1.9
Reserves	8.4	Mortgages	97.4
	121.2		121.2

Source: *Financial Statistics*, No. 300, April 1987, London: HMSO, Table 7.7.

As competition between building societies (and between building societies and other institutions) has intensified in recent years, building society shares have become much less homogeneous. Most building societies nowadays distinguish 'ordinary shares' (also called 'paid-up shares'), normally withdrawable on demand, from a large variety of differentiated share accounts that have been introduced to appeal to investors with differing requirements as to the liquidity of their assets. A large number of 'high interest' shares are now available where, in return for keeping certain minimum sums in their accounts, investors are paid interest rates above those available on ordinary shares; most of these share accounts are 'notice shares' which require some notice before funds can be withdrawn, or carry an interest penalty for immediate withdrawal, the periods of notice involved varying from seven days to typically around six months. A number of societies, however, offer high-interest shares which require minimum balances, but from which cash can be withdrawn on demand often through ATMs. In recent years a further innovation has been the introduction by some societies of high-interest shares linked to current accounts in banks. The first example of this was the Alliance 'bank save' account, operated in conjunction with the Bank of Scotland, introduced in 1984; in this instance a customer opens an account with the Alliance (the minimum sum required being £500), but £350 of this is transferred to a current account in the Bank of Scotland on which the customer can write cheques in the normal way; whenever the customer's current account falls below £350 funds are automatically transferred from his Alliance account. Additionally, building societies offer shares called 'term shares' (also called 'bonds') which have fixed terms offering even higher interest rates – terms usually run in discrete intervals of a year from one to five years. As a result of the introduction of such accounts with specialized features the proportion of total retail funds held in ordinary share accounts has fallen to around 30 per cent.

As well as operating share accounts where money can be deposited at the option of the holder, building societies have diversified into contractual savings schemes often called 'subscription shares', where the investor contracts to invest a given sum each month for a set period; such contractual schemes have often been operated in conjunction with insurance companies offering life assurance policies.[2]

The next item on the liabilities side of the balance sheet 'interest accrued but not credited' is a technical item arising from the fact that interest accrues to account holders on a day to day basis, but is only formally recorded as an addition to account holders' credit balances at discrete intervals of time. The following two items jointly reflect the recent movement of building societies away from purely retail funds raised through their branch networks to wholesale sources. In 1980, the Alliance first issued a yearling 'negotiable bond' and since 1983 some of the larger societies have bid for wholesale time deposits in the money market. The Finance Act of 1983 further extended the powers of the societies to attract wholesale funds by permitting them to issue certificates of deposit, while the Finance Act of 1985 enabled the societies to pay interest on Eurobonds to non-residents without withholding tax. The largest society, the Halifax, was the first to tap this source of funds with a £150 million Eurobond issue in the autumn of 1985. The 'reserves' item represents the accumulated surpluses of annual revenues over costs earned by the societies in their previous operations.

Turning to the assets side of the balance sheet, approximately 80 per cent of building society assets constitute mortgage loans, the vast majority of which are secured on owner-occupied houses. Clearly, as the term of a mortgage loan is very long in relation to the term of their liabilities, building societies have markedly mismatched balance sheets. The original term of a typical mortgage loan varies according to the preference of the borrower, but most societies are prepared to lend for periods up to thirty years. The average term to maturity of the stock of mortgage loans outstanding at any given time is, of course, much shorter, because the stock will include loans made some time ago which are nearing the end of their terms. Moreover, as individual homeowners tend to move house on average once every seven to eight years, the average term of an individual mortgage contract is considerably less than the nominal term; many mortgage loans in practice are rolled over on the basis of the security of a new property, but, technically, a building society could insist on the repayment of the loan when a house is sold.

The average maturity of the stock of a society's mortgage loans is also reduced by the contractual arrangements relating to the repayment of loans. The majority of mortgage loans are repaid on an annuity basis where the borrower (assuming a constant interest rate) pays a fixed sum each month large enough to pay the interest on the outstanding balance of his debt and to pay off the original loan over the stipulated term. Thus a borrower repays the principal of the loan continuously; his repayments are small initially as a fraction of the monthly payment but increase gradually as the end of the term is approached. The normal annuity method of repayment was amended in detail by most societies following a change in the arrangements relating to tax relief on mortgage interest, which was enacted in April 1983. Previously borrowers paid interest gross to a society and then claimed a personal tax allowance for the payments being made, so that as the fraction of the constant monthly payment constituting interest gradually declined, the borrower's net of tax monthly payments increased. The present arrangement for most taxpayers is known as the mortgage interest relief at source (MIRAS) scheme; with this scheme the borrower pays directly to the building society an interest payment net of tax at the basic rate of income tax and the society then claims the difference between this net of tax interest rate and its gross interest rate from the government. With the introduction of this scheme many societies revised their contractual repayment schemes to provide for a constant net monthly payment by spreading the tax relief evenly over the life of the mortgage; in effect, this scheme results in an increased inflow of funds to a building society in the early years of a mortgage loan.

With certain contractual arrangements, however, none of the principal of the loan is repaid before the end of the term. In this case a borrower arranges a mortgage loan and simultaneously contracts an endowment policy with a life assurance company to run for the same term as the loan. The borrower then pays monthly interest payments to the building society plus monthly insurance premiums (the building society typically collects the premiums from the borrower on behalf of the life assurance company) until the end of the term, when the endowment policy matures and yields a sum which normally suffices to repay the loan. Because their funds are tied up for a longer period, societies generally charge the borrower a higher interest rate on endowment-linked mortgage loans, but some societies have recently discontinued this practice.[3]

Most of the other assets of building societies constitute their liquid reserves. Until 1987 the societies were subject to a minimum liquidity ratio of 7½ per cent laid down by the Chief Registrar of the Friendly Societies. As can be seen from the table, at the end of 1985 the actual ratio of liquid assets, comprising short-term assets, British government securities and other marketable securities, amounted to 18.1 per cent of total assets. Within this average there were variations in the liquidity ratios of individual societies, the larger societies tended to operate with somewhat lower ratios. 'Short-term assets' comprised notes and coin (£105 million), bank deposits (£6,937 million), certificates of deposit (£1,291 million) and local authority temporary debt. Of the total of British government securities held, 91 per cent were of under five years to maturity. Building societies have generally held higher liquidity ratios than the stipulated minimum because the rate of withdrawals and inflows of funds can vary substantially over short periods of time. As borrowers the societies compete with a variety of other assets such as National Savings instruments, gilt-edged securities, unit trusts, etc., as well as with bank deposits and, at the margin, flows of funds into societies in practice have been very sensitive to the differentials between their interest rates and rates on competing assets.

Building society interest rates

Unlike similar institutions in the USA which make long-term mortgage loans at fixed-interest rates, building societies have avoided the interest rate risks involved in borrowing short and lending long by contractual arrangements which permit them to vary the interest rate on mortgage loans at their own discretion. None the less, for a long period (since 1939) the societies operated an interest rate cartel whereby most individual societies set a recommended rate on both shares and mortgage loans decided by the Building Societies' Association (BSA). Competition between individual societies took the form largely of non-price competition such as the creation of extensive branch networks (branches were often located in prime high street sites), advertising campaigns, etc. Because of the recommended rate system which necessitated individual societies reaching an agreement, interest rates often tended to be 'sticky' and tended to lag behind changes in other rates. This inflexibility in interest rates also reflected the fact that the societies generally regarded their business as having the social service objective of making home ownership available as cheaply as possible and were particularly reluctant, on occasion, to move interest rates upwards.

Consequently, net inflows of funds to the societies from quarter to quarter tended to vary markedly in response to changes in building society competitiveness, particularly when nominal interest rates became more volatile in the 1970s. The societies tended to absorb these variations in net inflows in the short run by variations in their liquidity ratios and also by various forms of non-price rationing of mortgage loans. Interest rates were adjusted eventually in response to persistent declines or increases in liquidity ratios, but for significant periods of time during the 1960s and 1970s, the interest rates set by the societies were at levels which resulted in mortgage queues.

In the early 1980s, however, the recommended rate cartel came under increasing strain. The dominant position of the societies as lenders in the mortgage market was threatened by the large-scale entry of the banks into the market, while at the same time they faced increased competition in the market for deposits. In particular, in order to facilitate non-bank funding of the PSBR, the government improved the interest rate terms available on non-marketable National Savings instruments while extending the availability of index-linked National Savings certificates to the whole population. Many societies responded to this situation by more explicit interest rate competition which took the form, as previously described, of the introduction of differentiated share accounts on which interest was paid above the recommended rate applying to ordinary shares, at the discretion of individual societies. Although a move was made by some societies, via the BSA, to extend the cartel arrangement to cover differential share accounts, in October 1981 the BSA formally limited its interest rate recommendation to the ordinary share rate alone.

While most societies thereafter still continued to adhere to this rate the process of differentiation meant that the recommended rate became progressively less meaningful, both as an administrative 'base' rate for the determination of a society's interest rate structure and as an indicator of the general level of building society interest rates; ordinary shares diminished rapidly as a proportion of retail liabilities and the average interest rate paid on all shares came to diverge markedly from the ordinary share rate. The effective disintegration of the interest rate cartel continued when in September 1983 the second largest society, the Abbey National, announced that it was withdrawing from the BSA arrangement and finally, in November 1984, the BSA Council formally decided that the practice of recommending or advising on any specific interest rates to members should cease. Collective discussion of interest rate policy has continued, but effectively the boards of individual societies now make independent and competitive decisions about the timing and extent of interest rate changes. Consequently, building society interest rates now exhibit a tendency to react more quickly to changes in interest rates elsewhere.

A further change in building society operations has stemmed from their entry into the wholesale certificate of deposit and time deposit markets. In the same way as for the retail banks, the wholesale markets provide extra flexibility for the societies in their lending activities. Traditionally in the short term, the societies concentrated on asset management, using their holdings of liquid assets as a buffer to stabilize the flow of mortgage lending against a background of fluctuations in retail net inflows. By using the wholesale markets to offset fluctuations in retail net inflows, the societies have adopted, in part, the techniques of liability management which, in the longer term, may enable them to operate with a lower ratio of liquid assets to mortgage loans. An increased reliance on wholesale funding again implies that interest rates on mortgage loans will, in the future, be more responsive to changes in interest rates elsewhere.

The 1987 Building Societies Act

We have already discussed certain changes in the services offered by building societies which are making them less distinguishable as institutions from banks. The tendency is likely to develop further following the passage of a new Act laying down the regulatory framework for building societies which became operative from 1 January 1987. The main provisions of the Act in summary are as follows:

1. The supervision of building societies is transferred from the Registrar of Friendly Societies to a new Building Societies Commission. There will also be a Building Societies Investor Protection Board responsible for administering a compensation scheme for building society investors and a Building Societies Ombudsman to adjudicate in disputes with customers.
2. Societies are permitted to hold up to 5 per cent of their assets in the form of unsecured loans not related to property with a limit on loans to individual borrowers of £5,000. This provision removes a previous impediment on the provision of cheque books for building society investors as, previously, societies could not issue cheque guarantee cards which within limits permitted individuals to overdraw on accounts.
3. Up to 90 per cent of a society's assets can be invested in mortgage loans and the societies are now able to lend in other member states of the EEC.
4. As a result of further amendment to the Act in 1988, societies are permitted to raise up to 40 per cent of their funds from wholesale markets.
5. Societies can offer full personal banking and money transmission services if they wish and are permitted, also, to provide ancillary services such as the provision of foreign currency and travellers cheques, insurance broking, the management of unit trusts, and the management of transactions in securities, as well as non-financed services such as estate agency. Additionally, societies have extended powers to engage in joint ventures, act in an agency capacity for other institutions, and to take equity interests in subsidiary companies.
6. Procedures are laid down whereby societies may convert to company status.

Within the limits of the new Act, therefore, societies have powers to emulate the clearing banks, in part, by becoming 'financial supermarkets'. From the broader viewpoint of the

monetary and financial system the Act extends the powers of
building societies to provide assets for individuals which, from a
portfolio choice viewpoint, will narrow still further the distinguishing characteristics between bank liabilities and building society
liabilities. For example, the Nationwide Society has already introduced in May 1987 a new 'flex account' which is an interest-
bearing current account with chequing facilities, a home-banking
facility, overdraft facilities and zero transaction charges even if
the account becomes overdrawn; clearing of cheques is handled
by the Co-operative Bank. Building societies are already
extending the provision of ATM services with facilities for both
cash withdrawals and cash deposits in network arrangements
whereby customers of a particular society will be able to use the
ATMs of any of the member societies in the network. The principal building society network is called Matrix, managed by a
company called Electronic Funds Transfer created under the
auspices of the BSA. A rival network is called Link which includes
the Abbey National, the Nationwide, and sixteen smaller
societies, and the Co-operative and Giro banks. Although, at the
time of writing, network arrangements are primarily confined to
cash withdrawals and deposits, it is envisaged that these systems
will eventually expand into electronic funds transfers at point of
sale systems. If retailers and other traders open accounts with
building societies and are prepared to accept direct book transfers
to their accounts from the building society accounts of customers,
then it is not beyond the bounds of possibility that building society
liabilities will evolve still further and circulate directly as a means
of payment.

Competition between building societies and the banks

In recent years considerable controversy has arisen as to the
nature of competition between building societies and the banks
and the extent to which the rapid growth in building society
liabilities has been at the expense of bank deposits.

One can make an initial distinction here between clearing bank
deposits and wholesale bank (or secondary bank) deposits. Both
wholesale bank deposits and building society deposits stand in a
tiered relationship to clearing bank deposits and, therefore, if
building societies can attract funds from non-bank depositors
which otherwise would have been held in the wholesale banks,
then building society deposits can increase directly at the expense
of bank deposits. Given the building societies' entry into the

wholesale markets in the 1980s there is thus more direct competition between the building societies and the wholesale banks.

However, the competitive mechanisms between the building societies and the clearing banks are more complex. If a depositor in an individual clearing bank switches funds into a building society which happens to bank with another clearing bank, then the bank concerned will lose deposits and cash and, therefore, any individual bank has an incentive to make its interest rates competitive with the rates being offered on building society deposits to avoid drains of deposits and cash to other banks. None the less, as the example we considered in Chapter 2 illustrates, unless the liquid reserves held by building societies substantially duplicate those held by the clearing banks, then such switches into building society deposits do not involve an immediate loss of deposits and cash for the clearing banks considered collectively.

In practice, there is some overlap in holdings of liquid assets in that building societies hold some assets in the form of notes and coin and, if the ratio of cash to deposits is fairly stable then, other things equal, a net switch by the public from clearing bank deposits into building society deposits would result in the societies withdrawing deposits from the banks to hold in the form of notes and coin. Equally, if individuals made net deposits of notes and coin in building societies, as opposed to the banks, then the growth of bank deposits would be likewise reduced. However, the amount of notes and coin held on average by the building societies is very small in relation to their total deposits. At the end of 1985, for example, in relation to 'retail' deposit liabilities of £104,870 million the societies held only £105 million in the form of notes and coin, a ratio of only 0.1 per cent. Thus cash leakages from the clearing banks following a net switch from bank deposits to building society deposits are unlikely to be particularly significant while, similarly, net deposits of notes and coin received by the societies will be largely deposited with the clearing banks for purposes of making payments or holding reserves.

Of the remainder of building society liquid assets £8,200 million were held in deposits with the UK monetary sector or certificates of deposit, while, approximately £10,900 million were held in the form of British government securities. In principle, building society acquisition of government securities might constitute a means whereby the bank might lose deposits following a switch to building society deposits, but the significance of such a direct mechanism in practice would depend on the policies being pursued by the government in the gilt-edged market. If, for example, the government had some target for interest rates in the gilt-edged market then sales of government securities would essentially be demand-determined; thus if building societies attracted deposits from the banks, the societies' demand for government securities might constitute a net addition to the total demand for government securities in relation to the government's borrowing requirement (hence reducing the government's residual financial deficit or increasing the overfunding of the borrowing requirement), thus directly reducing bank deposits compared to what they otherwise would have been. On the other hand, at the time of writing, the declared policy objective of the government is neither to overfund nor underfund the PSBR. Thus as public sector borrowing is now largely channelled through the central government, given the PSBR, the government needs to sell a fixed amount of debt in any period. In this instance, if building societies acquire more government securities, then the rest of the non-bank private sector will acquire fewer newly issued securities than they otherwise would have done and the end result as far as bank deposits is concerned is neutral; the total drain of deposits and cash from the banks consequent upon the purchase of newly issued government securities is given and the drain is fully offset by the matching government expenditure. Thus providing the government adheres to its current stated policy objectives then there is unlikely to be a substantial immediate loss of bank deposits following portfolio switches into building society deposits through this direct mechanism.

If deposit growth by the building societies as a group is to be at the expense of the deposits of the clearing banks as a group, then this is likely to come about in the long run through the sort of indirect mechanisms we have already alluded to when discussing competition between the clearing banks and the wholesale banks. Such indirect mechanisms will depend in detail on the sorts of monetary policy being pursued by the authorities.

1. Suppose the monetary authorities are pursuing a policy where they have a fixed target for the growth of a monetary aggregate comprised largely of clearing bank deposits. Assuming the target is achieved then the nominal stock of bank deposits is given, but suppose that building society deposits become more attractive as a form of holding wealth and individuals switch from bank deposits into building society deposits. In effect this is a symptom of a decrease in the community's stock demand for money and the resultant excess supply of money might as a consequence lead to an increase in aggregate monetary expenditure which drives up the general price level (the income velocity of circulation of money

increases). Thus although there is no immediate reduction in nominal bank deposits, there is a decline in the real value of the existing stock and in consequence a decline in the real value of the bank's profits.

2. The monetary authorities might be operating a flexible discretionary policy where they do not set any fixed monetary targets but aim to achieve a certain growth in aggregate monetary expenditure. If building societies, by deposit expansion, can initiate in aggregate monetary expenditure above what the authorities consider to be warranted, then the response of the authorities might be tighter credit and monetary policies which reduce the growth in nominal bank deposits below what it otherwise might have been.

3. If the monetary authorities set an intermediate target for the growth of a broader 'credit' aggregate which includes both building society deposits and bank deposits then, if building society deposits as a result of portfolio switches expand at a faster rate than that targeted, there is less scope for the growth of bank deposits. Portfolio switches into building society deposits which resulted in the target being exceeded might be followed by restrictive measures which would reduce the growth in nominal bank deposits.

Notes

1 For non-taxpayers, of course, building society deposits paying the same gross interest rate as elsewhere were an inferior investment, as they were not allowed to reclaim from the Inland Revenue the tax paid on their behalf. Despite this, many non-taxpayers continued investing in building societies as, even on a net of tax basis, building society deposits were for a long period competitive with such alternative investments as National Savings or Trustee Savings Bank deposits.

2 Prior to 1984 the linking of building society subscription shares to life assurance policies meant that advantage could be taken of tax privileges granted to savings via life assurance.

3 Indeed, following the introduction of the MIRAS scheme in 1983 many societies actively encouraged borrowers to switch to endowment-linked mortgages.

Further reading

Boleat, M. (August 1987) 'Building societies: the new supervisory framework' *National Westminster Bank Review*.

Harrington, R. L. (1974) 'The importance of competition for credit control', in Johnson, H. G. and Nobay, A. R. (eds) *Issues in Monetary Economics*, London: Oxford University Press.

Llewellyn, D. T. (January 1979) 'Do building societies take deposits away from banks?', *Lloyds Bank Review*.

Revell, J. (1973) *The British Financial System*, London: Macmillan, Chapter 14.

Struthers, J. and Speight, H. (1986) *Money: Institutions, Theory and Policy*, London: Longman, Chapter 5.

'The future of building societies – a central banker's view', *Bank of England Quarterly Bulletin*, June 1983.

'Housing finance', *Bank of England Quarterly Bulletin*, March 1985.

Chapter eleven

Investing institutions

Contractual savings institutions: life assurance and pension funds

The essential rationale of investing institutions as financial inter-mediaries is that they enable individuals to participate in collective investment funds which, by pooling a large number of individual contributions and acquiring widely diversified portfolios of financial and real assets, can reduce the risks associated with direct investment.

The main media for long-term contractual savings in the UK are life assurance policies and pension funds and, as we have already indicated in Chapter 3, these institutions have become particularly significant in the workings of the financial system. In 1985 contributions to life assurance and pension funds amounted to 45 per cent of gross personal sector savings and 38 per cent of the stock of gross personal sector financial assets; likewise life assurance and pension funds held significant amounts of the total holdings of marketable securities.

Under the terms of the Insurance Companies Act of 1982, the business of insurance companies is separated into two categories: long-term business and general business. The latter is concerned primarily with providing individuals with insurance against specific contingencies such as fire, damage to property, theft, or accidents for fixed periods of time. Although general insurance companies hold financial assets as reserves to meet their uncertain liabilities arising from potential claims, general insurance contracts relate to the purchase of a particular consumption service (indemnity against possible loss), the premium involved representing the price of this service. Since no borrowing or lending is involved this aspect of insurance company business can be regarded as non-financial.

In contrast, long-term business is concerned with extended contracts where, in return for a series of premiums or sometimes a single premium, payments are made on the death of the insured or on his survival to a certain age. In general, there are four types of life assurance policy:

1. *Term assurance*: in this case a payment of a certain sum is made only if the individual dies within a specified period covered by the policy. If the individual survives the specified period no payment is made.
2. *Whole-life policy*: under this contract the period covered is the remaining lifetime of the individual – a guaranteed sum is paid whenever the individual dies. For an individual whose lifetime exactly equals the average life expectancy, the payment of the guaranteed sum essentially boils down to a refunding of the premiums paid, enhanced by net earnings from the assets in which the premiums have been invested, and the policy has fulfilled the dual role of providing the individual with cover against premature death and also a vehicle for savings. Over the individual's remaining lifetime a stream of annual premiums is handed over to the insurance company which invests the fund built up on behalf of the insured.
3. *Endowment policy*: this policy is again a mixture of cover against premature death and an instrument for savings, and combines term assurance with the promise of a future payment if the individual survives to the end of the contract period. The guaranteed sum payable on premature death or on survival is known as the 'sum assured'. With some policies (without-profits policies) the sum assured is fixed at the outset, but with other policies (with-profits policies) the exact sums paid, while subject to some minimum sum assured, are conditional on the investment performance of the underlying funds. Under with-profits policies, bonuses, sometimes termed 'reversionary bonuses', are added to the guaranteed minimum sum assured during the life of a contract at the discretion of an actuary who calculates, using certain assumptions about future interest rates, mortality rates, etc., the discounted present value of a fund in relation to the discounted present value of future liabilities. If the fund has a surplus according to these calculations then reversionary bonuses are often declared which become a firm liability of the company from that point onwards. Part of the computed surplus is often distributed as a terminal bonus on policies that mature either on the death of the assured or on his survival to the end of the stipulated period.

The funds built up from the premiums paid on conventional contracts are invested at the discretion of the life office, normally being spread across a wide portfolio of assets. Some policies, however, are linked to specific funds such as unit trusts, the premiums paid being used to purchase units in a trust of the policyholder's choice. The sums paid on the maturity of such policies then depend on the performance of the unit trust to which the contract is linked.

4. *Annuities*: with this class of policy an initial lump sum is paid in return for the right to receive a stated income each year until death. A fund is thus created immediately and then gradually run down in annual payments to the policyholders.

Long-term insurance business that serves as a vehicle for contractual savings has become increasingly important relative to ordinary life cover. As far as individual savers are concerned, the financial claims held in the form of endowment policies are not particularly liquid assets. A saver can terminate a regular savings contract at his discretion and can demand repayment of funds, but there are penalties for so doing in that the surrender values of endowment policies are lower than the maturity values of policies for the same total premiums paid (a twenty-five-year policy surrendered after ten years would yield less than a ten-year policy maturing after ten years). The penalty for premature surrender is greatest in the early years of a contract and a policyholder might not receive even the premiums he has paid. An option often open to policyholders, however, is the possibility of obtaining loans against the security of such policies.

In 1984 there were 330 separate institutions authorized by the Department of Trade to carry out long-term insurance business, although a number of these were subsidiaries of larger groups. Some are proprietary companies with shareholders while others are 'mutual offices' in the same fashion as building societies. Proprietary companies generally undertake all types of insurance business, while mutual institutions tend to concentrate on life business. As with building societies, there is considerable variation in the size of the institutions and a considerable degree of concentration of total assets within the largest institutions. The Wilson Committee reported that the four largest companies held 30.6 per cent of total assets, while the ten largest held 50 per cent.[1]

Occupational pension schemes in the UK, although they date back to before 1914, have grown in importance mainly since 1945. In 1936 the number of employers belonging to private pension schemes was only 1.6 million; by 1967 this had increased to 8.1 million, although by 1983 this number had fallen back to 5.8 million, largely due to a reduction in the number of male manual workers covered. Some public sector pension schemes are unfunded or 'pay as you go schemes' where the cost of pension payments to retired members in a particular period is met from contributions received from working members and from other revenues within the period concerned. Funded private sector schemes, however, are in effect a combination of an endowment life assurance policy and an annuity; during the period of a person's employment, contributions from both the employee and the employer are used to accumulate an investment fund, the terminal amount of which is used to buy an annuity for the employee during his years of retirement. The contractual arrangements of pension funds vary; for some schemes the benefits eventually paid are calculated on some fraction of a person's final salary multiplied by the number of years for which contributions have been made, the maximum benefits obtainable under such schemes being limited by the Finance Act of 1970. In other instances there are no precisely defined benefits, instead the terminal sum accumulated is used to purchase formally an annuity for the beneficiary, so that the annual pension obtainable depends upon the annuity rates being offered at the time of retirement.

Funded pension schemes are normally set up as trust funds administered by a board of trustees and can be operated in several ways. They may be self-administered with the funds being managed by full-time investment managers, or the services of other financial institutions may be used. Where an individual fund might be considered too small to achieve adequate portfolio diversification, the trustees may join a pool of managed funds, and another method used by smaller private sector schemes is to operate via life assurance companies.

In addition to group schemes, life assurance companies operate personal pension plans for self-employed individuals and for employed individuals who receive non-pensionable income. Changes to the social security system planned for 1988, however, will make it possible for all employees to opt out of occupational group schemes and operate their own personal pension plans. Generally speaking, contributions to personal pension plans, like those to group schemes, are extremely illiquid assets from the individual's viewpoint in that the sums contributed are locked up until retirement when, in addition to an annuity, some terminal lump sum is often paid. Some life offices, though, do offer a loan facility whereby contributors to pension schemes can borrow against the lump sum to be received at the date of retirement.

The growth of life assurance and pension funds

Life assurance and pension funds have grown very rapidly over the last three decades. Between the end of 1962 and the end of 1985 life assurance companies' assets corresponding to long-term business (including pension schemes operated by life assurance companies) expanded from £7,339 million to £129,794 million.[2] Similarly, the total assets of self-administered private pension funds expanded from £2,460 million at the end of 1962 to £101,041 million by the end of 1985; if funded pension schemes in the public sector are included the total value of pension fund assets at the end of 1985 was £157,376 million. The year to year growth reflects, not only net inflows of money corresponding to an excess of contributions, interest and dividends, etc., over sums paid out, but also changes in the market value of the financial assets held in the funds (in 1973 and 1974, for example, when share prices fell heavily the growth in the value of assets was negative).

The growth in life assurance and pension funds reflects the increase in the personal sector savings ratio during the 1970s and also the fact that fiscal privileges have been attached to savings taking these forms. When an individual pays a contribution into a pension scheme, the whole of his contribution is treated as a deductible expense in the calculation of his income for income tax purposes. Suppose a person earns £19,000 per annum and that, of this gross salary, £1,000 is paid as a contribution to a pension scheme; in this case the income subject to a tax is at most £18,000 (there may of course be other allowances that can be set against tax) and the individual's pension contribution reduces his tax bill by £270 if his marginal rate of income tax is 27 per cent. The pension fund is then able to purchase £1,000, say, company securities on the individual's behalf, but the net cost of this for the individual is only £730, i.e. £1,000 minus the extra £270 he would have paid in income tax had he not contributed to the scheme. An individual wishing to buy £1,000 of company securities directly on his own behalf would have enjoyed no deduction from his taxable income and, hence, would have incurred a higher acquisition cost of the same bundle of securities. In addition, the interest, dividends, and capital gains accrued by a pension fund are also tax exempt, whereas the same gross returns earned by an individual on securities held directly would be subject to income tax and possibly capital gains tax.

Until recently income tax relief also applied to savings made via life assurance premiums – the income corresponding to such premiums was taxed at half the basic rate of income tax, thus again reducing the net cost of the premiums for savers. This concession, however, was withdrawn in March 1984, although there are still some tax advantages attached to savings via life assurance companies in that the income derived from a fund is taxed at a lower rate in the hands of a life office than it would be if the securities involved were held directly by an individual.

In recent years there has been increasing criticism of the fiscal privileges accorded to contractual savings via these financial intermediaries. From the point of view of the capital market, a particular criticism has been that it has resulted in a concentration of equity shares in the hands of large institutional shareholders to a much greater extent than is observable in countries comparable to the UK. In Germany, for example, in 1982 insurance companies and pension funds held less than 10 per cent of the ordinary shares of companies, whereas in the UK the comparable percentage was of the order of 43 per cent. Institutional shareholders, it is argued, tend to concentrate on the shares of large established companies which can be traded in large blocks without unduly affecting the market price, thus the effect is to channel equity funds away from smaller newer companies. This dominance of institutional shareholders in the capital market is plausibly a factor explaining why the concentration of production among large companies in the UK has gone beyond levels witnessed in other countries and which is difficult to justify on other economic grounds.

Recently the special income tax privileges attached to institutional savings have been modified in that income tax concessions have been extended to individuals undertaking certain financial investments directly on their own account. Under the Business Expansion Scheme, instigated in 1983, tax allowances are given to private individuals directly investing up to £40,000 in certain qualifying new or small companies. In January 1987 a scheme for personal equity plans (PEPs) was introduced whereby individuals could invest up to £200 per month (or £2,400 a year) in the shares of UK companies quoted on the Stock Exchange, with dividends and capital gains being tax-free provided the shares are held for a minimum of twelve months. Whether PEPs will do much to redress the imbalance between personal and institutional shareholdings remains to be seen, however, as the scheme also applies in part to investment schemes administered by institutions (a certain proportion of a PEP can be invested in unit trusts).

Insurance company and pension fund investment

Unlike deposit-taking institutions, the liabilities of assurance companies and pension funds for the most part are very long term. In whole life assurance the actual term depends on how long the policyholder survives after making the contract, but terms of fifty years or more are quite common. For endowment policies terms range from ten years upwards to around forty years. Pension funds generally have a liability from the time an employee enters a scheme (because some death benefit is usually involved) until his eventual death or the death of a dependent entitled to receive benefits.

A further difference is that, while deposit-taking institutions have a liability to redeem the face value merely of sums deposited plus any accrued interest, the committed liabilities of insurance companies and pension funds are greater than the contractual sums they can expect to receive by way of premiums and contributions, and are set in advance of the actual rates of return they will achieve on their investment funds. In the case of an endowment policy, for example, the guaranteed sum assured is derived from actuarial calculations based on assumptions about how the process of continual investment of received premiums and reinvestment of interest earnings will cause the value of a fund to grow over time, and the company will only be able to fulfil its obligations if the assumptions built into the calculation, regarding future mortality rates, interest rates, operating expenses, etc., are in fact eventually fulfilled in reality. Thus insurance companies and pension fund investment policies must attempt to achieve positive rates of return commensurate with the actuarial assumptions that have determined their future liabilities, while at the same time, their portfolio choices must reflect the associated risks involved in holding particular assets. While both life assurance companies and pension funds seek to reduce the specific investment risks involved in holding particular financial assets by appropriate policies of portfolio diversification, there are, however, some differences in their portfolio choices which stem from certain differences in the nature of the future liabilities involved.

Life assurance company contractual liabilities are usually specified in terms of future fixed sums of money, either as sums assured, in the case of without-profits policies, or minimum sums assured plus declared reversionary bonuses in the case of with-profits policies. An insurance company can therefore avoid the risk of failure to meet its contractual obligations by holding assets with terms to maturity which match the terms of its liabilities and which

215

also have a given yield if held to maturity, at least equal to the interest rate assumptions built into the relevant actuarial calculations of sums assured. Life assurance companies, therefore, have a preference in their investment strategies for holding a significant proportion of their asset portfolio in the form of fixed-interest gilt-edged securities with varying terms to maturity reflecting the term of their liabilities.

In principle, life companies might be able to meet their contractual obligations by holding entirely fixed-interest stocks, but in practice investors contributing to with-profits policies do so on the understanding that there is a reasonable expectation that the sums eventually paid out on maturity will exceed the minimum sums assured. Indeed, competition between different life companies for new business often focuses on the level of bonuses they have been able to achieve in past periods, so individual companies have some interest in achieving rates of return on their investments above the minimum required to meet their formal contractual obligations. For this reason, therefore, life companies mix investment in fixed-interest securities with investment in ordinary shares and property, in the hope that the returns will exceed what can be earned in fixed-interest stocks.

Pension funds, on the other hand, very often have contractual liabilities of a different form. Although many schemes in the past guaranteed benefits in money terms related to the number of contributions made, they have increasingly taken the form where the value of future pension rights is related to the final salary, or average earnings over some stipulated period, of the member, adjusted for the number of years for which the member has made contributions. As individuals' final salaries are not entirely predictable, there is, therefore, greater uncertainty as to the future obligations of the pension fund in money terms. Such uncertainty is compounded by the possibility of future inflation, which by increasing the money value of final salaries or average earnings, increases the money value of pensions to be paid from a fund which has been accumulated from lower money contributions in past periods. Additionally, the future monetary liabilities of some pension schemes are rendered even more uncertain by the fact that pensions to be paid in retirement are index-linked, usually to the retail price index, so that inflation after a member has retired increases still further the monetary obligations of the pension fund.

For this reason the concept of matching applying to insurance company investment is less relevant than to a pension fund. Pension funds must aim at achieving positive 'real' returns on their portfolio (i.e. returns in excess of the actual rates of inflation). They therefore typically hold high proportions of their portfolios in assets such as ordinary shares and property, the real yields on which are least vulnerable to inflation over the longer term. More recently, assets such as index-linked gilt-edged securities also enable pension funds to hedge against the risks of future inflation.

The broad composition of the various assets held by insurance companies in long-term funds and by private and public sector funded pension schemes at the end of 1985 is shown in Table 11.1. In the table 'short-term assets' refers to notes and coin, bank balances, certificates of deposit, and deposits in other financial institutions, which in both cases constituted less than 5 per cent of total assets. Insurance companies held 23 per cent of their total assets in the form of British government securities and 33.2 per cent in the form of UK ordinary shares. Reflecting their 'real' as opposed to monetary liabilities, pension funds held only 17 per cent in British government securities (of which 15.6 per cent were in index-linked stocks) and 50 per cent in UK ordinary shares. As can be seen, both institutions now hold significant fractions of their assets in the form of overseas securities. The sectorial composition of life assurance and pension fund assets varies considerably with time in response to changing conditions in the financial markets and in the general economy.

Table 11.1 Assets of life assurance companies and pension funds as at end of 1985

	Life assurance companies	Pension funds
	£ billion	£ billion
Short-term assets	3.2	5.8
British government securities	30.5	27.5
of which		
index-linked	(2.3)	(4.3)
5 to 15 years	(15.1)	(12.7)
over 15 years and undated	(11.5)	(9.9)
UK company securities	46.4	80.8
of which		
ordinary shares	(43.1)	(78.8)
UK land and property	20.1	13.2
Mortgages and loans	4.3	0.4
Unit trust units	8.0	1.2
Overseas	14.1	22.7
Other	3.2	5.8
Total assets	129.8	157.4

Source: *Financial Statistics*, No. 300, April 1987, London: HMSO, Tables 7.13 and 7.14.

Unit trusts

As the name implies, these institutions are legally constituted as trusts whereby a trustee holds all the assets of the unit trust on behalf of the beneficial owners, i.e. those individuals who have contributed funds. A fund is managed by a professional fund management company which is responsible for investment policy subject to the provisions of the trust deed. The formation and operation of unit trusts is controlled by the Department of Trade and Industry and stringent financial requirements are laid down as regards the institutions qualified to act as trustees; these tend in the majority of cases to be either banks or insurance companies. The ownership of unit trust management companies has been an area of diversification for a variety of types of parent financial institutions, including the retail banks, merchant banks, foreign banks, insurance companies, and stockbrokers, although a few companies are independent of other financial institutions. Almost all companies are members of the Unit Trust Association whose rules place limitations on the maximum commissions which individual companies can charge for their services.

The number of unit trusts in existence has grown rapidly in recent years. In 1960 there were 51 trusts in existence which by 1978 had increased to 375; by the end of 1986, however, this number had grown to slightly over 1,000 and there were 3.41 million individual holdings of units. There are a variety of types of trust with characteristics designed to appeal to the different preferences of individual investors. 'General' trusts aim at a balanced mixture of income and capital appreciation for unit-holders but certain trusts concentrate on the provision of regular income, or alternatively on capital appreciation. These days there are a large number of specialized trusts which limit the range of financial assets held; in particular, since the abolition of exchange controls in 1979, a number of funds have been established which specialize in investment in particular geographical areas such as North America, Europe, Japan, and the Far East. Since 1985 a new type of fund called a 'managed fund' has appeared; with this fund a management company invests across a range of specialized unit trusts which it operates, switching funds internally between individual trusts according to its judgement about investment prospects.

The essence of the operations of a unit trust is that there is always a direct relationship between the value of a unit and the total value of the fund, the fund being divided between unit-holders in proportion to the value of the units for which each holder has subscribed. The funds are open-ended, in the sense that the management company, at its discretion, can expand the fund by issuing more units identical in value at a particular point in time to the existing units. The management company also has a symmetrical obligation to repurchase units from any holder who wishes to redeem all, or part, of his investment; the value of each unit redeemed at a particular point in time must be equal to the value of each unit held by the continuing holders and the fund must contract in a pro-rata fashion. Units in funds are not tradeable to third parties.

When an investor buys units in a trust he pays the 'offer' price for units and when he sells units he receives the 'bid' price for the units redeemed. The offer price of units is calculated according to a formula until recently laid down by the Department of Trade and Industry and involves the following procedure. First, the underlying securities in the fund are valued at their Stock Exchange offer prices (the prices at which market makers are prepared to sell shares to investors) at the close of business on the previous day; to this total is added the accrued dividends and interest received by the trustee and a charge for dealing expenses and stamp duty. This total is then divided by the number of units issued to yield a basic appropriation price of units in the fund and, finally, to this is added on a certain percentage, constituting the management company's initial administrative charge – the resulting sum being the offer price of the units rounded up to the nearest tenth of a penny. The administrative charges are set out in each trust deed and are typically 5 per cent on the purchase of new units plus an annual fee as some percentage (0.375 per cent is common) of the fund. The bid price of units is calculated in a similar way to offer prices, except that securities are valued at their Stock Exchange bid prices (the prices which market makers quote for buying shares) minus dealing expenses, but without deduction of a management charge. Units in most trusts are revalued on a daily basis and their prices are published in the financial press. Given the way they are calculated, therefore, the prices of units reflect movements in the prices of the underlying securities in the fund and, thus, while investors can enjoy a reduction in risk by virtue of the diversified portfolio, they are still subject to the risk of general changes in quoted securities prices.

The spread between bid and offer prices calculated according to this formula can often be as much as 12 per cent. However, because fund managers do not immediately buy or sell the underlying securities every time they buy or sell units, but match a certain proportion of selling and buying orders, they can quote a narrower spread, usually around 6 per cent. If a fund is expanding and more units are being sold than redeemed, the fund will be priced at the upper end of the formula spread on what is known as an 'offer basis' – the fund managers will sell units at the formula offer price and redeem units at a price around 6 per cent lower. Conversely, if the fund is contracting the fund will be priced on a 'bid' basis at the lower end of the formula spread.

Under revised regulatory arrangements, the supervision of unit trusts is being transferred to the newly created Securities and Investments Board. At the time of writing, the SIB is proposing certain changes to unit-trust operations. Until now, unit-holders have been unable to tell whether quoted prices are on a bid or offer basis and one of the less controversial proposals is that the basis of the daily quoted prices should be made clearly known to investors. A more controversial proposal is that the dealing prices should be based on the calculation of units on the day after the receipt of an order. The argument here is that under the present rules unit-holders can buy units on a certain day at what is, effectively, yesterday's valuation of the fund. If the prices of the underlying shares rise during the day, a new purchaser of units or the fund manager himself can profit at the expense of sellers of units. The new proposals would mean, however, that customers will not know the exact price at which they have dealt until twenty-four hours later.

The economics of unit-trust operation mean that there are incentives for managers to seek expansion in their funds. The remuneration of fund managers is based on the initial charge for the creation of new units, plus the annual fees levied as a percentage of the total value of the fund; thus, if the fund is expanding, the management company's income increases. As administrative costs increase with the number of unit-holders and not with the value of the fund, the higher the average size of the individual holding, the higher will be the management company's profits and for this reason most unit trusts stipulate certain minima regarding the initial sums to be invested – these can be as high as £2,000. Increasingly, however, fund managers are offering regular savings plans with fairly low minimum monthly contributions permissible.

The distribution of the fund income to unit-holders utilizes two basic methods. With 'income' unit trusts, dividend or interest income is distributed to unit-holders, usually twice a year, in proportion to the number of units held. With 'accumulation' units the dividend or interest income is re-invested in the fund without the levy of the initial management charge, thereby augmenting the value of the fund; the investor can obtain income from the fund if necessary by selling some of his units back to the management company.

The total funds invested in unit trusts have expanded rapidly during the 1980s. At the end of 1981 total funds amounted in value to £5,902 million,[3] but by February 1987 this total had expanded to £37,245 million. Of this total, 2.8 per cent were held in the form of British government securities, 62.6 per cent in the form of UK company ordinary shares, preference shares, and debentures, and 34.1 per cent in the form of overseas company securities.

Investment trusts

Despite their name, investment trusts are not in fact trusts in the legal sense – rather they are public limited companies which raise funds in the same way as other companies and then use the funds to acquire other financial assets, largely the securities of other companies. At the end of 1986 there were around 200 companies recognized as investment trusts by the Inland Revenue for tax purposes, although the number of management groups is smaller, many management groups operating a number of formally separate companies. Some trusts are managed by specialist management companies, some of whom also manage unit trusts, while others are managed by merchant banks; the largest twenty-one groups account for approximately half the total assets. The shareholdings in investment trusts reflect the broader general patterns of shareholding – institutional shareholders such as insurance companies and pension funds own around 70 per cent of shares.

Because of their status as companies there are a number of differences between the operation of investment trusts and that of unit trusts:

1. An individual acquires an interest in an investment trust by subscribing to a new issue or by purchasing shares on the Stock Exchange; similarly, an individual divests of his interest by selling the shares to a third party. Shares are not bought back by the management company in the same way as units in unit trusts.
2. Investment trusts are not open funds in that, apart from new issues, their share capital is fixed.
3. Investment trusts can raise additional funds by the issue of debentures. The existence of debentures in the capital structure

of an investment trust means that if the value of the underlying securities held by a trust fluctuates there is a 'gearing' effect on the value of the ordinary shares of the trust.

This effect can be illustrated by a simple example. Suppose that an investment trust is established with an issued share capital of 4 million £1 ordinary shares and £2 million in the form of debentures. Suppose that the funds are invested in the ordinary shares of other companies so that the initial share portfolio has a value of £6 million. Suppose that subsequently the value of the share portfolio increases by 100 per cent to £12 million. The net assets of the company (i.e. its total assets minus its debt of £2 million to debenture holders) thus increases to £10 million. Divided by the 4 million shares this yields net assets per share of £2.50, i.e. an increase of 150 per cent. Because of this gearing effect, the shareholders of an investment trust are exposed to somewhat greater risk in relation to general movements in underlying ordinary share prices than is a holder of units in a unit trust. There is a similar gearing effect on the income of the shareholders in an investment trust in response to changes in earnings derived from the underlying shares.

At the end of 1985 investment trusts held assets amounting to £18,085 million in market value.[4] The proportions in various asset categories were: British government securities 5 per cent, UK listed company securities 41.5 per cent, UK unlisted company securities 4.6 per cent, and overseas securities 48.4 per cent.

Notes

1 Committee to Review the Functioning of Financial Institutions (1980) *Appendices*, Cmnd 7937, London: HMSO, Table 3.45.
2 The figures quoted are taken from the *Bank of England Quarterly Bulletin*, December 1986, p. 547, and *Financial Statistics*, no. 300, April 1987, London: HMSO, Tables 7.13 and 7.14.
3 The figures quoted are taken from *Financial Statistics*, ibid., Tables 7.10 and 7.11.
4 Ibid., Table 7.12.

Further reading

Bain, A. D. (1981) *The Economics of the Financial System*, Oxford: Martin Robertson, Chapter 11.
Committee to Review the Functioning of Financial Institutions (1980) *Appendices*, Cmnd 7937, London: HMSO, Appendices 3 VI, 3 VII, 3 VIII, and 3 IX.

Revell, J. (1973) *The British Financial System*, London: Macmillan, Chapters 15 and 16.

'Life assurance company and private pension fund investment, 1962–84', *Bank of England Quarterly Bulletin*, December 1986.

Part four

Monetary Policy

Chapter twelve

The role of monetary policy

In the remaining chapters we discuss discretionary monetary policy, i.e. why and how the monetary authorities in the UK (the Treasury, via the Bank of England) seek to exert an influence on what can be described loosely as 'monetary conditions'. Initially we discuss the general considerations which have underlain the use of monetary policy in the UK and then proceed in the following chapter to examine in more detail how policy is actually implemented.

The dictionary of monetary policy

At the outset it is useful to consider a taxonomy within which the discussion of monetary policy issues has increasingly come to be conducted.[1] It is postulated that what the monetary authorities are concerned with can usefully be divided into four categories:

1. *Ultimate objectives or goal variables*: these are things which 'really matter' in the minds of the authorities. Here it is common to cite such goals as the level of unemployment, the rate of economic growth and price level stability, although such a simple citation begs many fundamental questions regarding the compatibility of these objectives and the extent to which they are capable of being separately influenced by monetary policy, particularly in the long run.
2. *Instruments*: these are variables under the direct control of the monetary authorities, changes in which may ultimately exert an influence on the behaviour of the goal variables. Given the general constitutional powers of the UK government, the list of potential instruments is very long, but conventionally includes such things as changes in the Bank of England's implicit or explicit discount rate, open market operations by the Bank in the money and gilt-

edged security markets, the imposition and variation of ratios or other controls imposed on the commercial banks, etc.

3. *Targets or 'proximate' objectives*: these are intermediate variables, not of particular interest in their own right, which stand between instruments and the goal variables, but which may serve as the immediate focus for the use of policy instruments. The need for targets is said to arise because the authorities, given the complexity of the economy, may be in considerable ignorance as to the precise links, or 'transmission mechanisms', connecting their policy instruments to the behaviour of the goal variables. They may, however, have sufficient information about the behaviour of the economy to judge that certain intermediate variables have a subsequent predictable influence on the goal variables and, if they are also confident of their ability to influence such intermediate variables by the use of their policy instruments, then they may perceive tactical advantages in explicitly adopting a particular intermediate variable as a target for policy, through which they may seek to exert an ultimate influence on the goal variables.

In principle a particular variable might be suitable as a target variable if:

(i) it can be readily observed by the authorities with little or no lag;
(ii) it exerts a predictable influence on subsequent values of the goal variables;
(iii) it is amenable to control by the authorities, in that it is rapidly affected by the use of policy instruments.

Not all economists are agreed on the necessity for explicit intermediate targets in the monetary policy context and, even when they are, uncertainty about the way the economy works leads to differing recommendations as to appropriate targets. In the UK a wide variety of possible intermediate targets have been discussed, these include particular definitions of the money supply, the volume of bank credit, other credit aggregates, the level of interest rates, the sterling exchange rate, and the level of aggregate monetary expenditure. There is, however, more agreement on the principle that, if the authorities explicitly adopt a particular target, then the choice implicitly determines the value of other potential targets. If, for example, the authorities choose to target some money supply variable, then this choice implies a certain level of interest rates; the authorities, as a further intermediate step, may aim at controlling the money supply through interest rates, but they cannot then choose a separate target for interest rates independently of their money supply target. Similarly, if the authorities target the exchange rate, then this choice implicitly determines appropriate values for interest rates and the money supply consistent with the targeted values of the exchange rate.

While the conceptual distinction between targets and goal variables is clear in principle, in practice this distinction is not always easy for the external observer to make. At various junctures in the UK it is clear that 'low' interest rates have seemed to constitute an end objective in themselves, because of the presumed electoral consequences for governments of the effects of high interest rates on the budgets of homeowners, or because the authorities have been concerned to minimize the budgetary cost of interest payments on the national debt. Equally, the maintenance of the exchange rate at a particular value has often seemed to assume the status of an end objective in the minds of the authorities.

4. Indicators; these are intermediate variables, not directly targeted as such, which may be monitored by the authorities as a source of additional information in gauging their appropriate policy stance. The case for the use of indicators is related to the argument that the particular variable explicitly targeted may also be affected by non-policy factors, in a way which alters the quantitative relationship between the target variable and the goal variables. By monitoring other variables which are closely affected by their policy instruments, the authorities might be better able to detect when changes in other non-policy factors were influencing their target variable and so be better placed to gauge their appropriate policy stance.

For example, suppose the authorities had adopted interest rates as a target because of a belief that, other things being equal, investment spending and, hence, aggregate monetary expenditure have a predictable relationship to interest rates. Investment spending, however, is likely to depend also on other factors, such as the conjectures which businessmen form regarding the future profitability of investment projects. Suppose businessmen become more optimistic and plan to increase their investment at any given interest rate; the quantitative relationship between interest rates and investment spending would change and the change itself is likely to exert upward pressure on market interest rates. By focusing exclusively on interest rates as their target, the monetary authorities might mistakenly conclude that their policy stance was 'too tight' and pursue expansionary policies which the overall situation might not require. In these circumstances the monitoring of other indicators also affected by their policy instruments (such as money supply variables) might enable the authorities to detect such a change in the non-policy factors influencing interest rates, thus enabling them to amend their appropriate policy stance to allow for such factors.

Clearly those variables chosen as targets must also serve as indicators of policy to a large extent, since the target must be amenable to influence by the authorities' policy instruments, but not all indicators need be treated as targets. The authorities may simply monitor a particular variable and may use this information to adjust their policy stance without setting any precise targets for the variable in question.

Money and the economy

In the 1970s and 1980s discussion of monetary policy issues in the UK have been dominated by the expressed intention of the authorities to 'control the money supply'. This emphasis on the money supply as constituting an explicit target for the use of policy instruments is, historically speaking, a novel development which, at the same time, has been highly controversial. While consider-ations of space preclude here a detailed discussion of the theor-etical controversies involved, some understanding of the basic arguments is necessary to appreciate this changed emphasis. The core ideas stressing the importance of controlling the money supply are, of course, not new, but have a long ancestry traceable back to the writings of David Hume in the eighteenth century,[2] which were later formalized as the quantity theory of money. The modern writings in the quantity theory tradition have come to be termed as 'monetarist' theory.

The quantity theory of money

The quantity theory in its simplest forms is usually expressed in two distinct versions – the 'Cambridge' version (so-called because it was developed by economists such as A. Marshall and A.C. Pigou at Cambridge University around the turn of the twentieth century), and the 'equation of exchange' approach formalized by the American economist Irving Fisher at roughly the same time.

The Cambridge approach

This approach is basically an application of the general principles of demand and supply to monetary analysis. It assumes that it is reasonable to suppose that each individual economic unit has a determinate demand for money – meaning that they will desire to hold on average over time a certain stock of money balances. The demand for money arises because of the convenience properties which money possesses as a liquid asset and the Cambridge economists explicitly recognized that this would depend on a variety of influences. However, in formalizing their theory they simplified by assuming that, other things being equal, at the aggregate level the demand for money would be proportional to the level of nominal (or money) national income. Thus they wrote a demand equation for money as:

$$M_d = kPy \qquad (12.1)$$

where M_d is the quantity of money demanded, k is some fraction, P is the general price level as measured by some index, and y is aggregate real income (or real output of goods and services); the product Py therefore equals nominal national income. We should note that in this formulation the quantity of money demanded varies in proportion to the price level so that equation (12.1) is equivalent to saying that the demand for real money balances (i.e. money in terms of its purchasing power) is a certain fraction, k, of real income. If we divide equation (12.1) through by P we get:

$$\frac{M_d}{P} = ky \qquad (12.2)$$

where M_d/P can be interpreted as the demand for real money balances.

The second element in the model is an assumption that the supply of money is determined independently of the demand for money. In a closed economy the simplest assumption one can make is that M is determined as a result of the monetary policy of the authorities. (In a context where the money supply comprises bank deposits as well as notes and coin this assumes that the monetary authorities are in complete control of the commercial banking system, but relaxing this strict assumption does not affect the argument so long as the creation of bank deposits by the banking system is independent of the forces determining the demand for money.) Thus we can write:

$$M_s = M \qquad (12.3)$$

where M_s denotes the money supply and M is simply a given amount of money determined by the monetary authorities.

The final element in the model is an equilibrium condition which states that the quantity of money demanded must equal the supply of money (or that for a situation of monetary equilibrium or macroequilibrium to exist the money supply must be willingly held). Hence we can write:

$$M_d = M_s \qquad (12.4)$$

Therefore, by substituting equations (12.1) and (12.3) into equation (12.4) we obtain:

$$M = kPy \qquad (12.5)$$

Thus if, at any point in time, $M \neq kPY$, then there exists a situation of monetary disequilibrium and the variables on the right-hand side of equation (12.5) must adjust to ensure that the quantity of money demand is equal to the predetermined money supply.

As it stands, equation (12.5) is perfectly general and tells us nothing about the underlying cause of monetary disequilibrium or whether the adjustment to it will come about through a change in all, or some, of k, P or y. The assumption typically made by the quantity theorists was that the factors determining k would be likely to change only slowly over time and hence k could be regarded as being approximately constant for long periods. Further it was argued that the price mechanism (which included the interest rate) was able to co-ordinate the decisions being made by individual economic units in both goods and labour markets in such a way that the normal state of the economy would be at, or near, the full employment level of real income. While this might be growing slowly in time owing to technical progress, real capital formation, and the growth in the labour force, there was little reason to suppose that y would deviate much from its long-term growth path; therefore, as it was held that changes in M could occur at a rate substantially different from the trend changes in k or y, the most probable cause of monetary disequilibrium would be changes in M itself. Further, given the near constancy of k and y, then the adjustment to monetary disequilibrium would be largely concentrated on changes in P; thus the theory became a quantity of money theory of the general price level. If it is assumed that k and y are absolute constants over a certain time period, then changes in the price level will be strictly proportional to changes in the money supply (although it was doubtful whether anyone believed in the literal truth of this proposition).

The theory outlined thus far is a theory about the properties of equilibrium situations and does not explain the process whereby the economy moves from one equilibrium to another. The explanation of the transmission mechanism from changes in the money supply to changes in the prices ran broadly as follows. Suppose, at a given point in time there is an increase in the money supply in excess of the growth in real income. Economic units will find that their actual money balances exceed their desired money balances and, hence, they will try to reduce their actual money balances to desired levels by increasing their spending on goods and services. An individual economic unit can get rid of excess money balances in this way but, given the assumption of a closed economy, the economy as a whole cannot – someone must hold the given stock of money and all individual units can do is to pass money from one to another like the proverbial 'hot potato'. The attempt by individual units to reduce their money balances, however, directly increases the community's aggregate demand for goods and services and thus, assuming the economy is at full employment, at the initial money prices being set in the various 'micro'markets, the result is generalized excess demand for goods and services (i.e. shortages of finished commodities, the emergence of unfilled vacancies in the labour markets, etc.). In response to this situation there is upward pressure on the money prices being set for various goods and services and, hence, on the general price level; this process continues until real money balances have been reduced to their desired level.

Although the quantity theory relates to levels of the money supply and prices, rather than continuous changes as such, none the less a strong implication is that a sustained inflationary process can be explained as a reaction to a continual monetary disequilibrium caused by the money supply growing at a faster rate than real income or output.

The equation of exchange approach

The equation of exchange is an identity derived from the elementary fact that every transaction is between a buyer and seller, and hence the number of pounds spent to purchase something by a buyer necessarily equals the number of pounds received from the sale of that something by a seller; hence, at an aggregate level, the value of all purchases must equal the value of all sales. Now the value of all sales must be equal to the number of transactions multiplied by the average price at which they take place. Similarly, the value of all purchases must be equal to the amount of money

233

in circulation multiplied by the average number of times a given pound changes hands or turns over. Thus we can write an identity:

$$MV_T = PT \tag{12.6}$$

where M is the quantity of money in circulation, V_T is the average number of times a unit of money turns over in any period, P is the average price per transaction, and T is the volume of transactions.

Nothing follows in itself from equation (12.6), but the equation of exchange identity becomes a theory once certain assumptions are made about the determination of the four variables. It was generally held that V_T would be determined by the habits, customs, and payments technology of the community, and that these influences on velocity would change only slowly with time. Similarly, it was held again that T would be closely related to the level of real income and, as the economy would typically be in a full employment situation, T would again change relatively slowly with time. Hence with V_T and T assumed to be determined independently of M and changing relatively slowly, P_T will not change significantly unless M changes. More specifically, if V_T and T are regarded as being constants it is again implied that P is determined solely by and is proportional to M.

The equation of exchange version of the quantity theory is sometimes amended to relate explicitly to the set of prices usually measured in practice by price indices. Most prices indices usually refer to the prices of currently produced goods and services purchased by final buyers, whereas the price level referred to in equation (12.6) is the average of prices in all transactions, including transactions in existing assets (such as antiques and second-hand cars) and all intermediate transactions in partly finished goods and raw materials which take place between firms. Thus the equation of exchange version is often rewritten as

$$MV_Y = Py \tag{12.7}$$

where V_Y is now defined as the income velocity of circulation. (In terms of the simple circular flow diagram depicted in Chapter 3 it can be visualized as the average number of times a unit of money flows around the income circuit per period.) P now refers to the average price of goods sold to final buyers as measured by some index and y is real income.

By comparing equation (12.7) with equation (12.5) it can be seen that in a situation of monetary equilibrium then $V_Y = 1/k$. In other words, in equilibrium, the income velocity of circulation is the reciprocal of the fraction of nominal income that individual economic units desire to hold in the form of a stock of money balances – the higher is k the lower is V_Y, and vice-versa.

Monetarism

The term 'monetarism' describes generally the modern continuation of the quantity theory tradition in monetary economics, but, like many other 'ism' words, could be said to mislead as much as it describes in that there are now considerable variations on the basic theme.[3] Indeed it is possible to argue that the differences between different brands of monetarism are greater than the differences between some monetarists and certain of those who write in the alternative so-called 'Keynesian' tradition.

A group of economists commonly referred to as 'the new classical school', who have become influential in recent years, hold views with a very close affinity to the classical quantity theory (albeit with a radically different view of the transmission mechanism) in that it is asserted that perceived changes in the money supply will result in more or less immediate changes in the price level with little, if any, effect on real income. However, the weaker forms of monetarism in its closed-economy versions, such as that associated with Milton Friedman, amend the classical quantity theory in various ways.

First, in recognition of the observed real-world reality of business cycles, it is asserted that the money supply has a dominating influence on nominal national income (Py), or equivalently aggregate monetary expenditure, rather than specifically prices as such. In the short run, the exact division of a given change in nominal income into a change in prices and a change in real income is regarded as a highly complex matter, which will depend at any time on a variety of influences, including the level of unemployment, the degree to which expectations held by firms and households regarding future changes in the price level are reflected in actual price changes, and various autonomous shocks (such as bad harvests, which raise the level of food prices, or a change in oil prices). Thus it is recognized that in certain situations where, for example, unemployment is initially high and where, the general expectation is one of future price stability, a given increase in nominal income may be reflected largely in changes in real income rather than prices. In other situations where inflation has been on-going for some time and individuals expect future price level changes of a certain magnitude, then the actual change in prices may exceed the change in nominal income, thus leading to a combination of rising prices and falling real incomes.

None the less, it is asserted that if the rate of growth of the money supply is held stable and hence the rate of growth of nominal income is stable then, in the long run, prices will change such that the level of real income will tend to converge towards that level where there is a 'natural' rate of unemployment (which, of course, will not mean zero measured unemployment because of fruitional and structural unemployment, etc.). Hence, with real income at the natural rate of unemployment growing at a certain rate over time due to the real forces of technical progress, etc., then the rate of growth of the price level in the long run will be determined by the rate of growth of the money supply. Thus a major policy implication is that a long-run anti-inflationary strategy requires that the money supply grows broadly at the same rate of growth as real income.

The foregoing argument that the money supply dominates the determination of nominal income does, however, depend critically on the stability of k (or equivalently V_Y). Here, following Keynes' fundamental critique of the quantity theory in the general theory, most monetarists accept that, in reality, k is hardly likely to be literally constant. Keynes' basic argument was that, given the existence of a number of alternative assets that can serve as substitutes for money as a store of value, then the demand for money is likely to be related, not only to money income, but to the opportunity cost of holding money, i.e. the interest foregone by holding wealth in the form of money rather than in non-monetary financial assets. According to the Keynesian view, the response to an excess supply of money would take the form of portfolio switches into other financial assets which, in the process, would reduce interest rates and thus alter k. Other things being equal, the reduction in interest rates might then induce additional expenditure on real assets, so that by this route changes in the money supply could affect nominal income, but not in a proportionate fashion. Moreover, Keynes postulated that for various reasons the liquidity preference of the community might change (the demand for money function with respect to nominal income and interest rates might shift), so that k could alter independently of changes in the money supply.

Most monetarists now accept that the transmission mechanism linking changes in the money supply to nominal income will work, in part, via changes in interest rates as well as by direct changes in spending on real goods and services and that, in the process, there may be changes in k. However, a crucial element in their argument is the assertion that, as an empirical matter, the demand for money function is a highly stable function of a few critical variables, primarily nominal income and interest rates. This assertion implies that monetary disequilibrium will essentially be a phenomenon associated with changes in the money supply rather than changes in liquidity preference, so that changes in k will be a predictable effect of prior changes in the money supply. Further, it is asserted, again as an empirical matter, that the demand for money exhibits low elasticity with respect to interest rates, so that the response to monetary disequilibrium will not involve significant changes in k. These assertions, combined with a further assertion that expenditure on real assets is sensitive to changes in interest rates, imply that although changes in M may be offset to some extent by changes in k, the changes in k will not be significant enough to nullify the dominating influence of the money supply in the determination of nominal income.

Open economy monetarism

The quantity theory and many modern extensions of it refer primarily to a closed economy, but the analysis requires some additional modification if it is to be relevant to a highly open economy like the UK's. Of crucial importance here are the assumptions made regarding the policy of the monetary authorities with respect to the foreign exchange rate. If the authorities allow the exchange rate to be determined freely by market forces then the broad causational influences running from the supply of money to nominal income might still hold, although the transmission mechanisms considered in the closed economy case might need some amendment. On the other hand, if the authorities decide to peg the exchange rate at some fixed value in terms of foreign currency, then the causational influences may change fundamentally; in this case it may be more correct to assert that in the long run the money supply is determined by money income rather than the reverse, as in the closed economy case.

The reason for this difference in the fixed exchange rate case lies in the mechanisms through which the authorities implement their chosen policy. If the authorities decide to peg the exchange rate they must stand ready to intervene in the foreign exchange market, buying and selling foreign currency in exchange for domestic currency whenever excess demand or supply emerges which threatens to move the chosen rate. As was explained in Chapter 2, such intervention has direct effects on the domestic money supply – if the authorities are buying foreign currency their actions directly increase the money supply, if they sell foreign currency the money supply contracts. This commitment to maintain a given exchange rate means, therefore, that the authorities can no longer be regarded as having the ability to 'determine' the money supply at will as we assumed earlier; rather the behaviour of the domestic money supply is constrained in the long run by the need to maintain the fixed exchange rate.

Consider again equation (12.5), the equation defining the condition for monetary equilibrium in the Cambridge version of the quantity theory, i.e. $M = kPy$. The earlier argument was that if $M \neq kPy$ then the adjustment to monetary disequilibrium would have to take place by changes in the variables determining the demand for money, because M was fixed by the authorities. In the fixed exchange rate case this is no longer true and there are reasons to believe that the response to monetary disequilibrium will largely take the form of an adjustment in M itself.

The adoption of a fixed exchange rate may itself constrain P, in that, if domestic firms are competing with foreign firms in both domestic and international markets, then to remain competitive they must set prices in domestic currency terms which are broadly comparable to the prices in foreign currency terms being set by foreign firms. If, for example, the pound/US dollar exchange rate is pegged at $2 = £1 and US exporters can sell a certain product in the UK for $4 in terms of their own currency, then to remain competitive, UK producers cannot afford to price similar products at much more than £2 per unit. Not all domestically produced goods and services are traded internationally, so that some price movements are not directly constrained by foreign competition and one would not expect general price indices to move in a rigid relationship with general price indices in other countries. None the less, if domestic consumers regard non-traded goods as substitutes to some extent for internationally traded goods, then the ability of non-traded goods producers to raise their money prices relative to traded goods prices will, likewise, be constrained. Thus in a fixed exchange rate system it is possible to argue that the domestic price level, to a large extent, will be 'anchored' by the 'world' price level and cannot move freely in response to domestic monetary disequilibrium. Similarly, with reference to portfolio adjustments which lead to changes in domestic interest rates and hence to changes in k, we must now recognize the possibility that, if there are no restrictions on movements of financial funds to and from abroad and if domestic residents regard securities issued abroad as close substitutes for domestically issued securities, then domestic residents can reduce excess money balances by purchasing foreign as well as domestic securities. If, therefore, an excess supply of money leads initially to reductions in domestic interest rates relative to interest rates abroad, this will induce holders of domestic securities to switch into foreign securities, thus restraining the downward pressure on domestic interest rates. Hence, if the demand for money function is reasonably stable, there may not be much change in k in response to portfolio disequilibrium, but rather an outflow of financial funds to abroad.

Thus, suppose that the monetary authorities of an economy with a fixed exchange rate, initially in equilibrium, increased the domestic money supply. Individuals holding excess money balances attempt to adjust by increased purchases of real goods and financial assets. Depending on the initial level of real income there may be some scope for an increase in y, but once y approaches full employment, then continuing monetary disequilibrium will result in additional purchases of foreign goods (or domestically produced goods previously exported) as well as purchases of foreign financial assets. As a consequence, excess demand for foreign currency emerges on the foreign exchange market and to maintain the foreign exchange rate the authorities would have to sell foreign currency from the official reserves. This action in itself reduces the domestic money supply, but if the authorities' exchange reserves are limited, then to protect their reserves they may have to use their domestic policy instruments directly to the same effect. Thus monetary disequilibrium is removed by changes in M – the money supply itself – rather than primarily by changes in k, P, or y.

Hence, the inference is that, if the monetary authorities decide to peg the exchange rate, then they cannot independently determine the domestic money supply; in the short run a symptom of monetary disequilibrium will be balance of payments deficits or surpluses, while in the long run the money supply must be adjusted to the influences determining the demand for money rather than vice-versa. Similarly, domestic inflation cannot diverge much from inflation rates elsewhere (although at the 'world' level inflation may be a consequence of changes in the world money supply, i.e. by the consequences of the collective actions of the world's monetary authorities).

On the other hand, if the monetary authorities leave the exchange rate to be determined entirely by market forces, then it again becomes more realistic to assume that the domestic money supply can be determined in the long run by the domestic monetary authorities and that, as in the closed economy case, the adjustment to monetary disequilibrium must take the form of adjustments in the variables determining the demand for money. If the authorities do not intervene in the foreign exchange market then the domestic money supply cannot be adjusted via the mechanism of balance of payments deficits or surpluses. Equally, the rate of domestic inflation can now diverge from the rate of inflation occurring in the rest of the world, with the exchange rate in the long run moving to reconcile the domestic price level consequences of the chosen monetary policy with whatever is happening abroad.

However, although the broad direction of causation in the floating exchange rate case may now again flow from the money supply to money income, the transmission mechanisms inducing changes in the domestic price level may now be even more complex in an open economy. Suppose again that the domestic money supply is increased with the economy initially in equilibrium at or near full employment. In response to monetary disequilibrium the immediate impact might be downward pressure on domestic interest rates. This might induce a capital outflow, not only because interest rates on domestic securities may have fallen relative to interest rates on foreign securities, but because domestic securities are denominated in a currency whose purchasing power may be expected to decline, relative to that of the currencies in which foreign securities are denominated. This capital outflow puts immediate downward pressure on the foreign exchange rate and this exchange depreciation may have a direct effect causing the domestic price level to increase, as given world prices of internationally traded finished goods and raw materials (entering into the costs of production of domestic producers) are translated into higher domestic prices. These effects on the domestic price level stemming from exchange depreciation complement and, plausibly, precede the upward pressures arising from the closed economy transmission mechanisms working via increased aggregate demand for goods and services produced by domestic firms.

Given the trend over the post-war period towards liberalization of controls on international capital flows and the more integrated nature of the international financial system, there are reasons to believe that, for open economies such as the UK's, this element in the transmission mechanism from the money supply to the price level, working directly via the exchange rate, has increased in importance and results in an accelerated response of the price level to monetary disequilibrium.

The influence of monetarism on monetary policy in the UK

Monetarist ideas could be said to have first influenced monetary policy in the UK most explicitly during the mid-1970s when the authorities became wedded to a policy of announced quantitative targets for the growth of the money supply.

It is pertinent, however, to question why the UK authorities adopted this approach when previously, since around 1870 when the Bank of England first started to manipulate its policy instruments in a systematic way, the money supply, as such, rarely figured in the official vocabulary. Here it has to be remembered that for much of this period the UK authorities were committed to the gold standard system (where the value of the pound was fixed in terms of gold and hence, by extension, was fixed in terms of other currencies similarly linked to gold within a narrow band determined by the costs of shipping gold abroad) or latterly, in the post-war period from 1945 until 1972, to the 1944 Bretton–Woods Agreement whereby the foreign exchange value of the pound was maintained within a narrow band around a fixed parity to the US dollar. This commitment to maintain a particular exchange rate (as the analysis in the previous section suggests) placed an indirect constraint on the domestic monetary policy – policy with respect to the money supply was subsumed by this explicit exchange rate target.

For most of the early post-war period down to the mid-1970s the primary ultimate objective of the authorities was the maintenance of full employment[4] and the main instruments used by the authorities to manipulate aggregate monetary expenditure to this end were fiscal policy instruments, i.e. variations in tax rates and, to a lesser extent, variations in public expenditure. The core theory underlying the use of policy was the Keynesian income expenditure model and the money supply as such was not regarded as a significant short-run influence affecting expenditure. An independent concern of the monetary authorities at this juncture was that of maintaining general stability in the price of government debt in order to enhance the long-run saleability of such debt (it was believed that undue fluctuations in government bond prices rendered them less attractive as a means of holding wealth). Until 1958 the authorities' reaction to falling gilt-edged prices was simply to cease sales until the market had recovered, but in the period from 1958 until 1970 there was a more explicit policy of what was called 'leaning into the wind', whereby the authorities reacted to falling prices by open market purchases of securities. Although the authorities did not attempt to resist what were regarded as long-run trends in interest rates, this policy of stabilizing prices in the gilt-edged market meant that movements in the domestic money supply tended to mirror changes in the government's budgetary position; when fiscal policy became more expansionary and the budget deficit increased, the constraint on open market sales of government debt meant an increase in government borrowing from the banking system and hence direct increases in the money supply.

As the post-war period developed, however, there developed continual tension between the low-unemployment objective and the commitment to maintain the exchange rate at a fixed parity, and a standard criticism of economic policy at the time was that it tended to oscillate in what was termed a 'stop-go' cycle. In periods when unemployment was relatively high, the authorities were prompted to take action to increase aggregate monetary expenditure, but although policy was often successful in reducing unemployment, periods of low unemployment tended to coincide with balance of payments deficits on current account. Given the finite nature of the official exchange reserves the perpetuation of such deficits often prompted expectations of a sterling devaluation amongst foreign holders of UK short-term financial assets, and there resulted frequent foreign exchange crises where speculative capital outflows put considerable pressure on the exchange rate. The response to foreign exchange crises on the part of the authorities typically took the form of 'package deals' which produced a simultaneous tightening of fiscal and monetary policy. Tax rates tended to be adjusted upwards while the Bank of England took action to increase short-term interest rates with the short-run objective of influencing short-run capital flows. This action in raising short-term interest rates in the longer term tended to have a restraining effect on bank lending (as bank lending rates at the time were administratively fixed to Bank Rate), and this influence was also buttressed by more explicit controls on bank advances.

Thus, in the longer run the monetary authorities could not permit the domestic money supply to grow at a rate which was inconsistent with the chosen exchange rate. There was no particular requirement for quantitative money supply targets, the money supply was determined as a residual effect of the policies with respect to the maintenance of the exchange rate. Equally, it could be argued that in the 1950s and 1960s the fixed exchange rate provided a direct 'anchor' for the UK price level. During this period, 'world' prices of manufactured goods and raw materials were largely static or declining and this low rate of world inflation was reflected in the low UK inflation rate (on average, prices rose over this period at a rate of around 3.5 per cent per annum).

The watershed in the orientation of monetary policy instruments in the UK could be said to have occurred as a result of the experience of the economy in the early 1970s. In November 1967, as the culmination of a sequence of foreign exchange crises, the pound was devalued and fiscal and monetary policy entered a 'stop' phase. As part of the conditions for a loan from the International Monetary Fund, in 1968 in a letter of intent the authorities stated that money supply growth in that year was to be restricted to its estimated growth rate in 1967; this was the first example of the use of an explicit money supply target in the UK and this commitment was followed by a further commitment in 1969 which set a limit for domestic credit expansion (i.e., broadly the recorded growth in the money supply plus the balance of payments deficit). It is doubtful, however, whether the UK authorities were themselves convinced at this juncture that such targets were useful and, as the balance of payments eventually moved into surplus in 1970 and 1971, the practice was dropped. The restrictive fiscal and monetary policies pursued following the devaluation, though, resulted in a recession which saw the level of unemployment reach 3.8 per cent in early 1972 – a post-war record level. The years following 1967 also witnessed a significant acceleration in inflation, which in retrospect was probably explained by a post-devaluation adjustment of the UK price level to a world price level which was itself increasing more rapidly at this time.

Despite this acceleration of inflation, the fiscal and monetary stances of the authorities became markedly expansionary in 1972 and, significantly, the Chancellor announced in the Budget speech that, if necessary, the so-called balance of payments constraint on domestic demand management was to be overcome by allowing the exchange rate to float. In the event, the exchange rate was allowed to float in June 1972 while at the same time, in conjunction with the fiscal expansion, monetary growth accelerated substantially. There is some reason to believe that at this juncture the monetary authorities lost some control of the situation as these increases in the money supply followed a change in the control regime instigated in 1971 when previous controls on the banks were relaxed and the previous mandatory 8 per cent cash ratio and a 28 per cent liquidity ratio were replaced with a new mandatory ratio of 12½ per cent defined in relation to a bank's eligible liabilities. Following the 1971 changes there was a substantial increase in bank lending and the M_3 measure of money supply (to be described in more detail shortly) grew by 28 per cent in 1972 and 29 per cent in 1973. In response to this expansionary fiscal and monetary stance unemployment did fall (down to 2.9 per cent by the first quarter of 1973) but at the same time inflation, as measured by the increase in the RPI compared to its value twelve months earlier, accelerated dramatically from 6.5 per cent in mid-1972 to a peak of 26 per cent in mid-1975 – the worst bout of inflation recorded in UK peace-time history.

The causes of this inflationary episode were and are the subject of intense controversy, but the combination of high rates of monetary growth, a depreciating exchange rate (the effective sterling exchange rate against all currencies depreciated by approximately 26 per cent from June 1972 to the end of 1975), and accelerating inflation were obviously in broad correspondence to the monetarist view of the relationships between money, nominal income, and prices in a floating exchange rate economy. From 1973 onwards it is fairly clear that the authorities began to give control of the money supply a new significance in their operations, although initially any quantitative targets were undisclosed. At least partial acceptance by the authorities of monetarist policy recommendations was then confirmed by the instigation in December 1976 of formally announced annual targets for monetary growth. The official rationale for monetary targets was subsequently spelt out by the Governor of the Bank of England in a number of speeches made during 1977 and 1978.

First, there was some acceptance of a medium-term link stemming from prior changes in the money supply to nominal income and prices, and hence it was argued that some justification for monetary targets lay in their ability to prevent the initiation of future inflation.

'I would not want to suggest that there is always a direct simple chain of causation running from the money supply to the price level. . . . But though this causation may not be simple there is an observable statistical relation between monetary growth and the pace of inflation. . . . What is far more important is the relationship between growth and inflation over the longer term. A great deal of work has been devoted to the study of this relationship over long time periods and in many countries; and that there is such a relationship cannot I think be doubted.'[5]

Second, a clear role for announced monetary targets was seen as a way of damping down the on-going inflation.

'One purpose of announcing monetary targets is to serve notice that excessive increases in domestic costs will come up against resistance. If people believe that the money supply will be expanded to accommodate any rise in costs and prices, however fast, inflationary fears are likely to be increased. If, on the other hand, people are convinced that the rate of growth of the money supply will be held within well defined limits this should help to reduce inflationary expectations. Monetary policy should therefore aim to act in concert with other branches of policy, including incomes policy, in slowing down inflation.'[6]

As implied in this statement, the authorities initially did not place total reliance on monetary targets in their anti-inflationary strategy. The Labour Government in the late 1970s, while using a money supply target to constrain the growth in nominal income, also attempted to influence the price level directly by means of a voluntary incomes policy to constrain the growth in wage costs, together with controls on permissible increases in prices. By this combination it was hoped that, given the growth of nominal income, a reduction in the inflation rate would not involve adverse consequences for real income. This policy had some success in reducing inflation to a low of 7 per cent by mid-1978, but the prices and incomes element in the overall strategy effectively collapsed during the winter of 1978–9, when a number of wage settlements infringed the guidelines for money wage increases set by the government.

The policy of monetary targets was, however, continued by the newly elected Conservative government in 1979, and was developed further in the medium-term financial strategy (MTFS) announced in the March 1980 Budget. After the collapse of the voluntary incomes policy, the inflation rate again accelerated rapidly to over 20 per cent by mid-1980 and, as an anti-inflationary programme, the authorities announced in the MTFS a four-year plan of diminishing annual targets for monetary growth, together with associated diminishing targets for the PSBR expressed as a proportion of GDP. Although some fluctuations in the PSBR were to be tolerated in the light of variations in economic activity, it was stated in the accompanying financial statement and Budget report that 'there would be no question of departing from the money supply policy which is essential to the success of any anti-inflationary strategy'.

245

The problem of an 'operational' money supply

While the philosophy underlying the adoption of quantitative monetary targets is clear enough in principle, there are considerable practical problems involved in the implementation of any such policy. The first requirement is obviously that the authorities have a clear idea of what constitutes money and, hence, what they are seeking to control. Unfortunately, the generality of monetary theory in this instance is not of much assistance; often, for simplicity, it is assumed that an identifiable asset called money exists (i.e. that the problem of definition has been solved), which is sharply differentiated from other assets which are, again for simplicity, often aggregated into a single category called 'bonds'. In practice, however, the problem of defining money for control purposes and then controlling it once it has been defined is not an easy one.

In Chapter 1 we adopted a definition of money using an *a priori* functional criterion – the means of payment criterion; we specified this criterion and then asked the question 'what assets can be placed in the appropriate box?' This approach sufficed for purposes of describing the structure of the monetary and financial system, but it by no means follows that such an approach would provide the authorities with a suitable definition of money for their primary purpose, which is to influence nominal income. The reason why this is so is that, as we also emphasized in Chapter 1, there are in existence numerous alternative financial assets of varying degrees of liquidity, some of which are plausibly very close substitutes for the means of payment as a means of holding wealth. This being so, the demand for the narrowly defined means of payment may well be sensitive to changes in interest rate differentials or structural changes in the financial system and, hence, the relevant income velocity of circulation may be so unstable in the long run as to render this definition of money very unreliable as a predictor of nominal income.

To illustrate the problems involved in defining money for control purposes let us suppose hypothetically that the authorities, as a first approach, were considering attempting to control a monetary aggregate corresponding to the actual means of payment. The identification of money according to this criterion is not, as we have seen, entirely clear-cut, but suppose for the sake of argument that they included in this aggregate only notes and coins plus current account deposits in retail banks leaving out other bank deposits which are not technically a means of payment. Consider now the behaviour of an individual who, initially,

Figure 12.1 The time pattern of an individual's current account balance

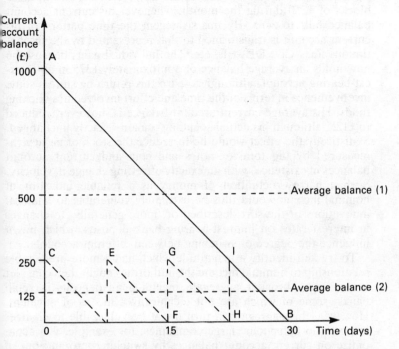

receives a net monthly salary of £1,000 paid into a current account which pays zero interest, on which he writes cheques to finance his purchases over the month, ending up at the end of the month with a zero balance. If we assume for simplicity he runs down his current account balance at a constant rate over the month, the time pattern of his current account balance can be illustrated in Figure 12.1. In the diagram the time pattern of his current account balance is portrayed by the line AB. On average the individual will hold a balance of £500, i.e. this is his stock demand for money.

Suppose, however, that his bank subsequently introduces a new interest-bearing account on which cheques cannot be written, and at the same time actively publicizes this new account (as the Midland Bank has done in practice with its 'Saver-Plus' account) as a means whereby individuals can economize on current account balances. Individuals are allowed to transfer funds on demand between this new account and their current accounts and suppose that the individual responds by converting £750 into this new account immediately on receipt of his monthly salary and then,

247

subsequently, converts funds bank to his current account in three blocks of £250 during the month, whenever his current account balance falls to zero. By this strategem the time pattern of his current account is transformed to that represented by the discontinuous lines CD, DE, EF, etc. The individual gains because he now holds an average balance of approximately £375 in an interest-bearing account, although to earn this return he suffers some inconvenience in terms of the time and effort involved in switching funds. His average current account balance is, however, reduced to £125, although his actual spending remains exactly unchanged. Statistically the effect would be to reduce the stock of money (as measured by the total of notes and coin and current account balances in existence) with an exactly offsetting change in velocity. Such a narrow definition of money as a reliable indicator of nominal income would thus be extremely vulnerable to financial innovations of the sort described or, more generally, to changes in interest rates on interest-bearing bank deposits, which might influence the degree of switching between different accounts.

To try and identify a magnitude which had a more predictable relationship to nominal income the authorities might then consider controlling a broader aggregate including all deposits in retail banks, some of which are not technically a means of payment. However, this aggregate in turn might be vulnerable to changes in portfolio behaviour; large companies, for example, can economize on current account balances by switching into and out of short-term deposits in wholesale banks, again with no change in their expenditure in any period. In this instance, although the total of retail bank deposits might not change much, the demand for such deposits and hence their velocity would again be affected. The authorities might then consider broadening their operational definition of money still further to include deposits in wholesale banks, on the grounds that the growth of such deposits might serve as a proxy for changes in the velocity of retail bank deposits, and that the velocity of this broader aggregate might itself be more stable.

However, once it is decided to expand the operational definition of money to encompass magnitudes other than the immediate means of payment, then there is no intrinsic reason why the dividing line should be drawn to include only the deposits of those institutions classified as banks. An individual can economize on current account deposits, or notes and coin, by using building society accounts or National Savings Bank accounts in essentially the same way as in our illustrative example, in the process, changing the velocity of a broader aggregate including all bank deposits. Therefore, there is an a-priori case for the inclusion of building society liabilities in a still broader aggregate, which might conceivably exhibit a more stable velocity than one based on bank deposits alone.

Once one departs from the conceptual definition of money as the means of payment there are thus a potentially large number of different aggregates which can be described as 'money' or 'monetary aggregates' for policy purposes.. The make-up of such aggregates can be based, not only on broad categories such as total bank or building society deposits, but on subdivisions of such categories, relating to deposits with less than certain terms to maturity, deposits below a certain maximum size, etc. Although one can discuss the merits of these aggregates in conceptual terms relating to their 'liquidity', or substitutability with regard to the means of payment, the choice of an appropriate aggregate (or aggregates) as monetary policy target is essentially a purely pragmatic one. The underlying philosophy can be illustrated by a quotation from Milton Friedman:[7] 'Money is not something in existence to be discovered like the American continent but a tentative scientific construct like "length" or "temperature" in physics'. In other words, the appropriate definition of money is considered to be that which best indicates or 'measures' subsequent changes in nominal income. This boils down to the question: which aggregate in practice seems to exhibit the most predictable income velocity of circulation?

This pragmatic approach to the definition of the money supply for policy purposes is, again, clear-cut enough in principle, but identifying a single aggregate with the desired properties has turned out to be far from straightforward and has constituted a major problem in the implementation of the policy of quantitative money supply targets.

The official monetary aggregates

Reflecting this uncertainty as to the appropriate definition of money for policy purposes, the Bank of England constructs a number of alternative aggregates. The classifications adopted have been subject to various changes over time and the aggregates outlined below are those identified in May 1987. The composition of those aggregates is as follows (in what follows 'banks' refer to all those institutions in the UK monetary sector, and the 'private sector' (PS) is the UK non-bank private sector):

M_0, the wide monetary base, comprises PS holdings of notes and coin plus bank holdings of notes and coin in tills plus bankers' deposits at the Bank of England (excluding cash ratio deposits). The largest component is PS holdings of notes and coin, over 95 per cent of the total.

M_1 comprises PS holdings of notes and coin, plus PS non-interest-bearing sterling sight deposits in banks, plus PS interest-bearing sterling sight deposits in banks. Non-interest-bearing sterling sight deposits are essentially current (chequeable) accounts. Interest-bearing sterling sight deposits comprise non-chequeable and 'high-interest' chequeable accounts held by individuals and large overnight balances held by companies or financial institutions.

M_2 comprises the non-interest-bearing component of M_1, plus PS interest-bearing retail sterling bank deposits, plus PS holdings of retail building society shares and deposits, and National Savings Bank ordinary accounts. Retail bank deposits refer to both sight and time deposits on which cheques can be written, or which are small (under £100,000) and short term (of maturity under one month). Retail building society shares and deposits are defined similarly.

M_3 (formerly, before May 1987, sterling M_3) comprises M_1, plus PS sterling time deposits in banks, plus PS holdings of sterling bank CDs.

$M_3(c)$ comprises M_3 plus PS holdings of foreign currency bank deposits.

M_4 comprises M_3, plus PS holdings of building society shares and deposits and sterling CDs, less building society holdings of notes and coin, bank deposits, and bank CDs.

M_5 comprises M_4 plus PS (non-building society) holdings of money market instruments (bank bills, Treasury bills, local authority deposits), certificates of tax deposit, and National Savings instruments (excluding certificates, Save as You Earn, and other long-term deposits).

Experience with monetary targets

The formal record with respect to the monetary targets announced since 1976 is set out in Table 12.1. The authorities chose initially to target M_3 and then soon afterwards sterling M_3 (£M_3), although there was some evidence to suggest that the short-run relationships between M_1 and nominal incomes and interest rates had been closer than had been the case with £M_3. On the other hand, the behaviour of the economy in the early 1970s strengthened the case for £M_3, as the time path of this aggregate did seem to be fairly closely reflected, after a two-year lag, by a similar time path in inflation and nominal income.

Table 12.1 Monetary targets and outcomes, as a percentage of the annual growth rate, seasonally adjusted

Date announced	Period	Aggregate	Target	Outcomes
12/76	4/76–4/77	£M$_3$	9–13	7.7
3/77	4/77–4/78	£M$_3$	9–13	16.0
3/78	4/78–4/79	£M$_3$	8–12	10.9
11/78	10/78–10/79	£M$_3$	8–12	13.3
6/79	6/79–4/80	£M$_3$	7–11	10.3
11/79	6/79–10/80	£M$_3$	7–11	17.8
3/80	2/80–4/81	£M$_3$	7–11	19.4
3/81	2/81–4/82	£M$_3$	6–10	13.0
3/82	2/82–4/83	£M$_3$	8–12	11.1
		M$_1$	8–12	12.1
		PSL$_1$ 2	8–12	11.0
3/83	2/83–4/84	£M$_3$	7–11	9.5
		M$_1$	7–11	14.0
		PSL 2	7–11	12.6
3/84	2/84–4/85	£M$_3$	6–10	9.5
		M$_0$	4–8	5.5
3/85	2/85–2/86	£M$_3$	5–9	14.8
		M$_0$	3–7	3.5
3/86	3/86–3/87	£M$_3$	11–15	25.4
		M$_0$	2–6	5.0

Source: *Bank of England Quarterly Bulletin*, various issues.

In the years immediately following 1976 the authorities were reasonably successful in restraining the growth of £M$_3$ to within the announced target range, but at the same time, it was argued by many commentators that there was a certain cosmetic element in this success. During this period the authorities placed much reliance on a particular control technique for restraining bank lending – namely the supplementary special deposits (SSD) scheme – which led to avoidance practices on the part of the banks with a consequential effect on the income velocity of £M$_3$ (the ratio of GDP to £M$_3$ on a quarterly basis rose from 3.1 in mid-1976 to 3.5 in mid-1980). Thus, while the authorities were able to restrain the growth of £M$_3$ formally, it was argued that the control techniques employed altered the relationship between £M$_3$ and nominal income, thus partially offsetting the constraint on nominal income growth intended by the introduction of the announced targets.

The real debâcle in the policy of targeting £M$_3$, however, arose during the period from 1979 to 1982 when, as can be seen from Table 12.1, the announced annual targets were overshot by considerable margins. Part of the reason for these overshoots may be attributable to the technical problems faced by the authorities in controlling £M₃, but there is little doubt also that the authorities tolerated such overshoots as a matter of policy. The strict guidelines laid down in the original MTFS were departed from, in that little attempt was made to claw back previous £M₃ overshoots (i.e. what was termed 'base drift' was allowed), and a sequence of such overshoots relative to the set targets was permitted. The point was that, despite the growth of £M₃ in excess of the announced targets, the growth rate of nominal income was declining in a way broadly intended by policy, although at a considerably faster rate than the gradual slowdown implicit in the MTFS. Within the time path of nominal income the absolute declines in real output of nearly 5 per cent between mid-1979 and mid-1980 and 3 per cent between mid-1980 and mid-1981 were certainly greater than anticipated, although the rate of inflation subsequently declined rapidly from a peak of around 20 per cent in mid-1980 to below 5 per cent by mid-1983.

It became apparent, therefore, that the previous perceived relationships between changes in £M₃ and nominal income no longer seemed to hold, and the upward trend in the income velocity of £M₃ prior to 1980 was sharply reversed (the ratio of £M₃ to GDP had fallen back to around 3.1 by the end of 1982 and fell further to 2.9 by the end of 1985). Moreover, the behaviour of other indicators such as the growth of M₁, interest rates, and the exchange rate, were suggesting that the stance of monetary policy was much tighter than that indicated by the growth of £M₃.

Part of this decrease in the velocity of £M₃ was attributable to a reversal of the changes induced by the SSD scheme after this was abandoned in 1980, but the change in velocity is also attributable to other factors, which highlight some of the practical problems referred to previously in the choice of a particular aggregate to be targeted. The problem with the £M₃ aggregate is that it comprises interest-bearing deposits, and the opportunity cost of holding such deposits is related, not to the general level of interest rates *per se*, but to the differential between the 'own' rates of interest on such deposits and interest rates on alternative financial assets. A narrowing of the average interest differential between bank deposits and other financial assets can thus increase the quantity of bank deposits demanded and thus the demand of £M₃ in relation to nominal incomes, regardless of the movements in the general level of interest rates. The velocity of £M₃ can thus

be affected by complex expectational and other factors determining the term structure of interest rates which are difficult for
the authorities to predict. A further difficulty with the £M$_3$ aggregate since 1980 has been financial innovation in the banking
industry, which has led to an increasing fraction of total bank
deposits bearing interest at rates much more closely related to
interest rates elsewhere; there has thus been a structural trend
tending to increase the general attractiveness of bank deposits in
relation to other assets, in the process reducing the velocity of
£M$_3$ in a fashion which, again, is difficult for the authorities to
predict.

The uncertainties surrounding the velocity of £M$_3$ prompted the
authorities in March 1982 formally to amend the policy laid down
in the 1980 MTFS. The money supply targets for £M$_3$ set out in
the MTFS relating to 1982–3 and succeeding years were revised
upwards and it was further stated in the financial and budget
report that 'the ranges for 1983–4 and 1984–5 will be reconsidered
nearer the time and will take account of structural and institutional
changes which may affect the economic significance of the
different aggregates'. In addition, targets for two other aggregates,
M$_1$ and PSL 2, were formally announced (PSL 2 was an aggregate
similar to the present M$_4$ aggregate) and it was stated that the
authorities would closely monitor the behaviour of a range of
other indicators in gauging their policy stance. The changed
approach was summed up in a speech 'setting monetary objectives'
delivered in New York in 1982 by J. Fforde, then an economic
advisor to the Bank.[8]

> In brief, the UK monetary authorities again confirmed that
> while the counter-inflationary strategy remained unaltered in
> substance, their presentation of the money supply as an inter-
> mediate target in pursuit of that strategy has been modified in
> the light of experience since 1979 . . . it recognises once more
> that the successful execution of monetary policy requires the
> exercise of judgement and of a constantly interpretative
> approach to the evolving pattern of evidence.

By and large, this more pragmatic and judgemental approach to
monetary policy has evolved further since 1982 with a progressive
downgrading in the role of formally announced monetary targets.
The M$_1$ target was retained for the fiscal year 1983–4, but after
this target was overshot was dropped, on the grounds that the
growth of interest-bearing sight deposits as a fraction of M$_1$ was
again influencing velocity in an unpredictable way (the PSL 2

target was also dropped at the same time). In the 1984 Budget an announced target was set for the growth of M_0 as well as for $£M_3$, with a lower target range for M_0 being set, on the grounds that the growth of interest-bearing sight deposits had an opposite effect on velocity compared to that of $£M_3$. Targets were similarly announced in March 1985 for both $£M_3$ and M_0, but the prospects of a substantial overshoot of the $£M_3$ target, combined with continuing doubts as to the behaviour of the velocity of $£M_3$, led to the abandonment of the formal target for the year 1985–6 in October 1985. A further target for $£M_3$ was re-introduced in March 1986 but, again, following a substantial overshoot, was finally abandoned in March 1987, leaving M_0 as the only formally announced target.

This downgrading of the significance of formally announced monetary targets in recent years has been accompanied by a growing emphasis on the exchange rate as an indicator, if not a formal target, influencing the use of monetary policy instruments. The strict logic of quantitative money supply targets implies leaving the determination of the exchange rate to market forces, and after 1978 the exchange rate in fact was allowed to float fairly clearly. However, the exchange rate appreciated rapidly during 1979 and 1980 and, in hindsight, this was widely regarded as an important element in the transmission mechanism contributing to the downturn in real output and the consequent rapid decline in the inflation rate in the early 1980s.

In the March 1982 Budget it was announced that the exchange rate was to be among the indicators which the authorities would monitor in gauging domestic monetary conditions. In principle, the behaviour of the exchange rate in a floating exchange rate economy can be an indication of a changing relationship between a given monetary aggregate and nominal income if, despite a monetary aggregate being on target, a changing demand for the aggregate leads to portfolio disequilibrium, resulting in capital flows which move the exchange rate. It is, of course, a relatively short step from using the exchange rate as an indicator to adjust the permitted growth of monetary aggregates in relation to their set targets, to adopting the exchange rate directly as a target and while, at the time of writing, no formal exchange rate target has been announced, there seems to have been a perceptible shift in the emphasis of policy in this direction. On a number of occasions, most conspicuously in early 1985 when the pound approached a value of unity against the dollar, the authorities have taken action to adjust short-term interest rates in response to movements in the exchange rate, rather than in response to movements in the monetary aggregates in relation to their set targets. This change in the status of the exchange rate was confirmed by the Chancellor in his Mansion House speech in October 1986, when it was made clear that the authorities would pay much closer attention in the future to maintaining a more stable exchange rate and much less to achieving explicitly targeted rates of the growth of the monetary aggregates. Further, the UK authorities have entered into collaborative arrangements with other countries with the intention of influencing exchange rates. This, of course, does not mean benign neglect on the part of the authorities in relation to the behaviour of domestic monetary aggregates; in the long run control over the growth of monetary aggregates is essentially implied by a policy of maintaining more stable exchange rates. None the less, it seems increasingly likely that, in the future, explicit money supply targets will be redundant in essentially the same fashion as they were under the Bretton Woods fixed exchange rate regime.

Notes

1 This taxonomy was originally formalized by Saving, T. R. (1967) in 'Monetary policy – targets and indicators', *Journal of Political Economy*, vol. 75, no. 4, pp. 446–56.
2 David Hume (1752) 'Of Money', in *Political Discourses*, Edinburgh:Fleming, pp. 41–59.
3 For a brief survey of the various strands of monetarism see, for example, Burton, J. (June 1982) 'The varieties of monetarism and their policy implications', *The Three Banks Review*, no. 134, pp. 14–31.
4 'Full employment' was never explicitly defined in terms of the measured unemployment statistics, but in practice unemployment rates in excess of 2 per cent come to be regarded as a departure from full employment.
5 'Reflections on the conduct of monetary policy', the first Mais lecture, given by the Governor of the Bank of England at the City University, London, 9 February 1978, reprinted (1984) in *The Development and Operation of Monetary Policy 1960–1983*, Oxford: Clarendon Press, pp. 51–8.
6 Extract from a speech by the Governor of the Bank of England given at the biennial dinner of the Institute of Bankers in Scotland on 17 January 1977, ibid., pp. 49–50.
7 Friedman, M. and Schwartz, A. A. (1970) *Monetary Statistics of the United States*, New York: Columbia University Press, p. 137.
8 Reprinted (1984) in *The Development and Operation of Monetary Policy 1960–83*, Oxford: Clarendon Press, pp. 65–73.

Further reading

Ball, R. J. (1982) *Money and Employment*, London: Macmillan.

Friedman, M. (1973) 'The quantity theory of money', in Walters, A. A. (ed.) *Money and Banking*, Harmondsworth: Penguin Education, pp. 36–64.

Goodhart, C. (December 1986) 'Financial innovation and monetary policy', *Oxford Review of Economic Policy*, vol. 2, no. 4, pp. 78–101.

Griffiths, B. and Wood, G. (eds) (1981) *Monetary Targets*, London: Macmillan, Chapters 1, 2, 3, and 4.

Smith, D. (1987) *The Rise and Fall of Monetarism*, Harmondsworth: Penguin Books.

Chapter thirteen

Techniques of monetary control

In the previous chapter, when discussing the broad issues underlying the use of monetary policy, we often simplified by assuming
that the monetary authorities could 'determine' the money supply.
This may have given the impression that monetary control is a
straightforward matter, but in reality this is far from being the
case. In the present chapter we consider the policy instruments
through which, in principle, the monetary authorities can attempt
to influence the behaviour of the monetary aggregates and the
way they have chosen to use such instruments in practice.

The framework of money supply control

The precise tactics employed by the authorities depend on the
particular monetary aggregate to be controlled, but if the authorities are seeking to control the behaviour of a broad money
aggregate like M_3, which is largely composed of bank deposits,
then they must obviously have a clear idea of the factors which
can determine the stock of bank deposits. (We have considered
previously in Chapter 2 the various influences which can affect
the stock of bank deposits.) In the UK the authorities' tactics for
the control of broad money aggregates have been based on an
accounting framework which seeks to summarize the influences
affecting the stock of bank deposits in terms of the 'credit counterparts', i.e. the changes affecting the assets side of the banks'
balance sheets which, by balance sheet identity, must be reflected
in a change in deposits. We outline below a simplified derivation
of the credit counterparts of M_3, until recently the preferred broad
money aggregate for which explicit targets were announced,
although the basic framework can be used to derive the counterparts of other broad monetary aggregates such as M_4, or to a
possible aggregate comprising the deposits of retail banks alone
(all that is required is a suitable redefinition of the term 'banks';

in the M_4 case 'banks' would mean banks included in the UK monetary sector plus building societies[1]). This framework, though, cannot be applied directly to the determination of a narrower aggregate such as M_1 because M_1 is an aggregate comprised of a subset of total bank deposits and, thus, bank assets can alter without there necessarily being a change in M_1.

The basic definition of M_3 is:

$$M_3 = C + D$$

where C denotes non-bank private sector holdings of notes and coin and D denotes non-bank private sector sterling bank deposits. Hence a change in M_3 (ΔM_3) can be written as:

$$\Delta M_3 = \Delta C + \Delta D \tag{13.1}$$

It follows by balance sheet idntity that the total assets of UK monetary sector banks must equal their total liabilities, but an increase in sterling bank deposits held by the UK non-bank private sector may not precisely equal the increase in the banks' sterling assets. There are three complicating factors which may cause divergences; firstly, on the liabilities side of the balance sheet non-deposit liabilities such as capital and resources are included; secondly, some sterling deposits are held by non-UK residents; thirdly, UK banks accept deposits and make loans in foreign currency and the matching of foreign currency deposits and loans is not perfect, so that an increase in the banks' sterling assets may correspond to an increase in foreign currency deposits. For simplicity we ignore these complications and assume that an increase in the banks' sterling assets broadly corresponds to an increase in sterling deposits held by the UK non-bank private sector. Hence we can write:

$$\Delta D = \Delta A \tag{13.2}$$

where ΔA denotes the increase in the banks' sterling assets. If we again ignore for simplicity the fact that the banks hold real assets, the assets held by the banks comprise financial claims. Thus (netting out inter-bank deposits) they can be formally described as loans either to the UK public sector or to the non-bank private sector. Thus we can write:

$$\Delta A = \Delta BLG + \Delta BLP \tag{13.3}$$

where BLG denotes bank lending to the public sector and BLP denotes bank lending to the non-bank private sector. Note in this framework that notes and coin are considered to be a non-interest-bearing debt of the government, thus if a bank is holding notes and coin it is considered to be lending to the government. From equations (13.2) and (13.3) we can write:

$$\Delta D = \Delta BLG + \Delta BLP \qquad (13.4)$$

Substituting (13.4) into (13.1) it follows that:

$$\Delta M_3 = \Delta C + \Delta BLG + \Delta BLP \qquad (13.5)$$

The public sector's need for sterling finance depends on the PSBR and the extent to which it is intervening in the foreign exchange market. The total amount of sterling finance required is termed the 'domestic borrowing requirement' (DBR) and hence we can write:

$$DBR = PSBR + \Delta R \qquad (13.6)$$

where ΔR denotes the increase in the foreign exchange reserves. The DBR can be financed either by the issue of notes and coin, by borrowing from the banking system, or by borrowing from the non-bank private sector by way of sales of marketable or non-marketable debt. Hence we can write:

$$DBR = \Delta C + \Delta BLG + \Delta PLG \qquad (13.7)$$

where PLG denotes non-bank private sector loans to the public sector. From equations (13.6) and (13.7) it follows that:

$$\Delta BLG = PSBR + \Delta R - \Delta C - \Delta PLG \qquad (13.8)$$

Substituting (13.8) into (13.5) we can write:

$$\Delta M_3 = \Delta C + (PSBR + \Delta R - \Delta C - \Delta PLG) + \Delta BLP$$

and thus simplifying:

$$\Delta M_3 = PSBR - \Delta PLG + \Delta BLP + \Delta R \qquad (13.9)$$

The items on the right-hand side of equation (13.9) are thus the summary credit counterparts corresponding to a given change in

259

M_3 where 'credit' is understood in this context as financial flows which affect the balance sheet position of the banks. From equation (13.9) it is common to write another identity:

$$\Delta M_3 = DCE + \Delta R \qquad (13.10)$$

where DCE equals 'domestic credit expansion' which is equal to $PSBR - \Delta PLG + BLP$. DCE can thus be regarded as the contribution to the growth of M_3 arising from bank lending to the domestic public and private sectors, net of the effect of official intervention in the foreign exchange market. If ΔR is negative then DCE exceeds the growth of M_3 and vice-versa.

It should be emphasized that equation (13.9) is derived from a series of accounting identities and is therefore itself an identity (true by definition) and it by no means follows that the separate credit counterparts can be regarded as being determined completely independently of each other. Numerous interactive mechanisms can be postulated as existing between them. For example, a change in bank lending to the non-bank private sector might change nominal incomes and hence savings and the sales of public sector debt to the non-bank private sector attainable at any given interest rate. Equally, it could be argued that if the PSBR was reduced by cutting bank public sector lending to private firms this might affect the demand for bank loans, etc.

None the less, what can be described as the dominant approach of the authorities to the control of broad money, has been to regard particular policy instruments as exerting a separate direct influence on each of the credit counterparts. Overall policy to restrain the growth of broad money then involves manipulating these instruments so that the sum total of these effects (ideally) adds up to produce a given final effect on M_3. Thus:

1. Fiscal policy instruments, more specifically variations in tax rates, transfer payment formulas, and public spending on goods and services are assigned to influencing the PSBR (in accounting terms, sales of public sector assets in the Conservative government's privatization programme have also had a side effect in reducing the nominal PSBR) thus restraining the potential borrowing by the public sector from the banking system.
2. Funding policy, or debt management policy, both with respect to sales of marketable or non-marketable debt influences ΔPLG, which has a direct contractionary effect on bank deposits.
3. Bank of England operations in the discount market are used to influence short-term money market interest rates, hence bank

lending rates, and hence the quantity of bank loans demanded by the non-bank private sector. Previous to 1980, policy with respect to the control of bank lending also relied heavily on direct controls designed to restrict the supply of bank loans.

4. ΔR is a matter of policy with respect to intervention in the foreign exchange market.

Obviously, in practice, there are important overlaps in the assignment of particular instruments to particular credit counter-parts. For example, action to increase short-term interest rates can lead to changed expectations regarding the movements in yields on longer-term gilt-edged securities and hence the willing-ness of the non-bank private sector to acquire such debt. Similarly, funding policy may affect long-term interest rates which react back on short-term money market interest rates.

The PSBR and debt management policy

A major and highly controversial element in the tactics of the authorities during the 1970s and 1980s has been the assignment of fiscal policy instruments specifically to purposes of monetary control rather than to a direct influence on income and expenditure flows (as was the case in the era of Keynesian demand management). This emphasis on the use of fiscal policy to constrain the PSBR for monetary control purposes was first made explicit in the UK in 1976 and was regarded as a key element in the later 1980 MTFS which set out a four-year declining path for the PSBR as a percentage of GDP simultaneously with the quantitative £M$_3$ targets; despite the problems with adherence to the published £M$_3$ targets, the actual PSBR expressed as a percentage of GDP has been gradually reduced in line with the MTFS since 1980.

It is clear from equation (13.9) that fiscal policy instruments need not necessarily be assigned to monetary control, at any rate in the short run, because the effect of a given PSBR on the monetary aggregate can always be neutralized by a sufficiently high level of sales of public sector debt to the non-bank private sector. Such neutralization implies, however, that interest rates must move to whatever level is necessary to persuade the non-bank private sector to take up the required quantity of debt. Despite their commitment to monetary control, the authorities in the UK have been somewhat reluctant to leave interest rates to be determined entirely by market forces, and this self-imposed constraint on debt management policy therefore implies a role for the direct management of the PSBR in the overall policy of controlling broad money. As the Governor of the Bank of England made clear in a statement explaining the choice of a broad money aggregate,[2]

> Unlike some other countries we have always thought in terms of a broad definition of money . . . it has the particular merit of being capable of analysis in terms of the counterpart sources of monetary growth which include the PSBR. This has helped considerably to focus attention on the vital need for consistency between fiscal and monetary policy. Thus we have attached particular attention to budgetary restraint which is essential if monetary control is to be effective without undue reliance on interest rates. For big changes in interest rates have serious economic effects of their own, for instance on exchange rates or on the viability of businesses, that are too important to ignore.

Thus the argument for reducing the PSBR is that it enables a given growth in M_3 to be achieved without, in the short run, undue fluctuations in interest rates which might be the consequence of the authorities having to sell large given quantities of debt in a certain period and without, in the longer run, the on-average higher (real) interest rates which would be necessary to induce the non-bank private sector to absorb an increasing quantity of public debt in their wealth portfolios.

This explicit use of fiscal policy for purposes of monetary control has drawn considerable criticism from economists with both a 'monetarist' and 'Keynesian' viewpoint. Monetarists often advocate an approach to monetary control known as 'monetary base control' which involves the authorities controlling M_0 as a means of influencing broader money aggregates. Of course, the higher the PSBR, the greater will be the required debt sales to restrain the growth of the monetary base, but control of the PSBR itself is regarded as an unnecessary element in monetary policy. Although monetarists do not generally regard the PSBR as having much direct effect on aggregate monetary expenditure, it is recognized that public borrowing may be an appropriate way of financing public investment and there is no necessary reason why such independent goals of fiscal policy should be subordinated to the dictates of monetary policy. Monetarists have often argued that the greater interest rate stability arising from a lower funding requirement is of dubious benefit as the financial system is capable of developing markets which allow private transactors to hedge against interest rate risks (as is evidenced by the growth of financial futures and option markets),[3] while in the UK context the argument regarding higher real interest rates in the longer run overlooks the fact that the capital market to which the authorities have access is international in scope.

Keynesian economists, of course, argue that a policy of setting targets for the PSBR as a proportion of GDP ignores the direct effects of the PSBR on aggregate monetary expenditure and, in consequence, involves the possibility of fiscal policy exacerbating cyclical fluctuations in real output and employment arising from other causes. Given that tax revenue is raised in the main by taxes on income and expenditure, and that transfer payments are also related to incomes, if economic activity declines, then the PSBR automatically increases as a proportion of GDP. If the authorities then respond by increasing tax rates or reducing government expenditure to reduce the PSBR, then the automatic stabilizing effects of the budget are over-ridden, causing fiscal policy to become procyclical rather than counter-cyclical in effect.

Given the gradual reduction in the PSBR in the 1980s, public borrowing from the non-bank private sector has generally been sufficient to fund the PSBR fully. Indeed, up to 1985 the authorities pursued a policy of overfunding the PSBR so that the net contribution of the PSBR to the growth of broad money was negative; since 1985 the net contribution has been broadly zero.

With respect to funding tactics, we have previously described in Chapter 7 the methods the authorities have employed to sell new gilt-edged securities. Since the late 1970s the authorities have further attempted to broaden the appeal of government debt by issuing securities other than traditional fixed-interest stocks. First, since March 1977 stock has been issued in 'partly paid' form, an initial subscription being followed by two further instalments, usually within three months; many partly paid issues have been made subsequently, their success resting on individuals' ability to subscribe to them at a time when they are temporarily short of liquid funds with which to make outright purchases. Second, the authorities have issued variable interest rate stocks whereby the coupons paid are adjusted in line with the average yields on Treasury bills; this adjustment reduces the nominal capital uncertainty involved in holding fixed coupon bonds in the face of changes in market interest rates. Third, since 1981 index-linked bonds have been introduced (originally restricted to pension funds and life assurance companies, but since made available to all purchasers) designed to reduce real capital uncertainty for their holders in the face of unpredictable future inflation. Part of the motivation for the introduction of index-linked bonds also reflected the authorities' concern in the early 1980s regarding the future real interest rate burden involved in issuing long-term fixed-interest stocks with coupons reflecting the then nominal interest rate of around 15 per cent, if the rate of inflation did subsequently return to single-digit figures (which in the event turned out to be the case). This concern also motivated the issue of convertible stocks, where the initial issue is a short-term stock, but the purchaser is offered the option to convert into long-term stock carrying a specified coupon at a fixed future date or range of dates. A further innovation has also been the issue of low-coupon stocks issued at a discount on their redemption values so that the yield on the stock accrues mainly in the form of a terminal capital gain. As capital gains on gilt-edged securities are exempt from capital gains tax, these issues were designed to appeal mainly to taxpayers with high marginal rates of income tax (a criticism of such issues on other grounds would be that the authorities are conniving in tax avoidance for wealthy taxpayers).

In the 1980s the authorities have also attempted to sell greater volumes of non-marketable debt, and the contribution of such debt to the funding of the PSBR has been much greater than previously. Previously, interest rates on non-marketable debt tended to lag behind movements in other interest rates, but the authorities now keep interest rates highly competitive with those of other assets. Additionally, index-linking has been applied to certain issues of National Savings certificates and also to the 'Save as You Earn' contractual savings scheme.

Control over bank lending

In practice, the primary credit counterpart explaining in an ex-post sense most of the growth in broad money aggregates has usually been bank lending to the non-bank private sector. In general there are three primary ways through which the authorities can attempt to control bank lending:

1. On the assumption that there is a predictable relationship between the quantity of reserve assets the banks are holding for prudential purposes and the quantity of non-reserve assets constituting loans to the non-bank private sector, the authorities can attempt to control the supply of reserve assets to the banking system, thereby exerting leverage effects over the banks' balance sheets as a whole. This form of influence might be complemented by the imposition of controls in the form of mandatory reserve ratios (with penalties for non-compliance) which reduce to some

extent the possibility of the banks offsetting the actions taken by the authorities in any given period by compensating adjustments in their reserve ratios. If mandatory ratios are imposed, a further possibility of control is via administrative variation in the required ratios. This form of control works through affecting the supply of bank lending.

2. Distinct from general ratio controls, the authorities may introduce controls which aim at specific elements in the banks' balance sheets. One possibility is to control bank loans directly by placing restrictions of some kind on the loans the banks are able to make. Another possibility is controls which place restrictions on the interest rates that banks are able to offer depositors relative to those on other financial assets, thus depriving the banks of the counterpart funds necessary to sustain increases in bank lending.

3. The authorities may attempt to influence the terms on which the banks are prepared to lend, thus influencing the quantity of bank loans demanded and, hence, the actual volume of bank lending transacted in any period.

By and large, the UK authorities have relied traditionally on the second and third approaches (and since 1980 primarily on the third approach), and this statement holds even in past periods when the authorities have imposed mandatory reserve ratios. In general, such ratios have not been used as a fulcrum to exert leverage effects directly on the whole balance sheet, but rather as a means of strengthening the Bank's ability to influence short-term interest rates. This particular choice of tactics has often been the subject of criticism from academic economists who often tend to favour variants of the first approach. As we indicated in the previous section, those economists who believe most strongly in monetary targeting typically recommend monetary base control which, it is claimed, would circumvent most of the problems experienced by the authorities in controlling bank lending in practice. We briefly outline this approach below and then contrast it with the actual approach pursued by the UK authorities.

Monetary base control

The underlying basis of monetary base control proposals is typically some variant of the 'bank credit multiplier' approach to bank behaviour, which involves the manipulation of identities to derive algebraic expressions summarizing the end result of a process of balance sheet expansion consequent upon a change in the banking system's holdings of reserve assets, similar to the

265

illustrative example employed in Chapter 2. That example, however, was very unrealistic in that it assumed that the general public would be prepared to hold all the additional bank deposits created as the banking system expanded and, hence, that the leakage of cash in the process of balance sheet expansion was zero. Thus, most formulations of the bank credit multiplier approach assume that the general public has some given desired ratio of cash to total bank deposits, and thus that there will be a drain of cash from the banking system via withdrawals of notes and coin by the non-bank public as bank deposits increase. We set out below a simple formulation of the bank credit multiplier approach incorporating this assumption. It is here assumed that the banks hold cash (i.e. notes and coin plus balances at the central bank) as a single reserve asset; cash in this sense is often alternatively described as 'high powered money'.

1. Assume that the non-bank public hold cash in some proportion (a) to their holdings of bank deposits. Hence:

$$C_p = aD \qquad (13.11)$$

where C_p denotes cash held by the non-bank public and D denotes bank deposits.

2. Assume that the banks hold cash as a reserve asset in some proportion (b) to their deposit liabilities – this can be a desired prudential ratio or a mandatory ratio. Hence:

$$C_b = bD \qquad (13.12)$$

where C_b denotes cash held by the banks.

3. The balance sheet of the banks can be expressed in simplified form as:

$$D = C_b + A \qquad (13.13)$$

where A denotes bank loans, broadly interpreted as the banking system's acquisition of financial assets issued by the non-bank private sector.

4. The total supply of cash or high-powered money (H) constituting the monetary base is held either by the banks or the non-bank public. Hence:

$$H = C_p + C_b \qquad (13.14)$$

From equations (13.11), (13.12), and (13.14) it follows that:

$$D = \left[\frac{1}{a+b} \right] H \qquad (13.15)$$

From equations (13.12), (13.13), and (13.15) it follows that:

$$A = \left[\frac{1-b}{a+b} \right] H \qquad (13.16)$$

Equation (13.16) is, of course, an identity and, as such, although it implies a predictable relationship between A and H if the parameters a and b are constant or highly stable, it tells us nothing about the direction of causation. If, however, it is assumed that the Central Bank is technically able to fix H at a predetermined level and chooses to do so, then it can be asserted that A will be determined by H. H, of course, corresponds to the liabilities in the Central Bank's balance sheet and the instrument through which they can technically determine their liabilities is via open market purchases and sales of financial assets. In terms of an industrial analogy, high-powered money can be thought of as an essential raw material that banks need for their business and the term in brackets is equivalent to a technical coefficient relating the 'output' of the banking system to the total supply of the necessary raw material. Thus, for example, if $b = 0.1$ and $a = 0.2$ the coefficient is equal to 3 and if the high-powered money supply is £10,000 million then the banking system can manufacture £30,000 million in the form of bank loans. The essential argument of many adherents of monetary base control is that the relevant technical coefficient is easily identifiable and stable enough in practice to permit fairly precise control over bank lending by the authorities (and hence over the supply of broad money) via their ability to determine the monetary base. If we write a further identity for broad money (M) as:

$$M = C_p + D \qquad (13.17)$$

then by similar manipulation of the identities one can derive an expression explicitly for broad money as:

$$M = \left[\frac{1+a}{a+b} \right] H \qquad (13.18)$$

We should note that controlling the total high-powered money

267

supply is not quite the same thing as explicitly controlling the cash reserves of the banking system, as the banks can acquire reserves through notes and coin deposited by the non-bank public. Control of the monetary base controls the potential reserves of the banking system rather than their actual reserves, but if the parameter *a* is stable, then monetary base control implicitly determines the cash available to the banks.

This simple approach, of course, does not precisely fit the present institutional situation in the UK where banks hold reserves in the form of call money and eligible bills, etc., as substitutes for cash; moreover, if we are thinking in terms of a broad money aggregate such as M_3 it is not directly applicable to the wholesale banks for whom cash is not an essential part of their business. However, under a strict form of monetary base control, the facilities which make it possible for banks to treat certain assets as very close substitutes for cash would not exist, while the multiplier approach can be extended, if necessary, to encompass wholesale banks by the introduction of further identities relating to the deposits of wholesale banks held by the non-bank public as a proportion of retail bank deposits and the proportion of their deposits which the wholesale banks keep as reserves in the form of retail bank deposits. Generally the same principles would hold – if the relevant ratios are assumed to be stable it can be asserted that the monetary base would determine a broader aggregate such as M_3.

The crux of the matter, though, is would such ratios be stable if monetary base control was attempted? Adherents of monetary base control tend to argue that while, in practice, the parameters *a* and *b* might not be literally constant and would display an inevitable degree of slippage (even in a system with a mandatory cash ratio, the banks might choose to hold excess reserves above the mandatory minimum), they would probably be stable enough to enable the authorities to exert a dominating influence on the growth of broad money via manipulation of the monetary base. The main difficulty in appraising this argument is that previous experience as to the stability or otherwise of such ratios provides little guidance as to their future behaviour in a monetary base regime, as the past behaviour of such ratios has been determined under an entirely different control regime. The basic *a priori* criticism of the multiplier approach is that the presumption of stable ratios ignores any element of choice in the portfolio behaviour of the banks or the public and is thus far too mechanical and simplistic to serve as a basis for policy. For example, even in the simplest formulation the assumption that the cash–deposit ratio of the public is stable ignores the institutional reality that many bank deposits are interest-bearing and that banks, if they deemed it profitable to do so, may actively induce the public to change their behaviour by raising interest rates. Equally, the multiplier approach implicitly assumes that there always exist willing borrowers to enable the banks to make the volume of loans determined by the algebraic expressions. One can always assume that the banks are always prepared to reduce their lending rates as necessary to ensure that the predetermined volume of loans is transacted, but this in turn would be to ignore the fact that banks are profit-making concerns who will only make additional loans if marginal revenue exceeds marginal cost. The bank credit multiplier approach implies, unrealistically, that the supply curve of bank loans is perfectly inelastic with respect to the rate of interest on bank loans, and that at the limit they would be prepared to lend at a rate of interest of zero.

In the face of such criticism, a somewhat weaker argument for monetary base control can be maintained by adopting a framework where the banking industry is regarded as essentially akin to any other competitive industry, where the supply curve of bank lending, in contradistinction to the multiplier approach, is portrayed as upward sloping in relation to price (i.e. the interest rate) in the usual manner. For banks which used cash as a reserve asset the supply curve at any time would be conditional on the monetary base; corresponding to a given stock of cash, other things being equal, there would be a unique supply curve, but its form would be determined by the portfolio preferences of the banks and the public. The upward slope of the curve is explained by the fact that, given their preferences for cash as a reserve asset, the banks would need to alter the cash–deposit ratio of the general public by offering higher interest rates on deposits if they were to expand their balance sheets collectively in the face of a constraint on the total supply of cash. Thus, as with any other competitive industry where there is a fixed supply of an essential raw material, the banking system is likely to be an increasing cost industry. This framework is illustrated in Figure 13.1.

In the diagram, the SS curve denotes the supply curve for bank lending, conditional on a given supply of high-powered money, while the DD curve is a demand curve for bank loans, again conditional on a variety of other factors, which would include factors influencing the total demand for credit, interest rates on other financial assets, etc. (structural changes like the banks' entry into the housing finance market could also be interpreted as shifting the effective demand curve). Both curves are to be inter-

Figure 13.1 The market for bank loans

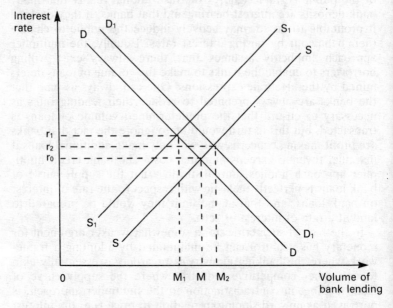

preted as long-run 'stock' supply and demand curves. Assuming the interest rate is free to adjust the equilibrium value of bank lending is thus determined at $0M$ at an interest rate of r_0.

In this framework monetary base control would work by influencing the supply curve; a reduction in the monetary base, for example, might shift the supply curve to S_1S_1 which, assuming the demand curve remain unchanged, would induce a contraction in bank lending – at the initial interest rate r_0 the banks are short of cash to support the volume of loans demanded and as they attempt to attract additional cash from the non-bank public there is a convergence to a new equilibrium where $0M_1$ loans are supplied at an interest rate r_1. (By extension it can be argued that an increase in retail bank interest rates would likewise shift a comparable supply curve for wholesale banks which are competing to attract retail bank deposits from the non-bank public.) Control over the monetary base in principle could still exert an influence on bank lending, but this would be much less predictable than that implied by the credit multiplier approach, as it would depend on the precise form and stability of the demand and supply curves; even with a given monetary base determining the supply curve as SS, for example, if the demand curve shifted to D_1D_1 the volume of bank lending could expand to $0M_2$. Thus certain adherents of monetary base control assert a weaker argument that, while short-run control of broad money would be technically difficult, control of the base in the long run (i.e. over a period of years) would be sufficient to ensure that 'no monetary aggregates can run away'.

Whatever the ultimate mechanisms through which monetary base control is assumed to influence bank lending, the basic assumption of course is that the monetary base can be controlled in a precise way by the monetary authorities for a reasonably short period, if not literally on a day to day basis. While most economists agree this would be technically possible, it does imply that the present framework of monetary control would be subsumed by such an approach, in that the authorities would have to relinquish any influence they might wish to exert on interest rates or on the foreign exchange rate. The authorities' tactics in the gilt-edged market would be dictated by the need to prevent an expansion of the cash base via the central government's borrowing requirement and the need to forestall holders of maturing government debt switching into bank deposits; equally, keeping the base on track implies a limitation on the authorities' intervention in the foreign exchange market.

Interest rate control

In contrast to monetary base control, by and large, the authorities in the UK have sought to exert control over bank lending by attempting to influence bank interest rates directly and hence the quantity of bank loans demanded (although at various junctures in the past interest rate control has been supplemented by additional, more direct controls). This is a persistent theme in the Bank of England's operations traceable back to the nineteenth century, and is explained by the Bank's perception of its other major role as lender of last resort to the banking system. An increased demand for cash on the part of the banking system can arise not only because the system is seeking to expand its lending and requires additional cash reserves to support the increased volume of deposits, but because the general public for some reason are making large net withdrawals of notes and coin from the banks. In order to maintain the convertibility of bank deposits into notes and coin and forestall the possibility of banking crises similar to those which occurred in the nineteenth century, the Bank has generally been willing to provide the banking system, usually via the institutional mechanism of the discount market, with high-powered money on demand, but at a 'price of its own choosing'.

Figure 13.2 Supply curves of high-powered money

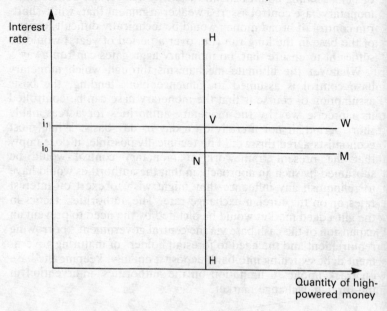

Effectively, therefore, this commitment has meant that, relative to the rate of interest on short-term assets held by the banking system, the supply curve of high-powered money at any time can be thought of as being more in the nature of a perfectly elastic curve in contrast to the perfectly inelastic curve which would apply in a system of strict monetary base control. Since 1981 this statement needs some qualification in that as long as short-term interest rates are within the unpublished band the supply of high-powered money can be regarded as fixed.

The contrast between the supply curve of high-powered money which would apply in a strict monetary base control system and that favoured by the UK authorities is illustrated in Figure 13.2. Under a monetary base system the supply curve of high-powered money at any time would be represented by a vertical line such as HH and control would be exerted by the authorities bodily shifting the curve to the left or right via open market operations. Previous to 1981, the effective supply curve would have been represented by a horizontal line such as i_0M, where the authorities ensured the convertibility between short-term liquid assets held by the banks and high-powered money at an interest rate of their own choosing i_0. The technique adopted by the authorities was to keep the discount houses continually dependent at the margin on finance from the Bank, which the Bank readily supplied at an explicitly announced interest rate. The Bank used various instruments to ensure that cash shortages in the discount market were the normal situation. These included open market sales of securities and calls for special deposits from the banks but, most importantly, since the discount houses were willing to cover the Treasury bill tender, the authorities developed the tactic of offering more Treasury bills for tender than was needed to cover the Exchequer's residual borrowing requirement (thus leaving the discount houses short of funds) and then subsequently relieving the shortage at a chosen interest rate. By this technique the Bank was able to influence short-term money market interest rates in a fairly precise fashion and was able to shift the horizontal supply curve bodily up or down at its discretion.

Since 1981 the authorities' tactics in the discount market have been amended in the way previously described in Chapter 7; the authorities no longer over-issue Treasury bills and aim to keep short-term interest within an unpublished band. Market forces will determine interest rates within the band, but at the limits set the supply of high-powered money again becomes infinitely elastic with respect to the interest rate. Thus if the interest rate band is hypothetically set between i_1 and i_0, the effective supply curve of high powered money becomes a kinked line of the form i_0NVW. In principle, if the interest rate band was very wide, the system would approximate monetary base control; the narrower the band the more the system approximates the previous system. In practice, the 1981 changes in operating procedures would not seem to have substantially amended the system in the direction of monetary base control. To quote from the Governor of the Bank of England in his seventh main lecture:[4]

> Some people have read into the changes in these arrangements that have occurred over the years – from Bank Rate to minimum lending rate to our present somewhat more flexible method of operation – much greater significance than is justified. While it is the case that the particular technical arrangements can provide for a greater or lesser degree of market or official influence and that the relative influence exerted by the market and the Bank can change with circumstances, both influences are always present.

In terms of the simple supply and demand framework depicted in Figure 13.1 this chosen method of operation, (subject to the qualification regarding a short-term interest rate band rather than

Monetary Policy

Figure 13.3 The market for bank loans if the authorities control bank rates

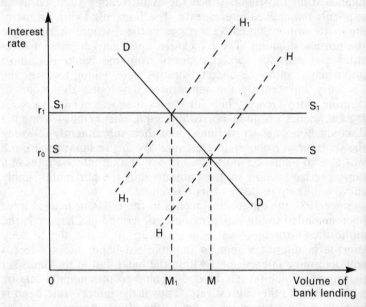

a precise level) transforms the effective supply curve of bank loans into a near perfectly elastic curve at a given interest rate. If, from any given point the banking system was seeking collectively to expand, with a given supply of high-powered money the symptom would be rising short-term interest rates in the money market. If the Bank did not wish to see interest rates rise above its unpublished band, it would need to relieve the cash shortage by conducting open market operations in the discount market on the appropriate terms – in effect providing the banking system with the cash it requires to support the increased volume of deposits. Thus, rather than constraining the banking system to move along a given supply curve of the form depicted in Figure 13.1, the Bank shifts the supply curves by varying the cash base, thus producing an effectively near-horizontal supply curve at its chosen interest rate.

The way in which interest rate control works in principle can thus be illustrated in Figure 13.3. Given a certain level of money market interest rates, the interest rate at which the banking system is able to supply additional loans is given at r_0 and the effective supply curve is SS. The volume of bank loans is thus determined

274

at 0M by the quantity of bank loans demanded at the given interest rate. In these circumstances, therefore, it would be correct to assert that the volume of bank lending determines the supply of high-powered money rather than the converse direction of causation implied by the credit multiplier approach. To influence the volume of bank loans the Bank can then use its operations in the discount market to influence money market interest rates and the terms on which the banking system is prepared to lend. For example, by manipulating money market interest rates, the Bank might shift the supply curve upwards to S_iS_i and if the demand curve remain unchanged, the quantity of bank loans demanded would contract to $0M_1$.

In principle, therefore, given the Bank's powers to influence short-term interest rates, control over the volume of bank lending could be quite precise if the authorities knew precisely the position and form of the demand curve for bank loans at any time, and if they were prepared to move interest rates to whatever level is necessary to achieve a given quantitative effect. In fact, if the authorities had full information as to the position and form of both the demand curve for bank loans and the supply curve of bank lending conditional on various levels of the monetary base, then there would be little to choose between interest rate control and monetary base control as techniques for influencing bank lending. With reference to Figure 13.3, for example, the authorities could have produced an equivalent result by shifting the dotted supply curve HH upwards to H_1H_1 by a contraction in the base. In both instances there would be a contractionary movement along the demand curve resulting in the same quantitative effect on bank lending, the only difference being that, in the monetary base control case, the rise in the bank lending rate would be a consequence of the response of the banks to a reduction in their cash base rather than a policy-induced change directly instigated by the authorities.

The basic criticism of interest rate control, however, relates to the fact that, in reality, the authorities have far from perfect information regarding the position and form of the demand curve for bank loans, and the response of bank lending to given changes in interest rates has been notoriously difficult for the authorities to predict. The implication drawn by many commentators is that the demand curve for bank lending is unstable over time and is liable to shift under the influence of various factors about which the authorities have imperfect knowledge. For example, the authorities can seek to influence the nominal interest rate on bank loans but the true cost of borrowing is the expected real rate;

275

Figure 13.4 The non-equivalence of monetary base and interest rate control

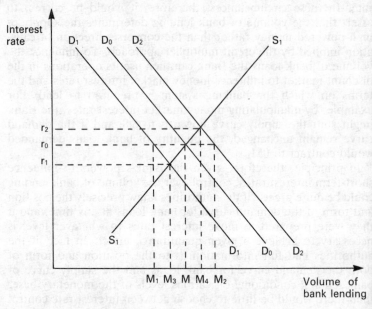

changes in inflationary expectations which are difficult for the authorities to gauge may therefore shift the demand curve drawn with respect to nominal interest rates in unpredictable ways. Again, if nominal interest rates on bonds rise (as in the 1970s) this may increase the demand for bank loans as firms seek shorter-term finance in place of the issue of long-term debentures. Structural changes such as the banks' entry into the housing mortgage market may also affect the demand for bank lending.

Given this fundamental uncertainty regarding the form and position of the demand curve for bank loans it is often argued, therefore, that although monetary base control similarly does not permit precise control of bank lending in such circumstances, compared to interest rate control it would reduce the possible errors likely to arise between actual and planned growth rates. This argument is illustrated in Figure 13.4.

Suppose the authorities are seeking to restrict bank lending consistent with their money supply objectives to a quantity 0M. Suppose the authorities believe that the 'true' demand curve at a given time is D_0D_0 and set an appropriate interest rate of r_0. If the true demand curve happened to be D_0D_0 the authorities would

276

achieve their objective, but suppose that the position of the true demand curve (which is unknown by the authorities) could lie in a range between that represented by D_1D_1 and D_2D_2. In the extreme cases of the demand curve turning out to be either D_1D_1 or D_2D_2 the quantity of bank lending would be either $0M_1$ or $0M_2$ and the authorities' quantitative objectives would be either undershot or overshot. Suppose, alternatively, that the authorities eschew interest rate control and hold the monetary base at a level which yields the supply curve S_1S_1. Given that the supply curve is not perfectly inelastic, the uncertainty regarding the position of the true demand curve also implies in this case that the authorities are unlikely to hit their precise target, but the dispersion of the actual outcomes from the desired outcome is likely to be less than wider interest rate control. In the case depicted, if the true demand curve turned out to be the extremes of D_1D_1 or D_2D_2, then the volume of bank lending would be $0M_3$ and $0M_4$ respectively. Clearly, monetary base control might enable the authorities to get closer to their quantitative objectives in circumstances where there is considerable uncertainty as to the quantity of bank loans that will be demanded at any given interest rate.

Direct controls

In practice, an important part of the authorities' technical problems in influencing the growth of broad money has stemmed from uncertainty regarding the demand for bank loans and hence an uncertain response to the authorities' manipulation of short-term interest rates. Consequently the UK authorities have often supplemented their basic approach with other direct controls. During the early post-war period the controls employed by the authorities took the form of 'lending requests' made by the Bank to individual clearing banks with the intention of directly restricting bank lending to within certain specified ceilings or to certain preferred categories of borrower. The problem with such controls, however, was that when they were in force for long periods, there was a diversion of traditional banking business to non-regulated channels and thus a progressive undermining of the real effectiveness of the restrictions in terms of the alternate effects on aggregate spending. To combat such avoidance of the controls in the later 1960s, non-clearing banks, finance houses, and to a limited extent bill finance were progressively included in the area covered by lending requests, but it was widely argued that the effect of the controls was to inhibit competition between financial institutions and to produce distortions and inequities in the allocation of funds to borrowers.

In response to such criticism, the arrangements embodied in the document 'Competition and Credit control' became operative in 1971 when the lending ceilings so frequently in operation during the 1960s were discontinued and the intention expressed by the authorities was henceforth to operate monetary policy via interest rate adjustments. The ending of lending requests, however, coincided with an upsurge of bank lending in the early 1970s and the authorities soon introduced another form of control, namely the supplementary special deposits (which became known in City jargon as the 'corset'). Under this scheme the authorities set guidelines for the growth in the interest-bearing eligible liabilities (IBELs) of each individual bank, and if an institution allowed its IBELs to grow faster than the stipulated rate it was required to place non-interest-bearing deposits with the Bank of England – in effect, a tax which reduced the profitability of balance sheet expansion. The required special deposits became steeply progressive as an institution's level of excess IBELs rose. The scheme undoubtedly exerted a restraining effect on the growth of broad money during the periods in which it operated, but had the obvious disadvantage of restricting competition between banks in a manner somewhat contradictory to the spirit of the reforms enacted in 1971. Moreover, the scheme, like the earlier requests, while statistically restraining the growth of M_3, had the disadvantage of encouraging avoidance devices on the part of the banks (commonly termed 'disintermediation' because the result is that ultimate borrowers and lenders by-pass the banks as intermediaries and transact in a direct fashion) which exerted a significant effect on the velocity of M_3 in an offsetting way. A principal form of avoidance was via the device of bank acceptances. An individual bank whose IBELs were at the stipulated maximum might, for example, be approached for a loan by a corporate borrower and as an alternative to making the loan itself the bank might induce the borrower to issue a bill of exchange, accepted by the bank, which it might then arrange to be discounted by a corporate non-bank lender in substitution for a deposit in the bank. Bank acceptances were thus a route by which the restraint on expenditure – the ultimate objective of controlling M_3 – could be avoided, while cosmetically M_3 was restrained.

So as regards regulations, Competition and Credit control turned out to be a much less important change in approach than was intended, and the corset restrictions led to the same blunting of competition and allocational inefficiencies as had the previous restrictions. However, the reduced recourse to controls intended in 1971 was more decisively undertaken in 1980. Exchange controls were completely abandoned in 1979 and this change opened up the possibility of offshore Eurosterling banking as a further method of avoiding the corset restrictions. The SSD scheme was thus discontinued in June 1980 and further deregulation of the banking system followed in 1981 when the mandatory reserve asset ratio applicable since 1971 was likewise abandoned.

Overfunding

Following the abandonment of the corset scheme, the continued uncertain response of the demand for bank lending with respect to interest rates led the authorities in the early 1980s to pursue a deliberate policy of 'overfunding' the PSBR (i.e. achieving sales of government debt to the non-bank private sector exceeding that required to fund the PSBR). From the flow of funds summary accounting identity (equation (13.9)) it can be seen that sales of debt to the non-bank public in excess of the PSBR exerts a direct contractionary impact on M_3 and can thus neutralize some of the effect of bank lending on the behaviour of the aggregate in any period.

The technical problem with overfunding from the authorities' point of view was that the resultant net flow of payments from the private sector to the central government led to persistent cash shortages in the discount market and, hence, to prevent short-term interest rates from rising above their targeted range the Bank was forced to be a consistent buyer of bills in open market operations. The accumulated volume of bill purchases by the Bank soon exceeded the banking system's holdings of Treasury bills and the Bank had to relieve the cash shortages by substantial purchases of eligible commercial bills; by 1985 the Bank's accumulated holdings of commercial bills had grown to in excess of £15 million. The build-up of the Bank's holdings of large stocks of commercial bills itself tended to perpetuate the persistent cash shortages as, when existing commercial bills mature, there is a flow of payments from the non-bank public to the government sector. The effects of this policy were therefore somewhat inconsistent with the authorities' declared intention (1981) of giving market forces more scope in the determination of short-term interest rates.

Some commentators argued that such tactics merely exacerbated the growth in bank lending in that the effect of the authorities' actions was to 'twist the yield curve' by increasing longer-term interest rates relative to shorter-term interest rates, thus

279

encouraging companies to seek finance by bank borrowing rather than the issue of long-term debentures. Others argued that the policy had a distorting effect on the velocity of M_3 as the authorities, in effect, were acquiescing in a form of disintermediation by borrowing long term via the issue of gilt-edged securities to finance the spending of those companies who were issuing commercial bills.

Coincidentally with the decision to abandon the M_3 target announced for the fiscal year 1985–6, in October 1985 the authorities decided to cease the deliberate policy of overfunding. This decision was justified in short-run terms by the continued decline in the velocity of M_3 stemming from continued changes in financial behaviour and an increasingly competitive and innovative financial system; the authorities argued that it would have been inappropriate to continue to pursue through funding policy the original path for M_3 growth, set on the basis of different assumptions about the relationship between money and nominal income. This decision means that the authorities are again reliant on the manipulation of short-term interest rates as their primary means of influencing the growth of broad money aggregates.

Monetary base control for the UK?

While monetary base control currently would not seem to be a live issue in the UK, in 1980 the authorities did publish a Green Paper in which a possible change to such a system was mooted and considerable debate ensued as to the practical feasibility of such a system.[5] In the event, in a note issued in November 1980, the Bank concluded that the uncertainties regarding the operation of monetary base control in practice and the degree of institutional change that would be involved were too great to justify the change, although it did not rule out entirely 'further evolution towards such a system'.[6] The new operating arrangements in the discount market introduced in 1981 were interpreted by some as a partial move in that direction, but subsequent experience has not indicated any substantial change in the Bank's operating methods in this direction. We briefly discuss below some of the main difficulties that have been cited in connection with the practical implementation of a monetary base control system.

1. Given that the monetary base is defined as notes and coin plus bankers' deposits at the Bank of England, there would be an initial problem of deciding whether banks would be allowed to choose freely their own prudential holdings of cash, or whether a

mandatory cash ratio would have to be imposed. Some advocates of monetary control have argued that mandatory cash ratios would be unnecessary.[7] Each bank would decide on its desired cash ratio depending on factors such as the maturity structure of its deposits, the frequency of cash withdrawals, the opportunity cost of cash as measured by day to day interest rates, and the bank's aversion to risk. These factors would differ from bank to bank and so would each bank's desired cash ratio, but, it is argued, all that is required for effective control is that each bank's demand for cash be reasonably stable. Other commentators have argued that if no mandatory ratios were imposed, then banks would be able to offset the action of the authorities by compensating variations in their cash ratios. Moreover, wholesale banks could operate with minimal cash, and control on their lending would have to operate indirectly through induced changes in interest rates. Some have concluded, therefore, that mandatory cash ratios would be required if monetary base control is to have predictable effects on broad money, but even in this case, depending on the penalties for non-adherence to the minimum ratios, banks might choose to hold excess reserves which again might be varied in an offsetting fashion (although it would be possible to stipulate penalties for exceeding as well as falling short of the officially specified ratios).

A further problem with mandatory ratios is that if they were set above the levels which individual banks would voluntarily choose to hold (as would probably be the case with wholesale banks) then the implicit tax might again re-introduce the discrimination against the banks inherent in previous controls; thus the problem of disintermediation or, in the continued absence of exchange controls, migration of sterling banking to offshore centres outside the controlled area might recur.

2. As noted previously, there is a potential conflict between strict control of the monetary base by the Bank of England and its role as lender of last resort to the banking system (strict control of the monetary base implies that the authorities would not alter the base in the face of substantial withdrawals of notes and coin from the banks). Many advocates of monetary base control argue, however, that the degree of conflict can be exaggerated. Most recognize that the existence of a lender of last resort is essential and that there would have to be a 'crisis over-ride' in the event of liquidity difficulties incurred by an individual bank (or banks). Providing, though, that the last resort loans are strictly temporary and made at a genuinely penal rate (so that it can never be profitable for a bank to make a loan on the expectation that, if necessary, cash will be provided by the authorities) it is argued

that over a period of, say, three months, the path of the monetary base need not be significantly affected by this central bank facility. Many critics have suggested that the difference between monetary base control and the present arrangements is that the Bank would need to act as a genuine lender of last resort instead of, as now, a lender of first resort.

3. In present institutional circumstances, owing to the short-run unpredictability of payments between the control government and the non-bank private sector, precise day to day control of the monetary base would be very difficult as the Bank could not gauge readily the offsetting open market operations necessary to neutralize such flows (although this technical problem could be avoided if the central government banked with the commercial banks rather than the Bank of England). The longer the particular time period adopted for control purposes, the more manageable becomes the technical problem of keeping the base on track but, even so, the changes in the Bank's operating procedures would imply that interest rates would be subject to greater short-run volatility than under present arrangements. This would be so, not only because open market operations would now have to be conducted to keep the base on track regardless of the consequences for interest rates in the gilt-edged market, but also because the absence of the Bank's smoothing function in the money market implies that the fluctuations in the demand for bank credit and, hence in the bank's demands for cash, will have a much more immediate impact on short-term interest rates.

There is a question here, however, concerning the magnitude of interest rate variations as opposed to their frequency. It has been suggested, for example, that although monetary base control would generate more frequent adjustments in interest rates, this would avoid the need for the less frequent, but much larger, changes in interest rates inherent in the present system.[8] In other words, in any system of monetary control, changes in interest rates are inevitable and the present regime is characterized by periods of interest rate stability followed by step-changes in interest rates; it is not obvious that, over the longer run, the present regime significantly reduces uncertainty compared to a system of more continually adjusting interest rates. In any case, monetarists tend to argue that the benefits of greater interest rate stability are not sufficient to justify the costs of erratic money supply growth.

4. A change to a monetary base system would involve structural changes in the banking system. The curtailment of lender of last resort facilities would reduce the liquidity of bank assets such as

bills, and the banks would respond (even without a mandatory requirement) by holding larger quantities of cash in relation to deposits than is currently the case. This would tend to raise the costs of financial intermediation by the banks, which would be reflected in widening margins between deposits and lending rates. A further development might be the curtailment of the overdraft system, as the banks would no longer be able to enter into open-ended commitments to make future loans if there was no guarantee of last resort cash from the authorities except at penal rates. The curtailment of the overdraft system, it is argued, might subsequently increase operating costs for private sector firms as the loss of these facilities might force them to hold larger quantities of liquid, but lower yielding, assets.

While for these and other reasons the UK authorities have hitherto rejected direct control of the monetary base, it is of course the case that (at the time of writing) M_0 remains as the only announced targeted aggregate, which on the face of it would seem to be somewhat contradictory. However, as the Chancellor of the Exchequer made clear at the time when the M_0 target was introduced, this did not imply any change in the Bank's operating methods. In principle, if the growth of M_0 was exceeding its targeted growth rate, this would be a signal for the Bank to manipulate money market interest rates upwards; the consequent effect on bank lending rates and hence on bank lending and the growth of broad money and nominal incomes, should then react back on the growth of M_0 if there is a reasonably stable relationship between nominal income and the quantity of notes and coin demanded by the general public. The targeting of M_0 should therefore be viewed as an indirect way of using interest rates ultimately to influence nominal income in a situation where the growth of broad money itself has become a much less reliable indicator of changes in nominal income.

Notes

1 The derivation of the credit counterparts of M_4 are outlined in 'Measures of Broad Money', *Bank of England Quarterly Bulletin*, May 1987.
2 'British economic policy over the last decade', *Bank of England Quarterly Bulletin*, June 1983.
3 For example, Laidler, D. (March 1985) 'Monetary policy in Britain: successes and shortcomings', *Oxford Review of Economic Policy*, vol. 1, no. 1, p. 39.

4 Reprinted in the *Bank of England Quarterly Bulletin*, August 1987, p. 369.
5 *Monetary Control*, Cmnd 7858, London: HMSO, March 1980.
6 This note is reprinted in the *Bank of England Quarterly Bulletin*, December 1980, p. 428.
7 For example, Griffiths, B. (October 1979) 'The reform of monetary control in the UK', *The City University Annual Monetary Review*, no. 1, p. 39.
8 See Griffiths, B., ibid., p. 35.

Further reading

Artis, M. J. and Lewis, M. K. (1981) *Monetary Control in the United Kingdom*, Dedington: Philip Allan, Chapters 3, 4, and 6.
Coghlan, R. *The Theory of Money and Finance*, Chapter 9.
Congdon, T. (1982) *Monetary Control in Britain*, London: Macmillan.
Llewellyn, D. T., Dennis, G. E. J., Hall, J. J. B., and Nellis, J. G. (1982) *The Framework of UK Monetary Policy*, London: Heinemann Educational Books, Chapters 2, 3, and 4.
Pierce, D. G. and Tysome, P. J. (1985) *Monetary Economics*, London: Butterworths, Chapters 4, 12, and 13.
'Monetary base control', *Bank of England Quarterly Bulletin*, June 1979.

Index

285

Index

Index